Studies in Natural Language Processing

Reference and computation

Studies in Natural Language Processing

This series publishes monographs, texts, and edited volumes within the interdisciplinary field of computational linguistics. It represents the range of topics of concern to the scholars working in this increasingly important field, whether their background is in formal linguistics, psycholinguistics, cognitive psychology or artificial intelligence.

Also in this series:

Reference and computation

An essay in applied philosophy of language

AMICHAI KRONFELD
Senior Staff Scientist, Natural Language Incorporated

Foreword by JOHN SEARLE

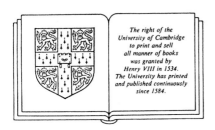

The right of the
University of Cambridge
to print and sell
all manner of books
was granted by
Henry VIII in 1534.
The University has printed
and published continuously
since 1584.

CAMBRIDGE UNIVERSITY PRESS

CAMBRIDGE

NEW YORK   PORT CHESTER

MELBOURNE   SYDNEY

Published by the Press Syndicate of the University of Cambridge
The Pitt Building, Trumpington Street, Cambridge CB2 1RP
40 West 20th Street, New York, NY 10011, USA
10 Stamford Road, Oakleigh, Melbourne 3166, Australia

© Cambridge University Press 1990

First published 1990

British Library cataloguing in publication data

Library of Congress cataloguing in publication data

ISBN 0 521 36636 4 hard covers
ISBN 0 521 39982 3 paperback

Transferred to digital printing 2000

For Chana
and Maya

"Nearly eleven o'clock," said Pooh happily. "You're just in time for a little smackerel of something," and he put his head into the cupboard. "And then we'll go out, Piglet, and sing my song to Eeyore."

"Which song, Pooh?"

"The one we're going to sing to Eeyore," explained Pooh.

A. A. Milne, *The House at Pooh Corner*

Contents

List of figures   xi

Foreword   xiii

Preface   xix

1 Methods and scope   1
   1.1 Internal and external perspectives   2
   1.2 Referring as planning   7
   1.3 Philosophical foundations   13
   1.4 Summary of Chapter 1   15

2 The descriptive approach   17
   2.1 The problem of reference   17
   2.2 The descriptive research program   20
   2.3 Objections   26
       The referential/attributive distinction   26
       Away with meanings   28
       In praise of singular propositions   30
       The status of *de re* beliefs   32
       Identification reconsidered   33
   2.4 Motivation   33
   2.5 Summary of Chapter 2   45

3 First steps   47
   3.1 Donnellan's distinction(s)   48
   3.2 Having a particular object in mind   50
   3.3 A three-tiered model of referring   57
       Individuating sets   58
       Referring intentions   60
       Choice of referring expressions   61

Contents

		Donnellan's distinction: final chord	62
	3.4	Summary of Chapter 3	65
4	**Referring intentions and goals**		**68**
	4.1	Communication intentions	68
	4.2	The literal goal of referring	71
	4.3	The discourse purpose of referring	75
	4.4	Summary of Chapter 4	82
5	**Conversationally relevant descriptions**		**85**
	5.1	Speaker's reference and indirect speech acts	86
	5.2	Functional and conversational relevance	91
	5.3	Descriptions as implicatures	97
		Recognizing conversational relevance	100
		Speaker's assertion	101
		Extensional and intensional justification	102
		The meaning of "must"	106
		Nonassertives and indefinite descriptions	110
	5.4	Summary of Chapter 5	113
6	**Thoughts and objects**		**116**
	6.1	The essential indexical	117
	6.2	The pragmatics of belief reports	123
		A conflict of interest	127
		The shortest spy revisited	129
		Causality and vividness	132
		Individuating sets and the descriptive view	134
	6.3	Summary of Chapter 6	137
7	**Computational models**		**141**
	7.1	General principles	141
	7.2	A Prolog experimental system	144
	7.3	Formalizing referring effects	149
		Mutual individuation	150
		Speech acts and rationality	156
		Referring and rationality	167
	7.4	Summary of Chapter 7	172
References			**175**
Index			**181**

Figures

2.1 Main aspects of the reference problem   18
2.2 Main postulates of the descriptive program   21

3.1 Aspects of Donnellan's distinction   57
3.2 Donnellan's distinction and its interpretation   64

5.1 Functional and conversational referring   97
5.2 Grice's conversational maxims   98

6.1 The Fregean view of *de re* thought   117
6.2 The Russellian view of *de re* thought   122
6.3 A descriptive theory of *de re* thought   137

7.1 A dialogue with **BERTRAND**   151
7.2 Declarative axiom   162
7.3 Imperative axiom   163
7.4 Referring axiom   168
7.5 Referring within a request   171

Foreword

by John R. Searle

Amichai Kronfeld's book, *Reference and Computation*, addresses one of the oldest problems in the philosophy of language, indeed, one of the oldest problems in Western philosophy: the nature of linguistic reference. Though the problem is old, the approach taken by Kronfeld is in many respects original, and in at least one respect, it is to my knowledge quite unique: Kronfeld's book is the only work known to me that joins a high level of philosophical sophistication in its discussion of the problem of reference with the beginnings of a a rigorous attempt at a computational implementation of the philosophical theory. Both philosophy and computer science benefit from this combination. On the one hand, you can't design a good natural language program unless you have a good philosophy of natural language to start with; on the other hand, the attempt to implement a theory of natural language computationally provides a rigorous form of testing the theory. The beauty of working with computers is that the computer will not allow you to fudge, avoid issues or theorize ambiguously.

Kronfeld sees, correctly in my view, that the most important current dispute in the philosophy of language concerning the nature of reference is between what he calls the "descriptive approach" on the one side, and on the other the "causal" or "externalist" theory of reference. On this issue, again in my view correctly, he sides with the descriptive approach. It is an odd fact about any causal or externalist theory of reference that it makes it incidental to the successful performance of the speech act of referring that the speaker and the hearer know, or even have any idea about, what they are talking about. On Kronfeld's view, contrary to the current orthodoxy, reference is achieved in virtue of denotation; that is, a speaker uses a referring expression to refer to an object and does so successfully because the speaker has a mental representation denoting what he believes to be a particular object, and if he succeeds in communicating his reference to the hearer, the hearer will come to have a mental representation denoting the same object. On Kronfeld's view linguistic reference is thus dependent on mental reference; and to say that is just to say that to talk about something you have to be able to think about the thing you are talking about. Thus, in a sense, linguistic reference is a special case of, an application of, mental reference. On this view, the function of certain sorts of noun phrases in discourse is to provide linguistic representations of the object referred to. Kronfeld explains how this is possible even in cases where the literal denotation of a noun phrase may differ from the intended reference, in cases where there is no literal denotation, and in cases where the noun phrase does not have a conventionally associated descriptive content.

Underlying this whole approach is the key insight that referring is a speech act, it is something that people do with words. So, though linguistic reference is dependent on mental reference, the speech act of referring is a goal-directed form of human behavior. And this assimilation of the act of referring to the theory of speech acts generally enables Kronfeld to apply computational accounts of goal-directed behavior to referring as a special case. In his final chapter, he provides us with a formalization in computational terms of a plan-based account of referring, where referring is seen as a planned activity intended to achieve particular goals. It is a consequence of Kronfeld's account of reference that the mental representation possessed by the hearer at the conclusion of the successful act of referring need not be identical with the mental representation possessed by the speaker, provided only that the representations denote the same object.

One of the most original portions of the book is his discussion of Donellan's alleged distinction between the attributive and referential occurrences of definite descriptions. I think Kronfeld's discussion of these issues is the best I have seen in the philosophical literature. Kronfeld points out that Donellan's distinction actually cuts across two different linguistic criteria for distinguishing referential from attributive. The first, which he calls the "denotational criterion," is based on the role played by the descriptive content of the referring expression in determining truth conditions. The second one has to do with the mental state of the speaker and what is involved in having a particular object in mind. Writers on this subject generally assume that what is referential according to one criterion should also be referential according to the other, but Kronfeld shows that this is not really the case. In his discussion of these issues he also makes important and original observations concerning the modal element in the original distinction. One sees this modal element most obviously in sentences containing "attributive" occurrences of definite descriptions. Thus, for example, in the attributive use of the definite description one is able to say either "The man who murdered Smith *is* insane" or "The man who murdered Smith *must be* insane." In the latter case, the modal auxiliary "must" makes explicit what was implied by the first utterance: It is *qua* murderer of Smith that the person referred to by the speaker is declared to be insane. The occurrence of the modal verb is an explicit rendering of the Gricean implicature of the first, and is itself subject to a further implicature: "Any such murderer of Smith is bound to be insane." Kronfeld thus uncovers a third aspect of Donellan's distinction. Besides the epistemic and the denotational, the distinction also has a modal feature. All of this is carefully worked out in Chapter 3.

The discussion of the attributive–referential distinction serves a double purpose. It is intended to cast light on certain crucial features of the speech act of referring, but it is also a defense of the descriptive program against one of the most common objections made to it. Other objections are dealt with in subsequent chapters. In this discussion Kronfeld accepts the current doctrines that there are essentially *de re* thoughts, singular propositions, and essentially indexical propositions. But he argues that the acceptance of these is not inconsistent with the descriptive program. The phenomena described in the philosophical literature as singular propositions, *de re* attitudes, and essential indexicals are standardly presented as difficulties or counterexamples to the descriptive analysis of the speech act of referring, but Kronfeld employs ideas from several philosophers, especially Russell, to show that these phenomena are easily accounted for in the descriptive framework. Marshalling Russell's distinction between "knowledge by acquaintance" and "knowledge by description," he says in this connection (p. 121):

> entities such as visual experiences and the self have
> a special ontological and epistemological status that
> enables the descriptive theorist to consider them as
> constituents of the content of beliefs. Accepting the

special status of such entities is not a rejection of the descriptive program, nor does it in any way involve a commitment to external reference fixing mechanisms of the sort insisted upon by the new theory of reference.

With this apparatus in hand, more or less in passing, he refutes Putnam's Twin Earth argument against the descriptive program.

In this brief introduction I will not try to summarize the whole book, but I want to conclude by calling attention to its synthesizing character: Kronfeld combines insights from the tradition of Frege and Russell with the work of speech act theorists such as myself and Austin together with Grice's theories of meaning and implication to give a general account of the relations between the intentions in the speaker's utterance, the hearer's understanding, the use of language that mediates the two, and the relations between mind, language, and the world that are involved in the entire process. And all of this is presented within a computational framework. Central to the whole theory is the Gricean idea that we achieve our communicational goals in speaking by getting our audiences to recognize our intentions to achieve those goals. In the case of reference this gives an elegant account of what Kronfeld calls "the literal goal" of the speech act of referring. Since an essential part of referring consists in invoking in the hearer's mind a representation of an object, the recognition by the hearer of such an intention automatically produces such a representation: as soon as the hearer recognizes that a noun phrase is being used as a referring expression he knows that the speaker is referring to a specific object he has in mind. But that is only the first step. The hearer must then come to possess an identification of *which* object the speaker has in mind, a process Kronfeld calls "pragmatic identification." At this point Frege's notion of a mode of presentation of the referent, together with Russell's distinction between acquaintance and description are used to explain the variety of ways of achieving success in identification.

The final chapter sketches the computational model of referring. Here the central concept is that of an individuating set, i.e. a set of representations that a speaker has which he believes uniquely specifies a particular object, the one he "has in mind." For computational purposes individuating sets can be treated as abstract data types. The philosophical account of reference is then implemented in a computational model where the performance of the speech act of referring in the utterance of a noun phrase is analyzed in terms of the speaker's intention to get the hearer to generate an individuating set which determines exactly the same object as is determined by the speaker's individuating set, and determines it in a particular way intended by the speaker. A major aim of the computational formalization is to assimilate an account of reference to a general account of speech acts and rationality. Only the beginnings are sketched in this chapter, but a foundation is provided for further work in this field.

Preface

When I began writing this book I was a philosopher. When an earlier draft was submitted for publication I was a computational linguist. Now I am a company staff scientist. The change in my title did not alter my main professional interests — then, as now, I earn my living working on natural language problems — but the shift in perspectives did bring with it a different sense of my intended audience. It also made me want to prove (first and foremost, to myself) that both philosophy and computational linguistics — even when quite technical — can be made accessible, relevant, and useful for people working on natural language problems in a variety of disciplines

Whether I achieved this goal is not for me to say. However, a conceptual map of the book could help readers with different backgrounds identify those segments of the book they may want to concentrate on or, alternately, avoid altogether.

Chapter 1 sets up the problem, and spells out in some detail three methodological assumptions that guide my entire approach.

Chapter 2 provides the philosophical background. Section 2.1 presents four aspects of the philosophical problem of reference. Section 2.2 characterizes what I call the *descriptive research program* — a theoretical framework that includes Frege, Russell, Strawson, and Searle, which I contrast with the *new* or *causal* theory of reference. Section 2.3 is a systematic presentation of the arguments against the descriptive program, and Section 2.4 explains why I think the descriptive program is the most promising theoretical framework available nevertheless. The discussion is not technical and, when appropriate, I include short summaries of leading philosophical theories.

Chapter 3 is the cornerstone of the entire study. It provides a detailed analysis of Donnellan's distinction between two types of referring expressions. All the other chapters further refine the computational model that emerges out of this analysis of Donnellan's distinction.

Chapter 4 defines the intentions and goals that characterize the speech act of referring. It combines the perspective of speech-act theory with a plan-based account of referring expressions.

In Chapter 5, I offer a computational interpretation of what I call *conversationally relevant descriptions* — i.e., descriptions that are used not only to indicate what is being discussed, but also to communicate something beyond that.

Chapter 6 brings us back into the philosophical domain. Using the conceptual apparatus developed in earlier chapters, I argue for the primacy of internal (i.e., mental) representations in establishing reference.

Chapter 7 concludes on a computational note. After summarizing the principles arrived at so far, I present two models which incorporate these principles. One is a Prolog program implementing a central idea which underlies a descriptive theory of reference. The other is an attempt at formalizing referring effects within the framework of a general theory of speech acts and rationality.

For the reader's convenience, each chapter includes its own summary.

* * *

My deepest intellectual debt is to John Searle and the late Paul Grice. They provided me, each in his own way, with the theoretical framework and tools for developing my own views.

While at the University of California at Berkeley, I had many long discussions about the problem of reference with Alan Code, George Lakoff, David Reier, and in particular, George Myro, whose untimely death saddened me very much. Possessing the sharpest of minds together with the most generous of spirits, he was an inspiration to work with.

Barbara Grosz was the first to encourage me to apply my philosophical views to computational linguistics. My research collaboration with Doug Appelt was crucial in the development of the computational perspective of this study. I am greatly indebted to both. Many thanks go also to other colleagues at SRI International who read segments of the manuscript: Phil Cohen, Jerry Hobbs, David Israel, Ray Perrault, Martha Pollack, and Stan Rosenschein.

Candy Sidner's careful comments and feedback were extremely helpful. Asa Kasher, a former teacher and an old friend, has been for years a constant source of insight and support.

Special thanks are due to the management of Natural Language Inc. for allowing me to typeset this book on their computers and for giving me the time off when deadlines were no longer flexible.

Savel Kliachko provided invaluable help with the stylistic preparation and editing of the manuscript, as did Orin Gensler and Eric Zakim. Ernie Limperis graciously offered help in reading the proofs. I am particularly grateful to Judith Ayling and Jenny Potts, my editors at Cambridge University Press, for their patience and expertise in seeing this project through. Thanks also to Methuen London for granting permission to use the lines from *The House at Pooh Corner* (©1928, pp. 2–3) as an epigraph.

Finally, I would like to thank Chana Kronfeld, who happens to be my chief editor, harshest critic, principal cheer-leader, and best friend. Now it is my turn to be all that for her. Let me tell you: she is a tough act to follow.

Berkeley, April 4, 1990.

1
Methods and scope

When two people talk to each other, they had better both know what they are talking about. This, I hasten to add, is not a condescending directive enjoining nonexperts to keep quiet. It is rather a general rationality constraint on our use of language. We frequently mention *things:* we may promise to return a book, request that a window be closed, remark that a certain tool is useful, and so on. But, as rational agents, we can expect such speech acts to be successful only if our addressee knows what book, window, or tool is being discussed. Thus the question arises: how do we let our audience know what we are talking about? How, in other words, do speaker and hearer form an agreement as to which entities are the subject of the conversation?

The question seems almost trivial: our hearer is expected to know what we are talking about because it is assumed that he understands the language we use and, moreover, we have already *told* him what is being discussed. If, say, we are talking about my mother, then I have presumably indicated that fact already by using an appropriate noun phrase, such as "my mother." Since my addressee understands English, he comprehends that the person I am talking about is my mother. Could anything be simpler?

Nonetheless, the ease with which a native speaker can *refer* — i.e., indicate what entity is being discussed — is deceptive. Like other mechanisms of language use, referring is easy to do but extremely difficult to explain or simulate. The case of "my mother" is indeed quite simple because the hearer knows that each and every person in the world has one and only one mother. Thus, the question, "Which of your mothers are you talking about?" never arises. But it is rather surprising that the act of referring is hardly ever that straightforward. "Did you find Maya's shirt?" my wife asks me, and I know she is talking about the shirt my daughter left in the playground. But my daughter is not the only girl named "Maya" and, besides, my daughter has more than one shirt. My wife's referring act is therefore successful, even though she never *tells* me explicitly what shirt she is talking about. In more complex cases, the success of the referring act is even more puzzling: "You know," I tell my wife while watching a couple at a party, "Jane's husband seems to be quite a romantic guy." "He is not her husband, you fool!" my wife answers. She, obviously, knows exactly who I am talking about, and I know that she does despite the fact that what I *told* her has to do with a different person entirely.

These two simple examples are neither unique nor exceptional. As a matter of fact, we hardly ever *tell* our hearers explicitly what we are talking about, although we expect them to figure it out. Indeed, in general, we are very good at providing hearers with just enough information — no more and no less than necessary — to enable them to understand the subject of the conversation. How do we do that? And how can we teach a computer to do it?

My goal in this book is to outline an answer to this question. Such an answer will ultimately take the form of a computational — i.e., algorithmic — model of referring, and a sketch of such a model is provided. In principle, it should be possible to implement such a model on a computer as part of a natural-language system. However, implementation is not my main concern here; the reader should not expect a blueprint for the construction of a specific program. Rather, my intention is to specify the general principles that ought to be incorporated in any particular implementation. These principles are derived from three methodological tenets that underlie this entire book. The first is that a theory of referring should explain how noun phrase usage is related to objects in the world, not how one use of a noun phrase is related to another. The second is that referring is a speech act. The third principle is that a theoretical account of referring must be firmly anchored in a well-defined, well-defended philosophical framework. In the next three sections I describe what exactly is meant by these three methodological tenets.

1.1   Internal and external perspectives

The act of referring is performed through the use and interpretation of noun phrases in a conversation. But we should be careful to distinguish between two perspectives — one *internal*, the other *external* with respect to the discourse.

2

From the internal perspective, our main interest is the relation of coreference among symbols. From the external perspective, on the other hand, what interests us is the relation between symbols and the objects they represent. Consider the following exchange between Representative Louis Stokes and Assistant Attorney General Charles J. Cooper during the Iran-Contra hearings:

Stokes: And lastly, when you and the Attorney General interviewed Colonel North, he was not under oath at that time, was he?

Cooper: No, he was not. (*New York Times*, June 26, 1987)

Although neither North nor the Attorney General, nor Cooper himself, was under oath when they met, it is clear that, when Cooper says "No, he was not," he means North. How do we know that? How is the connection between the expressions "Colonel North" and "he" established? These are the typical questions that are asked from the internal perspective. The questions that are asked from the external perspective, on the other hand, are different. How is the connection between the expression "Colonel North" and the *person* North established? What does it take for a hearer to recognize who the Attorney General is? When Stokes says "you," whom does he mean and how do we know what he means? This is what matters to us from the external perspective. Note that it is entirely possible that a native speaker of English would succeed in matching the expression "Colonel North" with the right occurrence of "he" without understanding at all who Colonel North is. His success must be explained from the internal perspective, his failure from the external one.

It is tempting to identify the internal/external dichotomy with the distinction between linguistic knowledge and world knowledge. This would be a mistake, however, although these types of knowledge may be characterized respectively as "internal" and "external." For example, the linguistic knowledge that proper names are capitalized in English is important to understanding that "North" stands for the person Oliver North. At the same time, the nonlinguistic ("external") knowledge to the effect that only when a man is *answering* questions does it matter whether or not he is under oath plays an important role in interpreting the pronoun "he" in Cooper's response: since no one else was answering questions in the situation described by Stokes, the query as to whether someone had been under oath must pertain to North. Thus, linguistic knowledge is relevant for explaining the connection between an expression and an object (the external perspective), while world knowledge is often used to disambiguate the anaphoric link of pronouns (the internal perspective). The crucial difference between the two perspectives is this: from the external perspective, the criterion of success for the hearer is correct identification of the object being discussed. From the internal perspective, the criterion of success is the right matching among symbols.

In the field of artificial intelligence (AI) there is a tendency to blur the distinction between these perspectives — partly, I think, because the external perspective is not well understood or appreciated. In all the natural-language systems with which I am familiar, reference to objects is handled under what may be called the *standard-name assumption*. According to this assumption, *all* objects in the domain have standard names that are known to all participants in the discourse. In such systems, the act of referring is successful when (and only when) the machine associates the right standard name with the noun phrase. For example, if a user types "The screwdriver is broken," referring to the object whose standard name is, say, the constant S_1, the referring act succeeds if and only if the machine associates the constant S_1 with the expression "the screwdriver." Given this approach to referring, it is easy to ignore the external perspective entirely. Since standard names are simply labels, we tend to take the relation between the standard name and its bearer for granted. All that is left for us to do is to show how one symbol (the noun phrase) is associated with another (the standard name). This places us firmly where our view is from the internal perspective.

But the external perspective is indispensable. First, most of the objects we talk about do not have standard names; hence labeling is hardly the right model for explaining how referring is done in natural language. Of course, we can always generate new labels whenever a new object is introduced, but we are still left with the problem of explaining how the object is identified in the first place. Therefore, if we are ever to explain how natural language is capable of representing reality for us, we must give up the standard-name assumption and pay closer attention not only to the way symbols are associated with one another, but also to the way they correspond to the objects they stand for. Furthermore, if we ignore the external perspective, we lose the basic rationale for the act of referring itself. Consider the following examples:

(1.1) The average farmer owns a donkey. He feeds it.

(1.2) The farmer down the road owns a donkey named
Buridan. He feeds it.

(1.3) If John owns a donkey, he feeds it.

(1.4) If a farmer owns a donkey, he feeds it.

In (1.2), in contrast with (1.1), the speaker has in mind a particular farmer and a particular donkey. But from the internal perspective, this fact is of limited interest, since both "the farmer down the road," and "the average farmer" have equal potential for initiating anaphoric chains. Similarly, in (1.3), there is a particular owner that the hearer is expected to identify. No such identification is required for the interpretation of (1.4). Still, from the internal perspective all three — "John," "a farmer," and "a donkey" are treated equally: they are assigned *discourse entities* (Webber 1983; Kamp 1984), which are basically "conceptual coathooks" on which a hearer "hangs" subsequent noun phrases in the anaphoric chain. Whether the discourse entity corresponds to a real object or not is immaterial as far as the internal perspective is concerned.

But the question of whether the noun phrase corresponds to a particular object that the hearer is expected to identify is of prime importance for a natural-language system. Consider a speaker who is attempting to achieve something by means of language. Suppose, for example, that Luke Skywalker of Star Wars instructs his trusted robot C3PO to look for Han Solo's spaceship. It makes a great deal of difference to Luke whether it is understood that he has a particular spaceship in mind and furthermore, whether the robot will be able to identify it. If the robot simply associates the phrase "Han Solo's spaceship" with the correct standard name and then switches itself off, Luke has not succeeded in his speech act. Any system that combines linguistic and nonlinguistic actions, and that is capable of cooperative behavior, must be able to talk about objects. It must distinguish when a noun phrase has a referent in the real world from when it does not, when a particular type of knowledge of the referent is required from when it is not, when knowledge of the referent is presupposed from when it should be actively sought. Without the external perspective, we cannot even ask these questions.

The present study examines reference from the external perspective. Quite bluntly, my own view is that *only* the external perspective is relevant to a theory of referring if such a theory is supposed to explain how expressions represent things, and how such representations can be used by a speaker for a specific purpose. This, of course, does not mean that the internal perspective is not important. On the contrary, the internal perspective is essential to our understanding of natural language. Moreover, although research from the internal perspective is largely independent of its external counterpart, the opposite is not true, since a theory of referring needs the constraints that a theory of anaphora resolution provides. Thus, if an internal theorist asks me why he should adopt the external perspective, my answer would be that he does not have to. There is enough to be done from the internal perspective for generations to come. If, on the other hand, I am asked why we need the external perspective at all, my answer would be that, without it, both semantics — in the sense of relating language to the world — and pragmatics — in the sense of correlating language with the purpose of its use — are impossible.

Throughout this section, I have talked about particular entities that a speaker may have in mind and a hearer is supposed to identify. Needless to say, there are many kinds of such entities. For example, *institutions* (the Supreme Court, the Presidency), *abstract entities* (the number 47, the theory of relativity), *events* (the shooting of J. F. Kennedy, World War II), and so on. We can talk about all such entities, and a comprehensive theory of referring should undoubtedly explain our ability to do so. Here, however, I concentrate on the familiar class of physical objects that, so to speak, are simply "out there" in the physical world for everyone to see: plants, cars, shirts, persons, houses, animals, etc. From now on, whenever I talk about objects, it is such physical objects that I have in mind. The problems associated with referring to other types of entities will be deliberately disregarded in the following discussion.

There are a number of related reasons for restricting ourselves in this way. From a theoretical point of view — as Strawson (1959) has argued — the category of physical objects is *basic* in the sense that, without it, identification of particular entities in other categories would be impossible (Strawson uses the term "material bodies"). From a practical point of view, a computer system that, among other things, is capable of referring is most likely to operate in a context in which the perception and manipulation of physical objects are of prime importance. But the main reason is essentially methodological. Physical objects of the type we are considering are more permanent than events and, unlike abstract and institutional entities, they can be perceived. Consequently, they can be recognized, identified, and reidentified in the most obvious and immediate manner. Focusing our attention on objects possessing such features simplifies the discussion significantly: we begin with a firm intuitive grasp of the category of things we are talking about, individuation is less of a problem (we all know what counts as one shirt or one person), and identification and reidentification are easier. When we shift to other kinds of entities, such as the Presidency, World War II, or the integer 3, it is much harder to understand the relation between a noun phrase and an intangible object because the latter is much more difficult to grasp. All in all, physical objects seem to provide a good point of departure. If a theory of referring cannot handle physical objects, it stands little chance of coping with anything else.

1.2 Referring as planning

The act of referring is done typically by means of noun phrases in conversation. However, not all noun phrases are intended to be used in this manner, not even those that have the form of a definite description. For example, in the sentence "The whale is a mammal" (uttered, say, in a biology class), the speaker is making a general statement in which no referring relation is presupposed between the noun phrase "the whale" and any individual whale. Let us reserve the term *referring expressions* for those instances of noun phrase usage that are intended to indicate that a *particular* object is being talked about. Note that one and the same noun phrase may sometimes function as a referring expression and at other times not. While discussing the whale at the Monterey aquarium, for example, I may comment "...but it costs a lot to feed the whale." Here, the noun phrase "the whale" is clearly used as a referring expression, in contrast to the above example.

Thus, whether or not a particular noun phrase is a referring expression depends on the way it is intended to be interpreted. A theory of referring, therefore, is not a theory of language but of language *use*. In general, theories of language use (that is to say, *pragmatic* theories) specify and explain the ability of humans to use language for some purpose. Consequently, an account of referring should specify and explain human competence in using referring expressions to achieve particular goals. Now, pragmatic theories have concentrated on two complementary aspects of language use. The first, which is at the heart of Grice's theory of meaning (1957; 1968; 1969), is this: when we use language, we typically achieve some of our goals by making our audience recognize our intentions to achieve them. For example, I can succeed in congratulating you simply by making you recognize my intention to do so. Once you have recognized my intention, you are thereby congratulated and nothing else is necessary. This is a unique feature of communication, as Grice was the first to notice. The second aspect of language use, which is a central element in Searle's speech acts theory is this: we make our audience recognize our intentions by following mutually known rules that determine what the utterance of a particular expression *counts as.* For example, underlying the recognition of an intention to pay one's debt is a rule that is mutually known by both speaker and hearer; this rule specifies that the utterance of "I hereby promise to pay my debt" *counts as* placing the speaker under the obligation of paying his debt (Searle 1969).[1]

These two general principles of language use determine the structure of pragmatic theories. For any communication act, such theories should state precisely what relevant speaker's goals are involved, and on what basis a speaker expects and intends these goals to be recognized (cf. Cohen and Perrault 1979). Moreover, since the relation between language use and a speaker's goals is what needs to be explained, it is natural, within the context of computational linguistics, to consider language use as a *planning* problem (Allen 1978; Appelt 1985b; Cohen 1978; Cohen and Perrault 1979). What underlies the *generation* of an utterance is a plan (constructed by the speaker) to achieve certain goals through available means (linguistic or otherwise). The *understanding* of the utterance involves the hearer's recognition of the goal, as well as of the plan itself (or perhaps just a part of it). By regarding language use as a special case of planning, we are provided with a large array of computational tools that have been developed within the field of AI in recent years. Moreover, since planning is a special form of rational behavior, the justification of rules for language use can be grounded upon a general theory of rationality, as shown by Kasher (1976; 1982) and others (Cohen and Levesque 1985).

Such a computational approach to language use governs the model of referring presented here. A plan-based account of referring is an integral part of a plan-based theory of speech acts. At a certain point in the planning of a speech act, it may become obvious that,

---

[1]This is the rule that defines the institution of promising — see ibid., 60. For a discussion of such rules (*constitutive rules,* as Searle calls them), see ibid., 33–42.

as a precondition for further steps in the plan, the speaker must make the hearer identify a particular object as being relevant to the conversation. To achieve this goal an act of referring then becomes necessary. Thus, a computational model of referring must show how the successful use of a referring expression in a given context is due to the solving of a planning problem — given also a goal, various rationality assumptions, and relevant linguistic institutions.

Note that, as is the case in other plan-based accounts of communication acts, the effects of referring are intended to be primarily on the hearer's model of the world, which naturally includes a representation of the speaker's model. In general, if my intention is that you recognize my goal, the typical way to satisfy my intention is to let you know what I think, hoping that I shall thereby alter your model of my mental state. The same reasoning applies to referring: by effecting changes in the hearer's model of the speaker's model, the speaker may be successful in his referring act. That is, he may succeed in making the hearer recognize which particular object is now relevant to the conversation. Of course, the speaker's model, in turn, includes a representation of the hearer's model; hence, by making the hearer recognize the object in question, the speaker's model itself changes. Thus, a model of referring — like other plan-based accounts — should describe how, after successful referring, the *hearer's* model of the speaker's mental state and the *speaker's* model of the hearer's mental state are both changed.

In sum, what I have been saying so far is this: a pragmatic theory of referring is one that specifies and explains human competence in using *referring expressions* to achieve certain goals. Since the relation between referring expressions and a speaker's goals is what must be explained, it is natural to consider referring as planned action. This, in turn, requires showing how the use of referring expressions is systematically related to changes in both the hearer's and speaker's mental states.

The view that the referring act is a planned effort to achieve certain goals through linguistic means simply follows from the fact that referring is a *speech act*, since all speech acts are attempts to achieve goals through linguistic means. Following Searle, I distinguish between two kinds of speech acts: *propositional* and *illocutionary*. There are two kinds of propositional acts, according to Searle, namely, referring and predicating, both of which are generally performed as parts of larger, complete speech acts. The latter constitute the illocutionary acts: promising, stating, requesting, congratulating, commanding, questioning, asserting, thanking, warning, advising, and the like. Now, although referring is a speech act, it is different from illocutionary acts in the following four important ways.

Literal goals. In performing one and the same speech act, a speaker may have many distinct goals. For example, by uttering "The house is on fire!" a speaker may intend to inform the hearer that the house is on fire, scare the hearer half to death, and/or make the hearer leave. Only the first goal, however, is what I call a *literal* one. Literal goals are the goals of Gricean communication intentions, i.e., they are intended to be achieved through recognition of the intention to achieve them.[2] Thanks to Austin, Grice, Searle and others, we have a fairly clear notion of what the literal goals of *illocutionary* acts are. For example, the literal goal of a promise is to let the hearer know that the speaker places himself under an obligation to do something. But it is not clear at all what the literal goal of referring is. Needless to say, without a clear notion of a literal goal, the task of treating referring as a planned speech act cannot even get off the ground.

Conditions of satisfaction. Illocutionary acts have *illocutionary force* and *propositional content*. An assertion that it is raining and a question whether it is raining share the same propositional content but have different illocutionary forces. A promise to come home early and a promise to pay one's debt have the same illocutionary force, but differ in propositional content. Part of the illocutionary force is the illocutionary *point* (Searle 1979c), which specifies the point or purpose of the (type of) act. The illocutionary point together with the propositional content determine what Searle (1983) calls the act's *conditions of satisfaction*: a request that a door be opened is satisfied if and only if the hearer indeed opens it; by the same token an assertion that the door is closed is satisfied (true) if and only if the door is indeed closed.

A referring act, however, has neither illocutionary force, nor propositional content, and although it obviously has a purpose, it is not clear what its conditions of satisfaction are. As with literal goals, we must have a clear notion of what it takes for a referring act to be satisfied if we want to view referring as a planned speech act.

---

[2]The term "literal goal" is taken from Kasher (1977), where literal *purposes* are introduced. Our use of the two terms is virtually the same, except that Kasher wishes to explain what literal purposes are in a way that is independent of Gricean intentions.

Note that specifying the conditions of satisfaction of a referring act is not the same as specifying its literal goal. The literal goal of a speech act and its conditions of satisfaction are usually distinct: if I tell you that I want the door closed and you understand me, the literal goal of my request has been achieved. But it is still up to you whether or not you will satisfy my request.

Compositionality. Speech acts can be combined with one another, creating new and more complex speech acts. For example, a question can be seen as a request to inform. It is also possible to either request a promise or promise to request. As Cohen and Perrault (1979) have shown, the appropriate planning of composite speech acts is a powerful adequacy test for a planning system that can generate speech acts. Now, since referring is not a complete speech act (that is, it is not an illocutionary act), one cannot refer to promise or refer to request (although one can refer to a *particular* promise or request). However, one can certainly request or promise a hearer that referring will be done, or refer and, at the same time, make an indirect request ("The envelope, please?"). Combining such speech acts is no less an adequacy test for a planning system than is the composition of *request* and *inform*. Viewed from this standpoint of speech act compositionality, referring is not different, in principle, from illocutionary acts.

But propositional acts (in particular, referring) *are* different from illocutionary acts. Seen from a certain perspective, propositional acts are related to illocutionary ones as the structure and meaning of noun and verb phrases are related to the structure and meaning of sentences. Referring and predicating are the building blocks out of which illocutionary acts are constructed; in pragmatics, as in syntax and semantics, it must be shown how the whole is a function of its parts. One way of stating the problem is in terms of *pragmatic presuppositions*. The pragmatic presuppositions of a speech act can roughly be described as the class of propositions that is characteristically associated with the felicitous performance of that speech act. The truth of these propositions is mutually believed to be taken for granted by the participants (Kasher 1985). Now, it is difficult to see how such a class of pragmatic presuppositions is generated unless the pragmatic presuppositions associated with illocutionary acts are largely a function of the pragmatic presuppositions associated with *parts* of the illocutionary acts. For example, a pragmatic presupposition of the command "Show me the letter!" is that it is mutually

believed that a certain letter exists and that both speaker and hearer
know which one it is. This pragmatic presupposition is generated,
in turn, through other presuppositions associated with the referring
act: for example, that it is mutually believed that the use of the definite article in this case signals, say, an anaphoric link with a referring
expression mentioned earlier.

In a planning system generating illocutionary acts, there would
be operators whose executions would correspond to the performance
of a particular speech act. Let us say that **REFER** is the operator
corresponding to the referring act. In such a system, the pragmatic
presuppositions generated by the act of referring will be represented
by the mutually known effects of the execution of **REFER**. One
way of capturing the relation between referring and complete speech
acts, then, would be to show how the mutually known effects of the
referring act contribute to the mutually known effects of illocutionary
acts.

Syntax and semantics. In [direct] illocutionary acts, we have a
fairly precise correlation between syntax and semantics, on the one
hand, and illocutionary point on the other. Assertions and com-
mands, for example, have their syntactic counterparts in declarative
and imperative sentences, while performative verbs represent those
illocutionary acts that are being performed. But whereas a serious
utterance of an imperative sentence is almost always taken as a directive type of speech act, the serious utterance of a noun phrase –
even a definite noun phrase – is not necessarily an act of referring,
as we have already seen. Similarly, one can promise, say, to pay
one's debt by stating "I hereby promise to pay my debt," but merely
uttering "I hereby refer to a friend of mine" is hardly satisfactory.
Hence, the semantic and syntactic clues that enable the hearer to
recognize an illocutionary act do not help much as far as referring is
concerned.

Thus, we have four problems with respect to referring acts that seem
harder to resolve than their counterparts in a theory of illocutionary
acts:

1. What is the literal goal of a referring act?

2. What are its conditions of satisfaction?

3. How does referring contribute to the success of illocutionary
   acts?

4. When is a use of a noun phrase a referring use?

Answers to the first and second questions are given in Chapter 4. To a limited degree, I also address the third question: I show how changes that take place in a hearer's mental state as a result of a referring act contribute to other changes resulting from a broader speech act (in particular, a request). The fourth question has two parts. First, there is the problem of specifying the algorithm by means of which a hearer recognizes a noun phrase as a referring expression. This is an extremely difficult question and I shall not be discussing it in this work. Second, there is the problem of specifying the mental state that underlies a speaker's use of a noun phrase as a referring expression. In a sense, this entire study addresses this problem, and my suggested solution is summarized in Chapter 7.

1.3   Philosophical foundations

Let us return to the external perspective. From its standpoint we have the object that the speaker is thinking of, we have the referring expression used by him, and we ask how a hearer makes the connection. Once the question is formulated in these terms, however, it is easily apparent that it masks a more general problem. Never mind how the hearer recognizes the connection between a referring expression and an object. How is this connection established in the first place? What does it mean to say that the speaker has a particular object in mind? Does it mean that he is able to identify that object when he sees it? Does it mean that he knows something that is true of that particular object and no other?

Such questions lead to what may be called the philosophical problem of *reference*, which can roughly be phrased as follows: "How can thoughts (and sentences that articulate them) be *about* objects?" The problem seems simple enough, but, as was the case with the *referring* problem (i.e., how do we let our audience know what we are talking about?), the simplicity is deceptive. In effect a solution to the problem of reference elucidates the general mechanism that enables the mind (and, derivatively, language) to represent the world for us. It is not surprising, therefore, that the problem of reference has occupied a central position in the philosophical debate that has been going on since the very beginning of this century. The question is whether anyone interested in a computational model of referring should get involved in the problem of reference, philosophical baggage and all.

What are the options? It should be obvious that the referring problem and the problem of reference are not mutually independent. We could avoid philosophy altogether and start from scratch. This has been done in AI on occasion — with lamentable results, however. On the other hand, philosophical debates drag on forever. Major philosophical problems may go in and out of fashion, but they are never really "solved." If a computational model is what we are after, it would be hopeless for us to wait for the philosophical discussion of reference to reach a consensus.

The way out of this impasse is to recognize that the philosophy of language and mind can offer *research programs.* The term was introduced by Lakatos (1970), as a rational synthesis of Kuhn's notion of a scientific paradigm and Popper's principle of falsification (Kuhn 1962; Popper 1959). It essentially denotes a general scientific framework that offers a methodological foundation for investigating certain scientific problems. When I say that philosophy can provide research programs for the study of language, I mean something very much like what Lakatos had in mind: a theoretical framework that, when stated explicitly, is invaluable as a source of general principles. Thus, rather than ignoring the philosophical debate or attempting to maintain "neutrality," we should scan the philosophical landscape for the most promising general approach to the problem at hand. Once we find it, we should isolate its central theses, systematically identify the main objections to it, and evaluate the possibility of modifying the program as to overcome these objections. If the program still looks promising, we should stay with it, using it as a general guide for computational research. This is indeed the method employed here, with a substantial amount of space devoted to the construction, articulation, and modification of the selected philosophical framework — so much space, in fact, that this book is as much a philosophical essay with a computational bias as it is a study in computational linguistics. Once the philosophical framework is made explicit, the computational model follows rather naturally from it.

There are three steps in making this philosophical framework explicit. First, I describe in some detail what I call the *descriptive* approach to the problem of reference. The essence of this approach is that reference is determined by facts about the mind itself (e.g., the nature of mental representations), rather than by facts about the world outside the mind (e.g., the existence of a causal chain between mind and object). Then the objections to the descriptive approach are enumerated. Finally, after weighing these objections, I consider which parts of the descriptive approach should be modified.

1.4   Summary of Chapter 1

We hardly ever *tell* our hearer explicitly what object we are talking about, although we expect him to figure it out. Indeed, in general, we are very good at providing hearers with just enough information to enable them to understand the subject of the conversation. How do we manage that? This is the central question motivating this study. My intention is to specify the general principles that any computational model of referring should incorporate. These principles are derived from three methodological tenets. The first is that a theory of referring should explain how noun phrase usage is related to objects in the world (the *external* perspective), not how the use of one noun phrase is related to another (the *internal* perspective). The second is that referring is a speech act. The third is that a theoretical account of referring must be firmly anchored in a well-defined, well-defended philosophical framework.

The distinction between the two perspectives — the internal and the external — should be carefully drawn in the study of discourse. From the internal perspective the main focus is on the relation of coreference among symbols. From the external perspective, what is of major interest is the relation between symbols and the objects they represent. In the field of AI there is a tendency to concentrate on the internal perspective, but the external perspective is indispensable. Any system that combines linguistic and nonlinguistic actions, and that is capable of cooperative behavior, must be able to distinguish when a noun phrase has a referent in the real world from when it does not, when a particular type of knowledge of the referent is required from when it is not, when knowledge of the referent is presupposed from when it should actively be sought. Without the external perspective, we cannot even ask these questions, and this is the perspective that is adopted in this study.

Since referring is a speech act, a theory of referring is a *pragmatic* theory: it specifies and explains human competence in using referring expressions to achieve certain goals. Since the relation between referring expressions and a speaker's goal is what must be explained, it is natural to consider referring as planned action. This, in turn, requires showing how the use of referring expressions is systematically related to changes in both the hearer's and speaker's mental states. But although referring is a speech act, it differs from illocutionary

15

acts in four important ways, and consequently referring acts present four problems that are harder to resolve than their counterparts in a theory of illocutionary acts: (1) What is the literal goal of a referring act? (2) What are its conditions of satisfaction? (3) How does referring contribute to the success of illocutionary acts? (4) When is a use of a noun phrase a referring use?

Returning to the external perspective, it is clear that the referring problem (how do we let our audience know what it is we are talking about?) is a special case of a more general problem: how can thoughts (and sentences that articulate them) be *about* objects at all? This is a problem that has occupied a central position in the philosophical debate in the twentieth century. We cannot ignore this important debate, but on the other hand, we cannot wait for a philosophical resolution. The way out of such an impasse is to recognize that the philosophy of language and mind can offer *research programs*: theoretical frameworks that, when stated explicitly, are invaluable as a source of general principles. We should, then, scan the philosophical landscape for the most promising general approach to the problem at hand. Once we find it, we should isolate its central theses, systematically identify the main objections to it, and evaluate the possibility of modifying the program so as to overcome these objections. If the program still looks promising, we should use it as a general guide for computational research. This is indeed the method employed here.

2
The descriptive approach

2.1 The problem of reference

Suppose I tell you that my cat is hungry. There are four distinct entities, each participating in, and contributing to this simple linguistic event. First, there is the *sentence* uttered, namely, the declarative "My cat is hungry." Second, there is the *proposition* expressed by the sentence (or rather, by its utterance). Third, there is the *belief* I am trying to convey. Finally, there is the *speech act* that ties everything together, namely, the speech act of asserting that my cat is hungry.

Each entity in this narrative is categorically different from the rest: the utterance of a declarative sentence is a string of sounds (or signs), a proposition is a theoretical abstraction, a belief is a mental state, and an assertion is an act. These four entities can be generalized further. Instead of limiting ourselves to declarative sentences, we can consider sentences of all types. Instead of just beliefs, we can take into account other *propositional attitudes* such as desires, fears, intentions, hopes, and the like. Assertions, of course, are only one type of illocutionary act among many, and the notion of a proposition, usually associated with declarative sentences and beliefs exclusively, can be generalized by introducing the notion of *propositional content*, which is the content of both illocutionary acts and propositional attitudes (Searle 1969; 1983) . Thus, within every linguistic event we can isolate the sentence uttered, the propositional content, the propositional attitude, and the speech act.

There are obvious relations among these four entities. If we consider the case of the hungry cat again, it is clear that the choice of that particular sentence was no accident. The content of my belief about the cat is a proposition that is true if and only if my cat is hungry, and the best way to express this proposition is by asserting it, which is done, in turn, by the literal utterance of the sentence "My cat is hungry." This sentence is a perfect candidate for performing, expressing, and conveying the appropriate speech act, proposition, and belief, respectively. Not every utterance of a sentence is associated with a unique speech act, propositional content, and propositional attitude, of course. Nevertheless, theoretically interesting relations among the four entities obviously do hold, and the study of each is relevant to the study of language and the mind.

As mentioned earlier, the problem of reference is to determine how thoughts and sentences can be about objects. In searching for a more precise formulation, we may start by identifying four elements that can be found in every linguistic event in which reference is made to a particular object, and that correspond to the four entities discussed above. If we take up the case of the hungry cat again, there is, first, the *referring expression* "my cat." Then there is the *constituent* of the proposition introduced by the referring expression. The third element is the *mental representation* of the cat. Finally, there is the *speech act of referring* itself that ties all these elements together. These four elements obviously correspond to expressions, propositions, beliefs, and speech acts, respectively, and each highlights a different aspect of the general problem of reference. These four aspects are presented, as questions, in Figure 2.1.

Expressions:
How are referring expressions related to objects?

Propositions:
What propositions are expressed by sentences containing referring expressions?

Beliefs:
What is the role of mental representation in beliefs about objects?

Speech acts:
What is the correct analysis of the speech act of referring?

Figure 2.1: Main aspects of the reference problem

Referring expressions. As an illustration of the kind of issue associated with the first question, let us consider the philosophical debate about the way proper names designate. Frege ([1892]1975) believed that all names must have a *sense* that mediates between them and the objects they stand for. Searle (1958) rejects Frege's claim, but insists that each name must be "backed by" a set of *identifying descriptions*. Kripke ([1972]1980), on the other hand, sees names as lacking any intrinsic sense or descriptive content. According to him, names are related to objects through a special sort of causal chain stretching from the moment a name is given, to any particular use of that name. These different accounts attempt to provide a partial answer to the first question.

Propositions. To illustrate the point of the second question, we must distinguish between *general* and *singular* propositions. Let us suppose that the statement "The queen of England is ill" expresses the proposition *there is one and only one thing with the property of being the queen of England, and it is ill*. Such a proposition is called "general" because all references to particular things has been eliminated, and all that we have instead (apart from predicates) is a quantifier ("there is"), and a bound variable (represented by "thing" and "it"). A statement such as "7 is prime," on the other hand, is said to express the proposition *7 is prime*, which is called "singular." Note the vast difference between "7" and "The queen of England" as far as their contribution to the logical structure of the proposition is concerned: the referring expression "7" simply introduces the integer 7 into the proposition, but whatever is introduced by the phrase "The queen of England" in the foregoing example is surely to be distinguished from Her Majesty herself. Deciding whether the use of a referring expression results in a singular or general proposition is a central issue as far as the second question is concerned.

Beliefs. A crucial distinction for understanding the third question is that between *de dicto* and *de re* beliefs. A belief *de dicto* is a belief that a certain general proposition (*dictum*) is true. A belief *de re* is a belief about a particular thing (*res*) that it has a certain property. My belief that there are spies is *de dicto* but not *de re* since it does not attribute the property of being a spy to anyone in particular. The belief I have about myself that I am left-handed is certainly *de re* since I am attributing left-handedness to a particular person (namely, myself). My belief that the president of the United States in 1987 is old seems to be both *de dicto* and *de re*. First, it is the belief that the proposition *the president of the United States in 1987 is old* is true, and hence it is *de dicto*. In addition, the content of the belief contains a representation of Ronald Reagan, and thus the belief is about the man himself. Hence, in holding this belief, I am attributing the property of being old to Reagan, and so the belief is *de re* as well.

The problem expressed by the third question is that of characterizing the relation between *de dicto* and *de re* beliefs. There are two parts to this question: (1) are *de re* beliefs a subclass of *de dicto* ones? (2) which *de dicto* beliefs are not also *de re*? We can express the same thing in terms of *individuating representations*. Let an individuating representation be a representation whose descriptive content is satisfied by one and only one object. The point of the third question is whether an individuating representation is *necessary* and *sufficient* for a belief containing it to be *de re*. Note that there are four possible ways to characterize the role of such representations in *de re* beliefs: they are either necessary or sufficient, or neither of these, or both.

Referring. Finally, we get to the fourth question about referring as a speech act. Many aspects of this problem were already addressed in Chapter 1. As mentioned earlier, the intuitive purpose of referring is to let the hearer know what is being discussed. The problem is how to provide a general account of how this is accomplished.

Each question brings a different perspective to the general problem of reference: the first question is a semantic one (in the sense of relating language to the world), the second has to do with logical form, the third belongs to cognitive psychology, and the fourth deals with the way language is actually *used*. Of course, any answer to one question has some immediate implications for the other three.

The formulation of these four questions makes it easier to characterize a general approach to the problem of reference that I call *the descriptive research program*.

2.2   The descriptive research program

If a rough statement of the problem of reference is "how can thoughts and sentences be about objects?" the descriptive solution would be, in a word, "descriptive content." But, as the formulation had to be distilled into four distinct questions, the descriptive solution must be spelled out in some detail as well. At the same time, I do not intend to present here a full account of the predominant theories.

All I do here is reconstruct, as precisely and as succinctly as I can, the *general principles* that have guided major philosophers in their attempts to provide answers to the four questions corresponding to sentences, propositions, beliefs, and speech acts, respectively. These principles are enumerated in Figure 2.2.

What do the theses in Figure 2.2 mean? Underlying each of them are two simple ideas. The first is that reference is a function of *internal* (i.e., mental) representation. In other words, to refer to an object — either in thought or in speech — is essentially to have or invoke a mental representation of that object. The second idea is that the relation between a sentence or a thought and the object they are about is the relation of *denotation*, which in turn is a function of *descriptive content.* That is, a sentence or a thought about an object contains a referring expression or a concept with a certain descriptive content and, if this content is true of or is satisfied by a unique object, the expression or the concept *denotes* that object. Thus, the crux of the descriptive program is that *reference is entirely a matter of associating a mental state with descriptive content.* What exactly is meant by descriptive content and how it can be associated with mental states depend on the particular theory within the descriptive program, but the principle remains the same. Let me illustrate how this principle is reflected in each individual thesis.

(E) **Expressions:**

    Reference is determined by meaning.

(P) **Propositions:**

    Singular propositions cannot be believed, expressed, or understood.

(B) **Beliefs:**

    Individuating representation is both necessary and sufficient for a belief to be *de re.*

(S) **Speech acts:**

    Referring is performed by means of identifying descriptions.

Figure 2.2: Main postulates of the descriptive program

Referring expressions. At the level of expressions, descriptive content is associated with *meaning*. The only way a referring expression and an object can be matched, according to the descriptive program, is through the relation of denotation; which object is denoted is determined by the descriptive content associated with the referring expression. Since the requirement for having descriptive content extends to *all* types of referring expression, one of the consequences of Thesis (**E**) is that proper names and demonstratives are, in one sense or another, disguised descriptions.

Propositions. At the level of propositions, descriptive content is part of the notion of individuating representation, i.e. representations that denote particular objects. Since singular propositions do not contain any individuating representation of such an object, but rather the object itself, the point of Thesis (**P**) is to assert that some sort of individuating representation is necessary for believing, expressing, and understanding propositions about particular objects. Note that propositions are taken by philosophers to be the content of both beliefs and utterances; it is tacitly assumed that whatever is true of propositions *qua* content of beliefs, is also true of propositions *qua* content of utterances. In particular, Thesis (**P**) implies not only that an individuating representation is *meant* whenever a speaker expresses a proposition about a particular object, but that it is crucial for determining whether the utterance is true or false.

Beliefs. At the level of beliefs, the notion of an individuating representation provides the perspective from which (and only from which) objects can be thought about. Insisting, as Thesis (**B**) does, that an individuating representation is both necessary and sufficient for a belief to be *de re* means that beliefs about particular objects always depend on individuating representations, which in turn depend on descriptive content.

Speech acts. The goal of the speech act of referring is to identify an object for the hearer. This is done by using *identifying descriptions*, i.e., descriptions that are satisfied uniquely by the object to which the speaker intends to refer. Of course, it is not necessary to utter a fully identifying description each time referring is done, but the speaker's ability to provide such a description is necessary for referring to a particular object. Moreover, within the descriptive approach, the literal utterance of an identifying description is sufficient for referring to succeed, given normal input and output conditions. Needless to say, a description is identifying by virtue of its descriptive content.

Among philosophers of language and mind today, it is Searle who most explicitly identifies himself as working within the descriptive program. But the program's founding father is undoubtedly Frege, whose theory of sense and reference underlies all the theses listed in Figure 2.2. The basic postulate in Frege's theory is that every expression possesses both a sense and a reference (the reference may be nil). Roughly interpreted, the Fregean sense of a referring expression is the mode in which the object is presented to the agent, while the Fregean reference is the object itself. Thus, in Frege's theory, two names of the same person share the same reference but have different senses.

The Fregean postulate that every expression has both a sense and a reference is accompanied by three principles: (1) reference is determined by sense; (2) the sense of a complex expression is a function of the senses of its parts; (3) a belief is a relation between an agent and a sense of a sentence. These three principles entail Theses (E), (P), and (B). Since the notion of referring as an *act* was introduced by Strawson only in 1950, Thesis (S) could not be a part of Frege's theory, nor was Frege much interested in the communicative function of language. But, as Searle, who incorporated Strawson's account of referring into his theory of speech acts, specifically acknowledges, the speech act theory of reference is clearly within the Fregean tradition (Searle 1969, 77).

So far I have hardly mentioned Russell, whose theory of descriptions has long dominated discussions of reference and, to a large extent, still continues to do so. Russell's relation to the descriptive program is an interesting one. Strictly speaking, he is not part of it, since his theory of proper names is inconsistent with all of the descriptive program's theses. Nevertheless, to exclude Russell from the program altogether would, in my opinion, be quite misleading. To understand why, we need to review briefly the essential elements of Russell's theory. This is particularly important because Russell's theory plays an important role in providing the modifications that enable the descriptive program to overcome its difficulties and serve as a foundation for the computational model.

Russell's account of reference has both an epistemological and a semantic segment, closely related to each other. The epistemological segment describes how knowledge of objects is possible. The semantic segment describes how referring expressions are to be interpreted. Crucial to Russell's epistemology is the distinction between *knowledge by acquaintance* and *knowledge by description*([1910]1953). One has knowledge by acquaintance of an object when one has a direct cognitive relation with it, that is, when one is directly aware of the object itself. One has knowledge by description of an object when one knows that there exists one and only one object having a certain property. For example, since I am directly aware of a pain in my left knee, Russell would say that I have knowledge by acquaintance of my pain. On the other hand, I am not acquainted with the twelfth president of the United States, but I know that there was one and only one person in the world who was the twelfth president of the United States. Thus, I have knowledge by description of him. It is important to note that Russell's theory of knowledge contains two postulates: (1) every proposition that we can understand must be composed of constituents with which we are acquainted; (2) we do not have knowledge by acquaintance of physical objects (in fact, the only objects with which we are acquainted, according to Russell, are *sense data*, and possibly the *self*[1]).

Russell's account of names and descriptions mirrors his epistemological distinction between knowledge by acquaintance and knowledge by descriptions. A proper name designates its object *directly*, but has no meaning apart from the designated object. Thus, when such a name is employed, the object *itself* is a constituent of the proposition, which, in turn, is a singular one. But since we are never acquainted with physical objects, they cannot participate in propositions we can understand; consequently, the proper names we use to designate physical objects (including, of course, names given to people) are not really proper names at all but abbreviated descriptions. In fact, as far as names of particulars are concerned, only the deictic words "this" and "I" are true proper names (*logically* proper names, as Russell calls them), corresponding to sense data and the self, respectively — the only particulars with which we can actually be acquainted.

A description, on the other hand, does not designate an object directly. Rather, it is capable of *denoting* an object that satisfies its descriptive content. The contribution made by a definite description to a proposition is rather complex, but, as was the case with proper names, the analysis reflects the epistemological distinction discussed earlier.[2] We have seen that to have knowledge by description is

---

[1] At one time Russell considered self-knowledge to be knowledge by acquaintance. Eventually he changed his mind (ibid., 211, n. 1).

[2] I am disregarding indefinite descriptions here.

to know that one and only one object possesses a certain property. Thus, if a definite description is part of a statement, the contribution of the description to the content of that statement is a logical structure asserting that one and only one object possesses a certain property. Such a logical structure is a propositional function. As a concrete example, consider the statement "The president is old." The contribution of the definite description to the proposition expressed by this statement is taken to be *x is the president and no one else is*. The predicate "is old" adds another propositional function, namely, *x is old*, while the statement as a whole simply asserts that, for some value *x*, the complex propositional function *x is the president and no one else is, and x is old* is true. In standard first-order logic, this is expressed as

$$(\exists x)(\mathbf{PRES(x)} \,\&\, (\forall y)(\mathbf{PRES(y)} \rightarrow x = y) \,\&\, \mathbf{OLD(x)})$$

Now it should be obvious why it would be quite misleading to exclude Russell's theory from the descriptive program. His account of logically proper names is indeed inconsistent with the descriptive theses, but, according to Russell, the only logically proper names for particulars are "this" and "I."[3] Since all other referring expressions are descriptions (abbreviated or not), what should really matter to us is whether Russell's theory of *descriptions* is part of the descriptive program. Let us consider each of the four theses in turn. For reasons that are essentially technical, Russell claims that descriptions are not meaningful in isolation, only within the context of a sentence (ibid., 215). Yet, he definitely recognizes that a description denotes by virtue of its descriptive content, which is a function of the meanings of the words that appear in that description. Hence, if reference to physical objects in Russell's theory exists by virtue of denotation, and denotation is a function of meaning, then Thesis (**E**) still holds. Moreover, since we are never acquainted with physical objects, we can never believe, express, or understand singular propositions about them. Hence, as far as physical objects are concerned, we have Thesis (**P**) and, since all *de re* beliefs about such objects are analyzed in terms of denoting descriptions, which in turn provide individuating representations, Thesis (**B**) is true as well. As for Thesis (**S**), Russell, like Frege, was not much interested in language as a system of communication, but he would have agreed that the

---

[3] If self-knowledge is indeed knowledge by acquaintance, *for each person*, that person's name is also a logically proper name.

purpose of using referring expressions in conversation is to identify an object for the hearer. I don't think he would have been very impressed by this fact, but he would surely not have denied it.

This discussion of Russell's theory concludes my characterization of the descriptive program. I now turn to arguments against it.

2.3   Objections

The descriptive research program, including Russell's theory of descriptions, has dominated the debate about reference for most of this century. However, in the last two decades or so, a new approach to the problem of reference has been developed. The new approach, to be sure, is not entirely separable from earlier theories. Nevertheless, it marks a radical departure from the descriptive program as a whole and, as a philosophical movement, it advocates an entirely new program. The new theory flatly rejects all four theses mentioned in Figure 2.2, but offers an alternative: if, according to the old program, *describing* the object is the way to reach it, the new approach takes *pointing* to be the central mechanism of reference. If the core of the old program is descriptive content, which mediates between object and mind, the core of the new one is the notion of a causal chain leading from the object directly to the agent. The most significant difference between the two, therefore, is this: according to the new approach, reference is determined by facts *outside* the mind, in contrast with the descriptive program, which seeks to explain reference in terms of properties of mental states.[4]

2.3.1   The referential/attributive distinction

The shift from the descriptive program to the new approach was initiated by Donnellan ([1966]1971), when he introduced a distinction between the *referential* and *attributive* uses of definite descriptions. Since the referential/attributive distinction (*Donnellan's distinction* for short) plays an important role in arguments against the descriptive program, it should be presented first. Here is how Donnellan himself first describes it.

> To illustrate [the] distinction, in the case of a single sentence, consider the sentence, "Smith's murderer

---

[4]The central architects of the new approach to reference are Donnellan ([1966]1971; 1970), Kaplan (1977; 1978), Kripke ([1972]1980), Perry (1977; 1979), and Putnam (1975).

is insane." Suppose first that we come upon poor Smith foully murdered. From the brutal manner of the killing and the fact that Smith was the most lovable person in the world, we might exclaim, "Smith's murderer is insane." I will assume, to make it a simpler case, that in a quite ordinary sense we do not know who murdered Smith (though this is not in the end essential to the case). This, I shall say, is an attributive use of the definite description.

The contrast with such a use of the sentence is one of those situations in which we expect and intend our audience to realize whom we have in mind when we speak of Smith's murderer and, most importantly, to know that it is this person about whom we are going to say something.

For example, suppose that Jones has been charged with Smith's murder and has been placed on trial. Imagine that there is a discussion of Jones's odd behavior at his trial. We might sum up our impression of his behavior by saying, "Smith's murderer is insane." If someone asks to whom we are referring, by using this description, the answer here is "Jones." This, I shall say, is a referential use of a definite description. (ibid., 198)

The intuitive presentation of Donnellan's distinction seems simple enough. Later on I shall argue that this simplicity is misleading; for the time being, at least, let us accept the distinction with no qualifications. The important features to note are as follows. In the referential use, the intended referent can be identified even though no single entity fits the description used or, alternatively, more than one does. The intended referent may also be identified even if something else altogether fits the description. In Donnellan's example, the speaker would have referred successfully to Jones in the trial even if Jones had not been the murderer. In the attributive use, on the other hand, if nothing fits the description, no entity can be said to have been picked out and referred to.

Consequently, if nothing fits the description in the referential use, the speech act may still be successful. If the speech act is an assertion, the speaker may still say something true with respect to his intended referent. If the speech act is a command regarding the intended referent, the command can still be obeyed — and so on for other speech acts as well. This is not the case, however, in the attributive use; if nothing fits the description, the assertion cannot be true of anything, the order cannot be obeyed, etc.

Thus, a description in referential usage is just a tool for identifying the referent; other descriptions that can perform the same task may also be employed. Those that are used attributively, on the other hand, can be deemed "essential." In a sense, they are indeed irreplaceable. The immediate, intuitive reason for this is that, in the referential usage, the speaker can be said to have a particular object in mind. There is a particular entity to be identified. In attributive usage, however, the speaker is referring to whoever or whatever fits the description and there is no particular entity to be identified apart from the description employed.

To the surprise of many, Donnellan's distinction turned out to play an important role in arguing against each of the four major theses of the descriptive program enumerated in Figure 2.2. Consequently, Donnellan's distinction will be used here as a methodological tool for the systematic presentation of general objections to the descriptive approach. This does not mean that all objections to the descriptive program are sustained or nullified by Donnellan's distinction. Kripke ([1972]1980), for example, has attacked significant parts of the descriptive program very forcefully, while at the same time rejecting some of the alleged consequences of Donnellan's distinction (Kripke 1977). But my purpose here is not to discuss arguments for or against particular elements of the descriptive program. My interest in the descriptive approach lies in its value as a research program, and Donnellan's distinction is an excellent tool for characterizing the general problems that the descriptive program has to resolve.

2.3.2 Away with meanings

At the level of referring expressions, the central postulate of the descriptive program is Thesis (**E**): reference is determined by meaning. The basic idea underlying this thesis is simply this: the only way to establish the required relation between a referring expression and an object is by having a descriptive content that is associated with both of them. This descriptive content is, in a loose sense, the meaning of the expression. But it seems that, in the referential uses of definite descriptions, the descriptive content plays no direct role in establishing the relation between the expression and the object. The expression "Smith's murderer" in its referential use refers (in Donnellan's example) to Jones, but the descriptive content seems irrelevant. The expression will refer to Jones whether he is the murderer or not.

But the challenge to Thesis (**E**) transcends the claim that, in some cases, reference is established independently of meaning. Underlying this thesis is a certain view of semantics that can be characterized by three general principles. The first is that meaning determines truth conditions. According to this principle, when one knows the meaning of a sentence, one also knows under what circumstances the sentence is true. A second principle is the Fregean dictum, already mentioned in a different form, which affirms that the meaning of a sentence as a whole is a function of the meaning of its parts. A third principle is that the meanings of individual words are determined by the general conventions of the language, no matter what the speaker wants them to mean. Combining these three principles, we arrive at the notion of semantic independence: with the exception of words that are by nature context-dependent (such as pronouns, demonstratives, and so on), the role of expressions in determining the truth conditions of what is said is independent of the speaker's intentions in using those expressions.

Such a view, however, seems to be inconsistent with Donnellan's distinction. For it seems that two literal utterances of the same sentence may differ in their truth conditions, depending on whether the definite description is used referentially or attributively. Compare, in Donnellan's example, the two utterances of "Smith's murderer is insane." In the first case, in which the description is used attributively, the speaker means *Smith's murderer, whoever he is*, and the statement will be true if and only if the one and only murderer of Smith is insane. In the second case, when the description is used referentially, the speaker means *Jones*, and whatever is said is true if and only if *Jones* is insane. Thus, in a limited sense, it seems that Humpty Dumpty was right after all: you can utter the words "Smith's murderer," and it is entirely up to you whether you meant *whoever murdered Smith*, or *Jones*. In other words, it seems that one and the same expression — "Smith's murderer" — plays a different role in forming the truth conditions of whatever is said, depending on whether the speaker intends to refer to a specific individual or just to the murderer of Smith, whoever he might be.[5]

---

[5] One way to maintain the independence of semantics in the face of Donnellan's distinction is to claim that definite descriptions are semantically ambiguous. But

2.3.3 *In praise of singular propositions*

The central postulate of the descriptive program at the level of propositions is Thesis (**P**): one cannot believe, express, or understand singular propositions. In other words, what a referring expression brings into the proposition is never the object itself — which is just a philosopher's fancy way of saying that an individuating representation of the object is essential for reference to take place, at least as far as physical objects are concerned. This view, however, is challenged by the referential use of definite descriptions. I shall illustrate the argument with respect to Russell's theory of descriptions. The same argument can be applied to other descriptive theories as well.

A standard objection to Russell's theory of descriptions is that, in many uses of definite descriptions, application of the theory yields the wrong results. When a speaker says "The computer is down," it is clear that he does *not* mean that there is one and only one computer in the world and that it is down. The standard reply is that the referring expression uttered is an elliptical form of a uniquely denoting description. What the speaker really means is, say, that the VAX-750 in Room EK247 at SRI International is not operational at the moment. There is no problem in applying the Russellian analysis to such a complete form of the description.

However, when we look at some referential uses of definite descriptions, it seems that the standard reply won't do as it stands. Consider again an utterance of "The computer is down," in which the definite description, "the computer," is used referentially. It is clear that the computer can be described more fully in many ways that are not equivalent — but which of these alternatives is the one actually meant by the speaker? In other words, which of them should be taken as part of the proposition that the speaker expressed?

First, it should be noted that in many cases the hearer may complete the description in a different way from the one originally intended by the speaker, and still it may not be clear that the hearer misunderstood what is said. For example, suppose a speaker uttered the above sentence, meaning "The computer in room EK247 is down," and that the hearer understands what is being said to mean "The computer used by the Natural-Language Group at SRI is down." Has the hearer misunderstood the speaker? It is by no means clear that he has: since the machine in EK247 *is* the one used

---

this is really a desperate move. As we shall see, there is a much better way to solve the problem.

by the Natural-Language Group, the hearer has identified the right computer and he now knows that it is down. Shouldn't this suffice?

Second, in many cases the speaker himself may not conceptualize a complete description at all; thus he would not know which complete description should be considered to be the one he really *meant*. A speaker may utter "The computer is down" without intending that the hearer pinpoint any *particular* individuating property of the computer.

Third, in the radical case of the referential use in which the description misses the mark entirely (e.g., "Smith's murderer" used in reference to Jones, who is innocent), "completing" the description is simply impossible. Moreover, when asked after the utterance which description he *really* meant, the speaker may be at a loss to respond. He would probably be inclined to say that he meant "Smith's murderer," but now, after realizing that Jones is not the murderer, he is no longer sure of what he did mean. This is not to say that the speaker is not readily capable, if challenged, of replacing "Smith's murderer" with a new, more accurate description, but it would not be what he *meant* before.

In any case, as these examples illustrate, it seems that the speaker would not care much *which* description he actually meant, or which was the accurate one, as long as the hearer was able to identify the right person or the right computer.

A natural conclusion to be drawn at this stage of the argument is that in referential usage, the only thing relevant to the proposition that the speaker is trying to express is the object per se, independently of any of its descriptions. In other words, in the referential case, it seems that the only thing relevant to the truth conditions of what the speaker is trying to express is the object itself; if this is indeed so, why not just take the object itself as a constituent of the proposition?

Thus we arrive at what Kaplan has called the semantics of *direct reference*, according to which referential uses of definite descriptions (as well as proper names and demonstratives) are rigid designators (i.e., expressions that designate the same object in all the possible worlds in which it would exist), and utterances containing such referring expressions express singular propositions. Such a semantics, of course, flies in the face of Thesis (**P**): singular propositions, according to this account, are frequently believed, expressed, and understood.

31

2.3.4 The status of de re beliefs

At the level of belief, the central postulate of the descriptive program is Thesis (**B**): individuating representations are both necessary and sufficient for a belief to be *de re*. The attempts to reject Thesis (**B**) and Donnellan's distinction are related first by a simple extension of Thesis (**P**): if the semantics of direct reference is accepted and singular propositions can be the content of beliefs, then such beliefs *de re* contain no individuating representations. But the connection between Donnellan's distinction and propositional attitudes goes beyond this. In fact, some philosophers would say that Donnellan's distinction and the *de re* vs. *de dicto* dichotomy are very closely related to each other (Hintikka 1967). The idea is simply this: when a speaker asserts that so-and-so is such-and-such, the belief he expresses, if he uses the definite description referentially, is *de re*. If, on the other hand, the definite description is used attributively, the belief expressed is *de dicto*, but not *de re*. Conversely, when a speaker wishes to express a *de re* belief, the referring expression he utters will be used referentially. If the belief is *de dicto* (and is concerned with a particular object), the referring expression uttered will be used attributively.[6]

Later on I shall examine the rationale for identifying Donnellan's distinction with the *de re* vs. *de dicto* dichotomy. For now, I'd like to point out how such an identification undermines Thesis (**B**): if indeed (the expression of) *de re* beliefs and referential usage always go hand in hand, and if, in referential usage, individuating representation is not relevant for what the speaker *means*, why should such representation be relevant to what he *believes*? In other words, if individuating representation is neither necessary nor sufficient for referential uses to be successful, it should be neither necessary nor sufficient for *de re* beliefs.[7]

---

[6] Kripke (1977) thinks that the identification of Donnellan's distinction with the *de dicto* vs. *de re* dichotomy is entirely without merit, but in my opinion, his argument misses the point. Kripke argues that in *de re* reports of beliefs — i.e., in constructions such as "Concerning Smith's murderer, Ralph believes that he is insane" — descriptions can be used *either* referentially or attributively. The same can be said with regard to *de dicto* reports of beliefs such as "Ralph believes that Smith's murderer is insane." This is true enough, but it does not affect the contention that, in *expressing* a *de re* belief (rather than reporting someone else's), a description is always used referentially and, whenever a description is used attributively, the belief *expressed* is *de dicto*.

[7] Cf. Burge (1977). Burge's argument that *de re* beliefs are not a subclass of the *de dicto* type is similar to Donnellan's argument that, at least in some

2.3.5 Identification reconsidered

At the level of speech acts, the main thesis of the descriptive program is Thesis (S): referring is performed by means of identifying descriptions. But when we use a description attributively, even though we are certainly trying to let the hearer know what we are talking about, we don't seem to *identify* anything for him. We don't seem to do that because, at least in a strong intuitive sense, we are not able to identify the object even for ourselves: when a speaker says "Smith's murderer, *whoever he is*, is insane," he is obviously talking about Smith's murderer. But, Donnellan would argue, there is no particular person whom he is able to identify as Smith's murderer, either for himself or for the hearer. Thus, on this account, Thesis (S) is at best misleading, since it ignores an important, nonidentifying function of referring expressions. On the other hand, Donnellan (1970) argues, even though in the referential use we do identify an object for the hearer, we do not necessarily do it by means of identifying descriptions — at least not in the sense intended by Strawson and Searle. Thus, Donnellan's argument forces a problem on the speech act theorist: if (as Strawson and Searle maintain) the central concept in the analysis of referring is identification by means of identifying descriptions, then in the referential use we seem to have identification without identifying descriptions, and in the attributive use we seem to have identifying descriptions (in the technical sense of speech acts theory) without identification. On the other hand, if we want a unified account of referring that includes both referential and attributive usage, we cannot take our intuitive understanding of the notion of identification for granted. We must specify precisely in what sense identification takes place in both types of usage.

Donnellan's rejection of the speech act thesis concludes this discussion of the descriptive program. What I have tried to do is to show how Donnellan's distinction plays a role in repudiation of the descriptive program as a whole. The question now is whether such a total rejection is justified.

2.4   Motivation

So far I have characterized in some detail the descriptive program, as well as some of its problems, and have introduced the program's

---

referential uses, no particular description can be picked out as the one *meant* by the speaker.

leading rival. At this point, a computational linguist or an artificial intelligence researcher might raise two important questions. First, given that what we are after is a computational model of referring, does it matter really which program we choose? Second, assuming that it does matter, why — given the objections that the descriptive program must respond to, and given the availability of an alternative — should we stay with the descriptive program?

In this section I answer these questions in a way that can be summarized as follows. For a computational model, it matters a great deal which approach is chosen because referring requires reasoning about the beliefs, desires, and intentions of other agents; this in turn requires an adequate account of the *content* of belief. It is precisely with respect to the content of belief (and other propositional attitudes) that the descriptive program and the new, or *causal*, approach differ radically. The descriptive program, no doubt, must undergo a fair amount of revision to eliminate its difficulties, but its main thrust stands unchallenged, in my opinion. Furthermore, upon closer scrutiny, it becomes clear that, as far as an accounting for the content of beliefs is concerned, the causal approach has so far had really very little to offer.

In order to make sense out of the behavior of others, we attribute to them beliefs, desires, intentions, and other propositional attitudes. For example, if you ask me why my neighbor gets into his car every morning, the most reasonable answer I can give you is that he *wants* to get to work and that he *believes* the car can take him there. Moreover, very frequently we attempt to achieve our goals by trying to change the beliefs and desires of others. This would be quite impossible if we did not have some idea to begin with as to the kind of beliefs and desires they possess. Thus, an important part of our model of the world around us is a representation of what we take to be the beliefs, desires, and intentions of others.

The role of propositional attitudes and their representations is particularly obvious when we try to model our linguistic behavior. As we have seen in Chapter 1, the central idea underlying computational speech act theory is that the performance of a speech act is the result of the speaker's planning to affect the hearer's conception of the speaker's intentions, beliefs, and desires. Thus, a computational model of any speech act, including that of referring, must be able to represent someone else's beliefs. But the notion of a belief makes no sense without a fairly precise notion of what the *content* of a belief is. It is the *content* of a particular belief that sets it apart from all others, and it makes no sense to represent that belief without somehow representing its content. Hence, a model of referring must begin with some notion of the contents of beliefs about particular objects, i.e., *de re* beliefs. Note, incidentally, that the term 'content' is used here to mean *whatever* individuates beliefs. That is, whatever the content of a belief, two beliefs are the same if and only if they have the same content.

Now, if the notion regarding the content of a *de re* belief is important for a model of referring, we cannot remain neutral with respect to choosing between the two research programs. According to the descriptive program, as we have seen, an essential component in the content of a *de re* belief is a representational entity that mediates between the belief and the object it is about. According to the causal approach, on the other hand, the relation between the belief and the object it is about is *direct*, and — at least according to the causal approach in its original form — the content of a *de re* belief is a *singular proposition* consisting of the object itself plus a propositional function. So, even at the level of formal representations of beliefs, the choice between the two programs is a significant decision. But much more is obviously at stake. The contrast between the two accounts of content is a reflection of the far more significant difference between the two programs. In the descriptive program, reference is determined by mental states: when the agent *apprehends* (Frege's term) the representational entity, reference is assured. In the causal approach, by contrast, reference is determined (at least in part) by the objective situation, quite independently of what the agent himself may think or believe.

The difference between the two positions has far-reaching implications not only for a general theory of mind, but for particular computational models as well. Imagine, for example, the initial steps in designing an intelligent system that is supposed to recognize, manipulate, and discuss objects in its environment. Such a system would have to have knowledge of objects, as well as the ability to represent and reason about the various beliefs, desires and expectations of other intelligent agents with which it is supposed to interact. If the system designer were to take the descriptive approach, he would assume that (1) internal representations of objects are essential for such a system; (2) a successful act of referring involves invocation of an internal representation in the hearer; and (3) these internal representations must be rich enough in descriptive content to provide a mechanism for reference to succeed. The main task of the designer, therefore, would be to look for appropriate data structures that play the same role as internal representations in various computational activities. Perhaps the most obvious choice at this stage of AI development is data structures that encode formulas of first-order logic, although this is by no means the only possible way.

On the other hand, if the designer takes a causal approach to reference, he would seek computational techniques that emphasize objective correlations between a world state in which, say, the Empire State Building exists, and a machine state that can be said to contain the information that the Empire State Building exists. A practical way to implement such an account of *de re* beliefs may be borrowed, perhaps, from the situated-automata approach to knowledge representation. According to that approach, a machine state S is said to contain the (true) information that P if and only if P is a world condition guaranteed to hold whenever the initial state of the machine is coupled to a world state W and an input string that is fed into the machine while the latter is in its initial state causes the machine to be in state S (Rosenschein 1985). It may be that the situated-automata approach to knowledge representation can be extended to representations of *belief* — in particular, *de re* belief.[8]

The difference between the two competing research programs is therefore computationally significant, and my contention is that a rational choice ought to favor the descriptive program. Obviously, I do not presume to "refute" the causal approach — I do not believe that research programs can be "refuted" — but I think that the causal approach suffers from a major weakness that, in my opinion, far outweighs the difficulties faced by the descriptive program. This weakness is related to the notion of the content of a belief. But before stating my case against the causal approach, I need to say at the outset why I do not regard the difficulties of the descriptive program to be as devastating as is commonly thought.

---

[8]There is no doubt that the characterization of a state in which an agent *knows* something must take into account not only the agent's internal state but also how the world is. After all, for an agent to know that P, P must be true. Thus, nothing prevents the descriptive theorist from adopting the situated-automata approach for knowledge representation. The dispute between the descriptive and the causal theorists is whether facts outside the mind are relevant to the characterization of *belief*. Incidentally, the descriptive theorist does not deny, of course, that causal explanations play an important role in understanding *why* someone holds a *de re* belief. For example, it is obvious that, in general, evidence is causally grounded. The descriptive theorist would insist, however, that what the belief is about is determined solely by its descriptive content.

The descriptive program can be interpreted as a general framework for two distinct (albeit related) projects. The first project is the attempt to provide a theory of meaning for singular terms. The second project is the attempt to construct a theory of mind. The arguments against the descriptive program are most powerful when the focus is on meaning: for example, it is widely accepted that Kripke's criticism of the descriptive theory of proper names (Kripke [1972]1980) is correct. But there is a tendency to extrapolate from problems of (linguistic) meaning to alleged inadequacies of the descriptive program as characterizing the general principles that underlie a theory of mind. Now, in trying to provide a model of referring, we are much more interested, for obvious reasons, in understanding the mind than we are in a theory of meaning. The latter per se cannot help us with questions of rationality, planning, actions, intentions, knowledge representation, and reasoning — topics of relevance to a computational account of communication (as well as to other cognitive models). Hence, as far as a model of referring is concerned, the main objections to the descriptive program are valid only if problems arising from a descriptive theory of meaning are indeed carried over to a theory of mind. I intend to argue that this is not the case.

Let us turn now to the problems that must be overcome by the causal approach if it is to be a real alternative to the descriptive program. I shall start by stating a premise that I take to be trivially true. I call it the *trivial principle*:

Trivial principle: It is impossible both to hold and not to hold the same belief.

It is important that the triviality of this claim be appreciated. This is not a characterization of our rationality. I am not actually claiming that it is impossible to hold both a belief and its negation. Although this is not particularly recommended, one can certainly hold the belief that P and, at the same time, hold the belief that not P. A belief and its negation are two distinct beliefs and, if one chooses to hold both, one is free to do so. But an agent cannot both hold and not hold the *same* belief any more than a geometric shape can be both a square and a circle.

Now, what is the content of a *de re* belief? Let us take a concrete example. Suppose Ralph believes of Wiley that he is a spy. Or — to attribute a *de re* belief to Ralph in a more dramatic way — let

37

Ralph himself point to Wiley and say: "I believe that this man is a spy!" Thus, there is no doubt that Ralph has a *de re* belief about Wiley, and its content, according to the causal theory (at least in its original form), is the singular proposition:

(2.1) Spy(*wiley*).

But the singular proposition cannot be the *complete* specification of the content of Ralph's belief because of the *trivial principle*. Suppose that, on a certain occasion (say, on the beach), Ralph points to Wiley and says "I believe this man is a spy." Suppose that at another time (say, in a supermarket), Ralph points to Wiley and says "I do not believe this man is a spy." Let us assume that Ralph is sincere on both occasions, and that his only problem is his failure to recognize Wiley in the supermarket as the man he saw earlier on the beach. If the *complete* content of Ralph's belief is a singular proposition, Ralph's first utterance shows that he holds a belief whose content is expressed by (2.1), while his second utterance shows that he does *not* hold the very same belief. But this is impossible according to the *trivial principle*.[9]

It is important not to confuse the problem this example poses for the causal theorist with that of the cognitive significance of *utterances*. Two utterances differ in their cognitive significance if a rational agent can accept one as true while rejecting the other. In the foregoing example, it is clear that an utterance on the beach of "This man is a spy" (coupled with a pointing gesture toward Wiley) would be accepted as true by Ralph, while the very same utterance and gesture in the supermarket would be rejected. Since, according to the causal theorist, the two utterances express the same proposition,

---

[9]Donnellan once suggested to me that (2.1) is indeed the complete content of Ralph's belief. When Ralph thinks to himself in the supermarket "I do not believe this man is a spy," Ralph is simply wrong. As a matter of fact, Donnellan suggested, Ralph *does* believe the man in the supermarket is a spy, but Ralph himself is not aware of this fact about himself (I do not know whether Donnellan still holds this view). Such a position, of course, amounts to abandoning the presumption of *positive introspection*, i.e., the presumption that, when an agent believes *P*, he also believes that he believes *P*. Note that Ralph's case can also be described in terms of *knowledge*: Ralph may know that the man he sees on the beach is a spy, while not knowing whether the man in the supermarket is one. Hence, if Donnellan's suggestion is to be maintained, Ralph may know something without knowing that he knows. Giving up positive introspection with respect to both knowledge and belief is not only extremely unintuitive, but, as Moore (1980, 16) notes, has dire consequences for formal accounts of planning.

it is not apparent what should account for the difference in cognitive significance. This is indeed a thorny problem for a causal theorist (Wettstein 1986), but the problem of the cognitive significance of *utterances* is not our concern. In fact, my point has nothing to do with natural language at all. If we could somehow grasp the content of Ralph's beliefs directly, we could have dispensed with Ralph's utterances altogether. My argument is simply this: (1) *believing* is a relation between an agent and a content; (2) Ralph cannot hold and yet not hold a belief any more than a beer bottle can both be in the cooler and not in it; (3) if the content of the belief attributing "spyhood" to Wiley is a singular proposition, Ralph would then have to both hold and not hold the same belief; hence, singular propositions cannot by themselves be contents of beliefs. Nothing here hinges on the cognitive significance of utterances.

If the singular proposition is not the complete content of Ralph's belief, some element of content is missing. Let Ralph's mode of presentation (of Wiley) be *by definition* that missing element. We do not know at this point what a mode of presentation is. What we do know is that a mode of presentation, in the sense described above, is necessary regardless of what one's theory of the content of *de re* beliefs is. The *trivial principle* simply requires it.

Several causal theorists have recognized that singular propositions do not suffice to individuate beliefs, and have suggested various remedies (Barwise and Perry 1983; Kaplan 1977; Perry 1977). But these remedies do not seem to me adequate, because they do not take seriously enough the need for modes of presentation. Whatever we take such modes to be, they must satisfy the following condition, which I call the *basic constraint*.

> **Basic constraint:** For every mode of presentation M_1 and M_2, if $M_1 = M_2$, then, if Ralph believes Wiley to be a spy under M_1, he also believes Wiley to be a spy under M_2.

I take the *basic constraint* to be as self-evident as the *trivial principle*. It is nothing more than an instantiation of Leibnitz's Law: if two things are identical, whatever is true of one is true of the other. However, if one feels uncomfortable applying Leibnitz's Law in a context of beliefs, all we need do for reassurance is to transform the *basic constraint* into its equivalent:

> **Basic constraint (second version):** For every mode of presentation M_1 and M_2, if Ralph believes Wiley to be a spy under M_1 and does *not* believe Wiley to be a spy under M_2, then $M_1 \neq M_2$.

In its second version, the *basic constraint* is simply a restatement of the initial motivation for introducing modes of presentation into the content of *de re* beliefs. If the constraint is not satisfied, it is easy to construct circumstances in which the *trivial principle* is violated.

Now, from the *basic constraint* on any theory of presentation modes it is possible to derive another principle, which I shall call the *individuation principle*. It is this:

> **Individuation principle:** If M is a mode of presentation under which Ralph believes Wiley to be a spy, then, in each possible world that is compatible with Ralph's beliefs, one and only one object is presented to Ralph under M.

What the *individuation principle* means is that modes of presentation — whatever they are — must carry out an individuation function within one's network of beliefs. In other words, if M, the mode of presentation under which Ralph believes Wiley to be a spy, is a concept, it is an individual concept instantiated by a unique object in each possible world compatible with Ralph's beliefs. If M is a description, it is a definite description denoting a unique object in each world compatible with Ralph's beliefs. If M is a causal chain, it "determines" a unique object in each world compatible with Ralph's belief, and so on with regard to anything a theory of presentation modes might come up with.

Incidentally, the argument for the *individuation principle* does not depend upon the concept of "possible worlds." States of affairs, alternative circumstances, situations, etc., would do equally well. As a matter of fact, as far as I am concerned, we can dispense with such terminology altogether and rephrase the *individuation principle* as follows: if M is a mode of presentation under which Ralph believes Wiley to be a spy, then Ralph believes that one and only one object is presented to him under M. This version, however, can be interpreted as implying that Ralph is aware of presentation modes, a claim that the causal theorist may deny (for example, by arguing that modes of presentation are really causal chains). In other words, phrasing the *individuation principle* in terms of possible worlds leaves open the question of whether the content of Ralph's belief is "in his head" or not. Another reason for using the apparatus of possible worlds is that the argument for the *individuation principle* is easier to state in this manner.

The argument for the *individuation principle* is, in essence, identical to the original motivation for modes of presentation. Let us suppose that the *individuation principle* is false and, to make the argument more concrete, let us assume that, in our theory of content, modes of presentation are nonindividuating *concepts*. Suppose, for example, that the mode of presentation under which Ralph believes Wiley to be a spy is *man on the beach*. Since Ralph takes Wiley to be a man on the beach, this concept is instantiated by at least one individual in every world compatible with Ralph's beliefs. As this is a nonindividuating concept, however, it is certainly possible for Ralph to believe that, at another time, he sees a different man on the beach; Ralph has no opinion as to whether or not he is a spy. Thus, on one occasion Ralph thinks to himself "I believe this man on the beach is a spy," whereas at another time he thinks "I do not believe this man on the beach is a spy." But suppose that on both occasions the man really is Wiley (although Ralph does not realize that). If the complete content of Ralph's belief is

(2.2) Spy(*wiley*) [under presentation mode: *man on beach*],

then we again find Ralph both holding and not holding the same belief. But this would be impossible, since it, too, violates the *trivial principle*.

I have borrowed this argument from Schiffer (1978), who uses it to show that nonindividuating concepts cannot be modes of presentation. But the same argument can be easily generalized to show that the *individuation principle* must be right, no matter what one takes modes of presentation to be. The schema of the argument is as follows. Let us assume that the *individuation principle* is false. There are then possible worlds compatible with Ralph's beliefs in which two distinct individuals are presented to Ralph under M. Nothing prevents Ralph from believing that one of them is a spy while *not* believing that the other is. But, since Ralph may fail to recognize that the man is Wiley in both cases, we have a situation in which Ralph believes Wiley to be a spy under M while *not* believing Wiley to be a spy under M. This contradicts the *basic constraint*, as well as, of course, the *trivial principle*. Hence, our hypothesis that the *individuation principle* is false must be incorrect.

The *individuation principle* holds no surprises for the descriptive theorist. The only thing missing there, he would say, is the realization that modes of presentation do not merely determine a unique object in worlds that are compatible with Ralph's beliefs. They determine the *referent*, i.e., what the belief is about in the *actual* world, whether this world is compatible with Ralph's beliefs or not. As this is, indeed, what modes of presentation are supposed to do in the descriptive program, we can begin to see why the latter is so attractive. Since the *individuation principle* holds in any case, individuating representations seem made to order for a theory of reference. Thus, in the descriptive program we have a stronger version of the *individuation principle*, which I call the *Fregean principle*:

> **Fregean principle:** Modes of presentation determine what a belief is about.

Now, according to the descriptive theory, whatever anchors a belief to the actual world is conceptual, or at least mental in nature. But the causal theorist insists that the object a *de re* belief is about is determined by a referential, presumably causal *chain*, beginning with the object outside Ralph's mind and — as if by a domino effect — progressing through Ralph's various mental states (perceiving Wiley, remembering him, etc.), and terminating in Ralph's belief state concerning Wiley and the property of being a spy. Given such a position, there are but two ways in which the causal theorist might incorporate the *individuation principle* into his account (which, in the last analysis, he must do). He can either accept the *Fregean principle* or reject it.

If the causal theorist accepts the *Fregean principle*, he must reinterpret causal chains as modes of presentation, which of course means that causal chains are part of the content of *de re* beliefs. I cannot imagine what this would mean in terms of, say, reasoning about the content of another agent's belief. But even if we can make sense out of this position, two of its consequences are (1) that a change in a causal chain should alter the corresponding belief and (2) that, when two causal chains are identical, so are the corresponding beliefs. This is extremely unintuitive. First, if Ralph had seen Wiley through a periscope, the causal chain from Wiley to Ralph would have been different, but it is hard to see why this should affect Ralph's belief. Second, suppose that the two causal chains that are responsible for two of Ralph's beliefs concerning Wiley are identical replicas of each other — right down to the subatomic level. Unless we adopt a very crude version of mechanical behaviorism, it still does not follow that the beliefs must be the same. To verify this, just imagine that, in spite of the identity of his two visual experiences, Ralph fails to recognize the same person in both. Finally, consider cases in which the causal chain is totally absent (for example, in cases of illusion). Let the entire scene on the beach be a massive hallucination. Ralph indeed no longer has a *de re* belief about Wiley (or anybody else, for that matter), and many causal theorists would argue that the content of Ralph's belief in this case is an "incomplete" proposition (one with a "gap"). But Ralph's belief seems to be the same whether he is under an illusion or not.

If, on the other hand, causal chains are not modes of presentation, the only alternative left for the causal theorist is to reject the *Fregean principle*. Modes of presentation are needed no matter what one's theory is and, in each possible world compatible with Ralph's beliefs, the mode of presentation determines a unique individual. But, the causal theorist would claim, the mode of presentation need not pick out a unique individual in the *actual* world. Even if it does pick out a unique individual, it does not have to pick out the right one. Let us suppose that modes of presentation are individual concepts. Given that premise, there is an individual concept under which Ralph believes Wiley to be a spy, and this concept is instantiated by a unique individual in each possible world compatible with Ralph's beliefs. But this concept may be one that *in fact* does not fit Wiley at all. Nevertheless, Ralph's belief may still be about Wiley by virtue of the causal connection between the person Wiley and Ralph's mental state.

This position is derived from referential usage of definite descriptions. When I say "Smith's murderer is insane," referring to Jones at the dock, my utterance is about Jones whether he is guilty or not. Similarly, the causal theorist may argue, my *belief* that Smith's murderer is insane may still be about Jones no matter who really murdered Smith. In such a case, the mode of presentation (roughly, the property of being the murderer of Smith) indeed determines a unique individual in all possible worlds that are compatible with my beliefs, in accordance with the *individuation principle*. However, whom in the *actual* world my belief is about is determined not by the mode of presentation, but by something else entirely.

But the inference from utterances to beliefs is very misleading in this case. Even though the description "Smith's murderer" does not apply, I can still use it precisely because I can identify Jones independently of his being the murderer of Smith. In other words, I have more than enough modes of presentation that pick out Jones in the *actual* world. To make the current suggestion plausible, it must be shown that, despite my inability to identify Jones independently of the concept *Smith's murderer*, and despite the fact that Jones is *not* the murderer, my belief can still be said to be about Jones. What we are asked to imagine, indeed, is the following: I believe that Smith's murderer is insane; I cannot associate any other mode of presentation with the person I take to be Smith's murderer; Jones is *not* the murderer; but my belief is still about Jones. Donnellan (1970) has attempted to show that this is indeed possible, but, as we shall see in Chapter 6, his argument does not work.

The *Fregean principle* certainly does not follow from the *individuation principle*, but surely a mere assertion to that effect is insufficient. The least the causal theorist should do is sketch out a plausible theory in which modes of presentation satisfy both the *basic constraint* and the *individuation principle*, and in which reference is nevertheless determined by something entirely outside the content of belief. I do not think any such theory is forthcoming, especially since the notion of a causal chain as determining reference is so hopelessly vague at this point.

As I have said earlier, this is not an attempt to "refute" the causal approach. My only point is that the *individuation principle* makes the descriptive research program more promising. Modes of presentation are needed no matter what one's theory of the content of beliefs is, and modes of presentation, whatever they may be, must individuate objects for agents. Given these facts, the ease with which the notion of individuating representation can accommodate them, and the difficulties of incorporating a theory of modes of presentation within the causal approach, it seems to me that the descriptive approach is the logical choice.

The proof of the pudding, however, is in the eating. The most convincing argument for the descriptive program is made by showing that its adoption as a philosophical foundation represents a productive step in developing a computational model. This is what the rest of this study is all about.[10]

---

[10]I am greatly indebted to Robert Stalnaker for incisive comments on an earlier draft of this section.

2.5   Summary of Chapter 2

In every linguistic event in which reference is made to a particular object we can identify the referring expression, the constituent of the proposition introduced by the referring expression, the mental representation of the object, and the speech act of referring per se. Each of these four elements contributes a different question to the general problem of reference (see Figure 2.1).

Armed with these questions, we can characterize a general approach to the problem of reference that I call the descriptive research program. Its main theses are presented in Figure 2.2, and they all express two central ideas. The first idea is that to refer to an object — in thought or in speech — is, essentially, to have or invoke a mental representation of that object. The second idea is that the relation between a sentence or a thought and the object they are about is that of denotation, which in turn is a function of descriptive content. Thus, the crux of the descriptive program is that reference is entirely a matter of associating a mental state with descriptive content.

Among philosophers of language and mind today, it is Searle who most explicitly identifies himself as working within the descriptive program. But the program's founding father is indubitably Frege. Russell too can be seen as adopting the same approach. Indeed, his celebrated theory of descriptions is the epitome of a successful theory within the descriptive program.

For the past two decades or so, a causal approach to the problem of reference has been developed that marks a radical departure from the descriptive program as a whole. If the core of the old program was the notion of a descriptive content that mediates between object and mind, the core of its causal counterpart is the notion of a causal chain leading from the object directly to the agent. The most significant difference between the two, therefore, is this: according to the causal approach, reference is determined by facts that exist *outside* the mind, in contrast to the descriptive program, which seeks to explain reference in terms of properties of mental states.

Donnellan's distinction between the referential and attributive uses of definite descriptions plays an important role in shaping arguments against the descriptive program on each of the four levels of expressions, propositions, beliefs, and speech acts. Consequently, Donnellan's distinction is used in this chapter as a methodological tool for raising general but systematically exposed objections to the descriptive approach.

Two questions remain. First, why should we have to choose between the two competing programs? Second, if we must make a choice, why should we remain committed to the descriptive approach? My response is that our decision has considerable importance for a computational model because referring requires reasoning about the beliefs, desires, and intentions of other agents, which in turn requires an adequate account of the *content* of beliefs. It is precisely with respect to the content of beliefs (and other propositional attitudes) that the descriptive program and the causal approach differ radically from each other. Furthermore, we should stay with the descriptive program both because its main thrust stands unchallenged, and because, on closer scrutiny, it becomes clear that the causal approach so far has really very little to offer regarding our need for an effective theory that can account for the content of belief.

3
First steps

Let us recall the two crucial features of Donnellan's distinction: whereas, in the attributive use, the description must be satisfied for reference to succeed, in the referential use this is not so. In the latter case, moreover, the speaker has a particular object in mind, while in the attributive he does not.

As we have seen, Donnellan's distinction is used extensively in arguments against the descriptive program. But opinions differ sharply as to its true significance. Chastain (1975), for example, thinks that the paper in which Donnellan's distinction is introduced is "the first significant advance beyond Russell" (196). Castañeda (1977), on the other hand, takes such enthusiasm to be "too much ado about practically nothing" (186). Even those who accept Donnellan's distinction simply as characterizing interesting linguistic behavior disagree strongly among themselves as to how it should be interpreted or represented in a computational model. For Cohen (1984), the speaker's intention that the hearer identify the referent constitutes a crucial difference between the referential and the attributive. Barwise and Perry (1983), on the other hand, take the referential use to be an instance of a definite description whose interpretation is *value-loaded*. That is, its denotation is a particular object in a particular situation that is "accessible" to participants in the conversation. However, as is pointed out by Grosz *et al.* (1983), Barwise and Perry's analysis ignores an essential aspect of the referential use, namely, the speaker's ability to refer to an object, whether or not that object satisfies the description at all.[1]

---

[1]In fairness to Barwise and Perry, they do acknowledge that their notion of the value-loaded use of a definite description does not entirely account for the referential use (Barwise and Perry 1983, 152 n. 3).

In this chapter, I provide an analysis of the cognitive structures that underlie referential and attributive uses of definite descriptions. This endeavor should be worthwhile in and of itself, but it is also intended here as a means toward another end. As we shall see, this analysis of Donnellan's distinction represents the initial step toward attaining our goal: the referring model.

3.1 Donnellan's distinction(s)

Let us now consider a new version of an old example. John, a police investigator, finds Smith's body. It is an unnerving sight, but John is a well-trained officer and, though repelled by his discovery, is determined to do his job. Finding the murder weapon, a knife, he checks it for fingerprints. Fortunately, the apparent culprit has left clear fingerprints on the handle. At this point John utters in total revulsion: "The man whose fingerprints these are, whoever he is, whoever he may be, is insane!"

As it happens, Smith's murderer is quite sane and he was careful to wear gloves during the murder. Moreover, the fingerprints are actually those of another man, Max, who used the knife an hour before the murder, and by a strange twist of fate, this Max (Mad Max) is known to be insane, having spent most of his life in an asylum.

Now, does John use the description "The man whose fingerprints these are" referentially or attributively? Let's look at the facts. John intended to speak about Smith's murderer, not about Max, and what he said about Smith's murderer was that he was insane. Hence he said something true or false about Smith's murderer regardless of whether Smith's murderer was in fact the man whose fingerprints were found on the murder weapon. Thus, John must have been using the description *referentially*. On the other hand, John had no particular person in mind. He said what he said about Smith's murderer, whoever he might be. Thus, the description must have been used *attributively*.

The problem is that Donnellan's distinction between the referential and the attributive uses of definite descriptions cuts across the boundaries of two independent linguistic parameters:

- Sometimes an object must uniquely fit the description used if the utterance is to be about anything, while, at other times, it does not.

- Sometimes a speaker refers to a particular object he has in mind — one that may or may not satisfy the description employed. At other times, the speaker has no particular object in mind at all.

These facts provide two intuitive criteria for deciding whether a particular use of a definite description is referential or attributive. The first criterion is based on the role of the descriptive content of the referring expression in determining truth conditions. I shall call it the *denotation criterion:*

> **Denotation criterion:** If the description must denote one and only one object for the utterance to be about anything, its use is attributive. Otherwise, it is referential.

The second criterion is based on an intuitive (and rather vague) characterization of the speaker's mental state:

> **Mental-state criterion:** If the speaker has a particular object in mind when he refers, his use of the referring expression is taken to be referential. Otherwise it is attributive.

Whenever Donnellan's distinction is discussed, it is tacitly assumed that the two criteria are equivalent: any use of a definite description that is referential according to the denotation criterion should also be classified as referential according to the mental-state criterion and similarly as regards the attributive use. But this is simply not the case. As my example shows, some uses are attributive according to one criterion, referential according to the other. The two criteria, along with the underlying linguistic phenomena, are indeed in need of elucidation, but there is no reason to lump them together. It is therefore misleading to talk about *the* referential/attributive distinction, since there are actually two distinctions: there is Donnellan's distinction as interpreted by the denotation criterion, and there is Donnellan's distinction as interpreted by the mental-state criterion. Each is logically independent of the other.[2]

The denotation criterion itself is quite clear; what remains to be seen is how to interpret the phenomena it characterizes within a

---

[2] A similar point is made by both Loar (1976) and Wettstein (1981). Their analysis of Donnellan's distinction, however, is entirely different from mine.

computational model of referring. The mental-state criterion, on the other hand, is much less tangible. All we have at this stage is an intuition and a metaphor to express it, namely, the metaphor of "having a particular object in mind." Definite descriptions can be used (so it is claimed) either while the speaker is in a mental state that is directed toward a particular object, or while the speaker is not in any such state. But what could such a mental state be? An answer to this question requires that we untangle two conflicting interpretations that are employed indiscriminately in formal characterizations of *de re* beliefs.

3.2 Having a particular object in mind

We have seen (Chapter 2) that there is a tendency to associate the referential use with *de re* propositional attitudes. If a description is used referentially to convey a belief, that belief, it is claimed, is *de re*. This idea clearly reflects the mental-state criterion: to have an object "in mind" is to have a *de re* attitude toward it. But what is it for an agent to have a *de re* attitude? Many have tried to answer this question by studying the conditions under which *de re reports* of attitudes are true. Suppose I report Ralph's belief by saying

(3.1) Ralph believes that someone is a spy.

My report is open to two interpretations. I may have meant to say that Ralph believes that spies exist, or that there is a *particular* person whom Ralph suspects of being a spy. The former interpretation is a *de dicto* report of belief, while the latter is *de re*. We can characterize the *de re* interpretation by saying that Ralph has a particular person in mind whom he suspects of being a spy. This is why we regard the study of *de re* reports as being relevant for understanding the mental-state criterion.

Formally, we obtain *de re* reports of beliefs by a simple application of existential generalization. From the truth of

(3.2) Ralph believes that Saul Kripke is a philosopher,

we should be able to conclude that

(3.3) There is a person about whom Ralph believes that he is a philosopher,

which is a *de re* report of Ralph's belief. But, as Quine ([1956]1972) has pointed out, constructions such as (3.3) lead to serious difficulties. For, although the move from (3.2) to (3.3) is justified, a similar move from

(3.4) Ralph believes that Santa Claus lives at the North Pole

to

(3.5) There is a person about whom Ralph believes that he lives at the North Pole

is not so justified, since Ralph's belief in Santa Claus is not enough to bring Santa Claus into existence. Similarly, from the obviously true statement,

(3.6) Ralph believes that Smith's murderer is Smith's murderer,

it would be highly misleading to say

(3.7) There is a person about whom Ralph believes that he murdered Smith,

since Ralph may have no idea who the murderer might be. Note that, if we substitute "Jones" for one occurrence of "Smith's murderer" in (3.6), the resulting sentence,

(3.8) Ralph believes that Jones is Smith's murderer,

may very well be false even if Jones is indeed the culprit. Thus, not only existential generalization fails; substitution of coreferring terms also does not work.

The problem is well known. Reports of beliefs are *intensional*: they create contexts in which the laws of substitution and existential generalization are not guaranteed to be valid forms of inference. What should be ascertained, therefore, is when existential generalization and substitution work in *de re* reports of beliefs, and when they do not. The various suggested solutions to this problem originate in two distinct ideas that should be carefully separated.[3]

The first idea is that existential generalization and substitution are allowable only if the agent's conception of the referent is "vivid" enough (Kaplan [1968]1975). The strongest version of this requirement specifies that the agent should know *who* or *what object* the

---

[3] Intensional contexts such as belief reports give rise to a host of other problems. Why do existential generalization and substitution sometimes fail? Do words in intensional contexts change their meaning? What values can be assigned to free variables in such contexts? Important as they are, these questions are not relevant to our concern, namely, determining when an agent can be said to "have a particular object in mind."

referent is (Hintikka 1962). This is supported by the fact that the more the agent knows about the object of his belief, the more comfortable we feel in substituting other referring expressions for the one used by the agent when we report his belief. As we have seen, it would be preposterous, on the basis of Ralph's belief in (3.6) and the fact that Jones is the murderer, to assert (3.8). Yet, had Ralph known who the murderer was, we would have then felt perfectly comfortable in asserting either (3.7) or (3.8). Such considerations I call the *epistemic* intuition underlying *de re* reports of belief.

In contrast to the epistemic intuition, we have what I call the *modal* intuition. This idea stems from a consideration of what is logically possible: from an intuitive standpoint, it makes sense to ask not only whether a true proposition could have been false under different circumstances, but also whether a given person could have been different from the way he or she is. For example, Saul Kripke is the author of *Naming and Necessity*, but surely he might not have been. That is, although Saul Kripke in fact has the property of being the author of *Naming and Necessity*, we can easily conceive of alternative circumstances in which he would lack this property. Note that for any property that Kripke may possess, it makes sense to *ask* whether he might not possess it. The *answers* to such questions may vary: some of Kripke's properties are perhaps essential to his identity. Nevertheless, no matter what the answers are, the questions themselves are not meaningless.

When we ask such questions about Kripke, what we are doing is this: through a mental process of abstraction, we regard Kripke not as being the author of *Naming and Necessity*, or as someone named "Saul Kripke," or, for that matter, as anything else. We simply focus our attention upon *him* and, for a while, ignore any attributes he in fact has. The ability to do this is what I call the modal intuition, of which Kripke himself has provided an eloquent presentation ([1972]1980). The modal intuition does not mean, of course, that there really exists such an entity as Kripke-without-properties to whom all of Kripke's attributes are affixed. Although this view has a long and respected history, I do not share it, nor does it really matter for our purpose whether in the last analysis, it is right or wrong. My only point is that, when we contemplate an object, we are capable of considering *this very object* without, necessarily, reflecting upon any particular property that the object may have. It is the modal intuition that enables us to make sense of expressions such as

(3.9) The inventor of the light bulb might not have been the inventor of the light bulb.

In this particular case, the first occurrence of "the inventor of the light bulb" only *fixes the reference* (to use Kripke's term). Once the reference has been fixed, we consider Edison himself — not as being the inventor or as being anything else — and we ask ourselves whether there could have been a world in which Edison were *not* the inventor. This is the modal intuition at work, and the way it expresses itself in natural language is through the use of what Kripke has called *rigid designators* — i.e. referring expressions that designate the same object in each possible world in which the object exists. Note that the converse of the modal intuition is consideration of the referent *qua* having a certain property. In some circumstances, we may be interested not so much in Kripke himself, but in Kripke only in so far as he is the author of *Naming and Necessity*. We may refer to Kripke during a discussion of the causal theory of proper names, but it is obvious that, if *Naming and Necessity* had been written by Gödel, we would have been talking about Gödel, instead of Kripke.

Now, the modal intuition plays a role similar to that of the epistemic intuition in interpreting *de re* reports of belief. To see how, note first that the modal notions of necessity and possibility create intensional contexts in the same way as do belief reports. For example, the statement

(3.10) Necessarily Smith's murderer is Smith's murderer

is surely true, since nothing can fail to be identical to itself. But from (3.10) we cannot conclude that

(3.11) There is a person who is necessarily the one that murdered Smith,

since it is hardly plausible to assume that being a murderer is a necessary property of the actual killer. Note the similarity in structure between the failure to derive (3.11) from (3.10) and the failure to derive (3.7) from (3.6). At the same time, as was the case in belief reports, there are occasions when existential generalization does work. For example, from the true statement

(3.12) Necessarily the number 9 is odd,

we can certainly conclude that

(3.13) There is a number that is necessarily odd.

Existential generalization works here for reasons that clearly have nothing to do with the epistemic intuition. They have to do rather with our *modal* intuition, i.e., with the fact that the numeral "9" in (3.12) is a rigid designator. When using the numeral "9", we are not considering the integer 9 as being, say, the number of planets, the square root of 81, or anything else, but are regarding it rather as a thing "in itself," so to speak. Since statement (3.12) is true, the proposition *9 is odd* will be true in all possible worlds. Since "9" is a rigid designator, one and the same number (i.e., the number 9) will be odd in all possible worlds; hence (3.13) is true as well.

Thus, two distinct ideas are employed to justify applying existential generalization within intensional contexts. The epistemic intuition requires that the agent have knowledge of the object if a *de re* report of his belief is correct. The modal intuition requires that a rigid designator be used if existential generalization is to be allowed. Characterized in this manner, the two notions appear to exhibit a natural "division of labor." The modal intuition is applied to the explication of necessity and possibility, while the epistemic intuition is applied to beliefs (cf. Kaplan 1968). But as the logic of modal concepts and the logic of belief are both couched in terms of possible-world semantics, *both* intuitions serve as a basis for applying existential generalization to reports of beliefs. Consider the formula

(3.14) $(\exists x)\mathrm{BEL}_{\mathrm{ralph}}(\mathrm{INSANE}(x))$,

which roughly states that there is someone Ralph believes to be insane. Under the standard possible-world interpretation, (3.14) is true just in case there is a person (at least one) such that, in each possible world compatible with Ralph's beliefs, that very same person is insane. Now suppose that the following statement is a correct report of Ralph's belief:

(3.15) Ralph believes that Smith's murderer is insane.

If Ralph knows who the murderer is, then, in each possible world compatible with Ralph's beliefs, Ralph can identify the man who actually murdered Smith, and in each such world that man is insane

— which means that the conditions under which (3.14) is true are satisfied. Obviously, this is a manifestation of the epistemic intuition. But now consider the statement

(3.16) Ralph believes that Jones is insane.

If Kripke is right, the name "Jones" is a rigid designator. That is, it picks out the same individual in every possible world in which that individual exists, independently of any property he may have. This, of course, is the modal intuition at work. Suppose that Ralph does *not* know who Jones is. Nevertheless, since "Jones" is a rigid designator, it denotes the same individual (i.e., Jones) in each possible world in which Jones exists. Since Ralph believes that Jones exists, it follows that Jones does indeed exist in every possible world compatible with Ralph's belief, and that, in each such world, Jones (i.e., whoever the use of the name "Jones" in (3.16) designates) is insane. Thus, we can again conclude that (3.14) is true, even though Ralph does not know who Jones is. The move from (3.15) to the formula in (3.14) is justified on epistemological grounds, while the same move from (3.16) is justified on modal grounds.

Let us first consider the modal intuition and its relation to Donnellan's distinction. The class of referring expressions most frequently associated with the property of rigid designation is the class of proper names, but Kaplan (1977; 1978) has argued that demonstratives are also endowed with this property. Moreover, we can use a definite description as a verbal mode of pointing the sole purpose of which is to help "fix the referent." This stratagem turns definite descriptions into rigid designators; consequently, when a definite description is employed in this manner, we can report what is said by using the *de re* form. Kaplan introduces the artificial operator **DTHAT** to mark a definite description that is used merely as a verbal way of pointing. For example, the sentence

(3.17) The inventor of the light bulb was a genius

is about whoever invented the light bulb. But the sentence

(3.18) **DTHAT**("The inventor of the light bulb") was a genius

is about Edison. The difference between the two is this: in a possible world in which the light bulb was invented by Einstein and in which Edison was the village idiot, (3.17) is true, whereas (3.18) is false.

As Kaplan acknowledges (1978, 234, 238), there is a close relation between the referential use and his treatment of definite descriptions as demonstratives. When a speaker uses a description referentially, he uses it as a rigid designator. But which of the two criteria of Donnellan's distinction should be so characterized? In the fingerprint example (p. 48 above), the description "The man whose fingerprints these are" is classified as referential according to the denotation criterion. Since it is *not* being used as a rigid designator (in every possible world the referent is the murderer, whoever he or she may be in that world), the analysis of the referential use in terms of rigid designation is *not* an explication of the denotation criterion. Hence it is somehow connected to the mental-state criterion (which is not surprising, given the close relation between rigid designation, the modal intuition, and the semantics of *de re* reports of belief). But the *epistemic* intuition is surely relevant to the mental-state criterion as well. According to the epistemic intuition, knowledge of the referent is a necessary condition for having the referent "in mind." Note that one cannot simply decide to possess knowledge, so that the question of whether a given definite description is used referentially (in the original, intuitive sense of "referential") is not entirely a function of the speaker's intention. At the same time, Kaplan's **DTHAT**, shows that a speaker is always free to decide whether or not to use a referring expression as a rigid designator.[4]

Thus, the mental-state criterion has two separate aspects. According to the epistemic aspect, knowledge of the referent is essential for a description to be used referentially. According to the modal aspect, the intention to use a definite description as a rigid designator is the defining feature of referential usage. If we add these two aspects to the *denotation criterion*, we get *three* aspects of Donnellan's distinction — the epistemic, the modal, and the denotational — that are conceptually independent of one another. They can be expressed in terms of three dichotomies:

- **Mental-state criterion (epistemic aspect)**: Knowing who or what the referent is, or at least having knowledge

---

[4] In discussions about the formal representation of knowledge, it is sometimes argued that an agent knows who a certain person is if the agent possesses a referring expression that rigidly designates that person. This view confuses the epistemic with the modal intuition: as Kaplan's **DTHAT** shows, any referring expression can be turned into a rigid designator, but this has nothing to do with knowing who the referent is.

of the referent (referential use), in contrast to lacking such knowledge (attributive use).

- **Mental-state criterion (modal aspect):** Intending the referring expression to be interpreted as a rigid designator (referential use) in contrast to considering the referent *qua* having a particular property (attributive use).

- **Denotation criterion (denotational aspect):** Using a definite description "the so-and-so," to refer to whoever is the so-and-so; if nothing is, the speech act cannot succeed (attributive use). This is in contrast to using a definite description to refer to an object x, whether or not x is indeed denoted by that description (referential use).

These three aspects are summarized in Figure 3.1.

3.3   A three-tiered model of referring

The three aspects of Donnellan's distinction — the epistemic, the modal, and the denotational — are conceptually independent of one another. Yet they must all be bound together in an obvious way, or else Donnellan's distinction would not have such a persuasive ring to it. What needs to be explained, therefore, is the intuitive immediacy of the distinction, given its complexity. How is it that there is in fact a single referential/attributive distinction and not three?

The answer, no doubt, must lie in the way the three aspects interact with one another. To show how this is done, I propose to cor-

DONNELLAN'S DISTINCTION					
Mental-state criterion				Denotation criterion	
Epistemic aspect		Modal aspect		Denotational aspect	
<u>Referential</u>	<u>Attributive</u>	<u>Referential</u>	<u>Attributive</u>	<u>Referential</u>	<u>Attributive</u>
Knowledge of the referent	No knowledge of the referent	Rigid designation	Nonrigid designation	Reference without denotation	No reference without denotation

Figure 3.1:   Aspects of Donnellan's distinction

relate aspects of Donnellan's distinction with the logical components that a plan-based model of referring must possess. Any such model must contain the following elements: (1) a *database* that includes representations of objects, (2) a *planner* that constructs strategies for carrying out referring intentions, and (3) an *utterance generator* that produces referring expressions. I show how each aspect of Donnellan's distinction could be represented in the corresponding computational component. Then, by demonstrating how each component interacts with the others in the course of a speech act, we can see how mind and language cooperate to produce what we call the referential and the attributive uses of definite descriptions. Then, leaving Donnellan's distinction behind us, we can concentrate on each of its aspects and the emergent referring model.

3.3.1 Individuating sets

According to the *individuation principle* (p. 40 above), if an agent has a belief about a particular object under a presentation mode, the latter determines a unique object in all possible worlds that are compatible with the agent's beliefs. It is not yet clear what, precisely, presentation modes are supposed to be. Yet, given the fact that, whatever they are, they must satisfy the individuation principle, the most plausible accounts take them to be some sort of internal representations. Such internal representations serve as a mechanism through which an agent can individuate objects within his conceptual scheme. This is done, under such an interpretation, by the relation of denotation: each presentation mode is believed by the agent to denote one and only one object.

Such a view sounds very much in line with the descriptive program of reference, but it need not be. First, as we have seen, the causal theorist can accept such an account of presentation modes while insisting that they alone do not determine the actual referent. Second, it is still left open to question whether *every* belief must contain a mode of presentation. All that the individuation principle entails is that, *whenever* a mode of presentation is needed, the agent must believe that it individuates an object. A causal theorist can still claim that some *de re* beliefs are special in that they do not require presentation modes. To a limited extent, as we shall see later on, he is indeed right. Third, to say that modes of presentation should be interpreted as internal representations still does not tell us what kind of representations they are. They need not individuate objects, for example, by means of general terms alone. Some modes of presentation may very well individuate objects only relative to other objects. Thus, as far as I can see, nothing prevents a causal theorist from accepting an account of modes of presentation as internal representations. Doing so, however, does not mean that presentation modes can always be articulated as linguistic descriptions. Nor should the claim that a presentation mode is believed by the agent to denote a unique object be taken too literally. It does not mean, for example, that we are always *aware* of the presentation modes under which we have beliefs about particular objects. Sometimes we are, but certainly not always.

We thus have modes of presentation, each believed by the agent to denote a particular thing. Let an *individuating set* be an exhaustive list of presentation modes, all taken by the agent to denote the same object. For example, the set

$$\{author \ of \ the \ \text{Odyssey}, \ author \ of \ the \ \text{Iliad}\}$$

is an individuating set for me, since (1) I happen to believe that one and only one person composed both the *Odyssey* and the *Iliad*, and (2) I must admit that I do not know of any other fact that *individuates* that Greek author.[5]

Individuating sets vary a great deal in informational content. The singleton {*shortest spy*} is an individuating set representing the shortest spy for me. On the other hand, the rich cluster of images and definite descriptions representing my mother for me is also an individuating set, although I could not even begin to enumerate all the presentation modes it contains. When all is well, and the presentation modes in a particular individuating set do denote a unique object, I shall say that the individuating set *determines* that object. But many things can go wrong. A speaker may possess two distinct individuating sets that, unbeknown to him, determine the same object (e.g., Oedipus' distinct conceptions of his mother and his wife). On the other hand, an agent may possess an individuating set containing two presentation modes that actually denote different objects (e.g., when a person mistakenly thinks that the author of *Sense and Sensibility* also wrote *How to Do Things with Words*). Of course,

---

[5]This is not entirely accurate. I do, in fact, have other modes of presentation for the Greek Homer: for example, *person believed by my mother to have composed both the Iliad and the Odyssey*. My concern here, however, is with an abstract data structure for modes of presentation, whatever they are. I am not interested at this point in the correct enumeration of presentation modes.

some individuating sets may include presentation modes that do not denote anything (e.g., an individuating set containing *present king of France*), while some individuating sets may determine nothing at all (e.g., a child's conception of Santa Claus).

Whether or not an agent can have knowledge of an object, or knows who or what the referent is (the epistemic aspect of Donnellan's distinction) depends on the relevant individuating set. On first approximation, the richer in content the individuating set, the more likely it is that the agent knows who or what the referent is. This, however, is far from being universally true. Some modes of presentation may be *privileged*, depending on circumstances (Boër and Lycan 1986). For the purpose of discussing computation theory, I can say that I know who Stephen Cook is: he is the person who proved that the satisfiability problem is **NP**-complete. For most other purposes (e.g., introducing him at a party), I cannot claim to know who he is, since I have never made his acquaintance. Nevertheless, as we shall see, the different contextual requirements can be expressed as constraints on the relevant individuating set.

Individuating sets are part of the database, and this is where the epistemic aspect of Donnellan's distinction should be represented.

3.3.2   Referring intentions

Individuating sets, per se, have nothing to do with speech. Nevertheless, they become involved when a speaker plans to make a hearer recognize what the speaker is talking about. We should distinguish, though, between two ways in which individuating sets are employed in the process of such planning, corresponding to two types of referring intentions. First, a speaker may select a mode of presentation from the relevant individuating set, intending that this particular presentation mode be recognized by the hearer. Second, the speaker may intend to refer to an object determined by an individuating set, but without at the same time intending that any *particular* presentation mode from the set be part of the proposition he wishes to express. Consider, for example, the following two statements:

(**3.19**) The author of *Othello* wrote the best play about jealousy.

(**3.20**) Shakespeare was born in Stratford-upon-Avon.

In making both statements, a speaker would normally be referring to Shakespeare. But note the difference between the two referring

intentions. In statement (3.19), the speaker selects a particular presentation mode of Shakespeare, namely, that he is the author of *Othello*, and intends to make the hearer think of Shakespeare in terms of
this presentation mode. If the hearer fails to do so, he will miss the
whole point. In statement (3.20), on the other hand, the speaker does
not select any particular presentation mode of Shakespeare from the
relevant individuating set. Indeed, he may not care at all *how* the
hearer makes the connection between the name "Shakespeare" and
the referent, as long as he appropriately identifies who the speaker
is talking about.

In Chapter 5, the difference between these two types of referring
intentions is spelled out more precisely. Even at this preliminary
stage, however, it should be clear that the two types of intentions result in two distinct types of propositions that a speaker may express.
In (3.19), the presentation mode is a constituent of the proposition
expressed. In (3.20), no particular mode of presentation is meant;
consequently, we may say that the proposition expressed is a *singular* one, involving, as it were, (1) the property of being born in
Stratford and (2) Shakespeare himself. This seems to me the most
natural interpretation of singular propositions in terms of speech act
theory.[6]

The two types of referring intentions correspond to the modal
aspect of Donnellan's distinction. In (3.19), the hearer is supposed
to think of Shakespeare *qua* being the author of *Othello*. In (3.20),
the hearer is expected to interpret the referring expression as a rigid
designator. Since the planner is where referring intentions (as well as
the procedures for carrying them out) are represented, this is where
the modal aspect belongs. Note that the two types of referring intentions can be described as intentions to impose various constraints
(including the null constraint) on the way the hearer should think
of the referent. Later on we shall see how this can be generalized to
other referring intentions — for example, to the intention that the
hearer identify appropriately what is being talked about.

3.3.3 Choice of referring expressions

Once the speaker knows what particular mode of presentation (if
any) he means, he must pick out a referring expression to be used in

---

[6]A hard-line descriptive theorist might be tempted to say that the mode of
presentation associated with "Shakespeare" in Statement (3.20) is the entire individuating set. But a speaker cannot *mean* such a mode of presentation, since
the individuating set is not accessible to the hearer.

the speech act. It is natural to assume that if, say, the mode of presentation is *author of Othello*, the definite description "the author of *Othello*" would be a natural choice; if no particular presentation mode is relevant, a proper name would be most appropriate. But this, obviously, is not at all necessary. It would be very tiresome for the speaker to keep saying "the author of *Othello*" over and over again whenever reference to Shakespeare is called for. Conversely, even if it makes no difference to the speaker how his audience comes to think of the referent, he may surmise that no one around is familiar with any of the names he might offer, and that a definite description would better serve his communication goals. In any case, whether or not a definite description must denote one and only one object for the speech act to succeed (the *denotation criterion*) depends on the relation between that description and the particular presentation mode (if any) that the speaker regards as important. If the description expresses that same presentation mode, unique denotation is required. If the relevant presentation mode is only implied (as was the case in the fingerprint example), or if no particular mode of presentation is meant, denotation is superfluous.

As the choice of the actual referring expressions to be used is made within the utterance generator, it is there that the denotational aspect of Donnellan's distinction should be represented.

3.3.4 Donnellan's distinction: final chord

We end up with a correspondence between Donnellan's distinction and an outline of a referring model. The nature of the relevant individuating set, the type of referring intention, and the actual choice of a referring expression correspond to the epistemic, modal, and denotational aspects, respectively. Such a correlation is not a coincidence, of course. It is another reflection of the three-tiered structure of beliefs, propositions, and expressions that was described at the beginning of Chapter 2. It should not be too surprising, then, that the epistemic aspect of Donellan's distinction is concerned with representations of objects in the mind, that the modal aspect is manifested by the structure of the proposition that a speaker intends to express, that the denotational aspect is concerned with utterances of referring expressions, and that Donnellan's distinction itself is a formulation of two natural ways in which mental representations, propositions, and utterances are interrelated in the course of a speech act. We can now utilize this correspondence among Donnellan's distinction, cognitive elements in the production of a speech act, and the computational components in explaining the structures underlying typical referential and attributive uses of definite descriptions.

In the paradigmatic examples of attributive usage, the speaker selects a *particular* mode of presentation (the modal aspect) and, not surprisingly, chooses a definite description that expresses that presentation mode (hence the denotational aspect). As Donnellan himself notes ([1966]1971), *lack* of knowledge concerning the referent (the epistemic aspect) is not a prerequisite of attributive usage. One can know who murdered Smith, but still insist that *anyone* who would have murdered Smith in such a brutal way must be insane. Nevertheless, the attributive use typically occurs when the identity of the referent is not known, because, under such circumstances, the intention to refer to an object *qua* being the such-and-such is easier to recognize. When the identity of the referent is well known to all participants in the conversation, the speaker must frequently make his intention to refer to the object *qua* having a certain property more explicit. Moreover, when the speaker has no knowledge of the referent whatsoever, his use of a definite description is not likely to be intended as a rigid designator. The pragmatic reasons for all these conclusions are discussed further in Chapter 5, but we can already see why the attributive side of Donnellan's distinction encompasses a natural category of uses of definite descriptions. Nonrigid designation tends to accompany a particular choice of a definite description, usually when knowledge of the referent is lacking.

In the paradigmatic examples of referential usage, on the other hand, knowledge of the referent must be possessed; at the same time, the speaker does not take any *particular* mode of presentation to be of importance. The speaker's goal is simply to have the hearer identify appropriately what is being talked about, a task for which any well-suited referring expression will be acceptable. Moreover, when knowledge of the referent exists, identification can be achieved, to a large extent, apart from the descriptive content of the referring expression. Hence, strict denotation is frequently unnecessary.

This completes my analysis of Donnellan's distinction. Figure 3.2 shows the correspondence between Donnellan's distinction and the proposed outline of a referring model. The first column lists the three aspects of Donnellan's distinction; the second summarizes how these aspects are to be interpreted; the third enumerates the corresponding cognitive elements that contribute to the production of a speech act; the fourth shows the computational components of the model.

In Chapter 2, Donnellan's distinction served as a methodological tool in presenting objections to the descriptive program. The role its analysis plays in the present chapter is twofold. First, because of the attention accorded to Donnellan's distinction in both computational linguistics and philosophy, an understanding of its underlying cognitive structure is valuable in itself. Second, the process of dissecting the various aspects of referential and attributive usage provides an outline of a computational model of referring whose main data structure is that of an individuating set and in which the three aspects of Donnellan's distinction can be represented.

From the standpoint of this study, however, Donnellan's distinction cannot be regarded as an end in itself. We do have bigger fish to fry. The real point is not to represent a complex distinction, but rather to formulate general principles of a computational model of referring. We must therefore shift our perspective; instead of assigning central stage to referential and attributive usage, we can treat Donnellan's distinction as a *test case* for a putative theory of referring as a speech act. Any such theory must take Donnellan's distinction into account. That is, it must at least specify (1) what it takes for

Donnellan's distinction	Theoretical interpretation	Cognitive element	System component
Epistemic aspect	Type of individuating set	Propositional attitude	Data-base
Modal aspect	Type of referring intentions	Propositional content	Planner
Denotational aspect	Choice of noun phrase	Expression	Utterance generator

Figure 3.2: Donnellan's distinction and its interpretation

an agent to have *de re* beliefs, (2) what makes an agent express a general proposition rather than a singular one (or vice versa), and (3) what the reasons are for preferring one referring expression to another. If a theory of referring as a speech act cannot handle these questions, it stands little chance of being adequate.

My contention is that the three-tiered structure proposed in this chapter is a suitable outline for such a computational theory of referring. That a theory based on this structure is likely to handle Donnellan's distinction correctly may not be very surprising. After all, the foregoing questions are precisely the ones that motivated the three-tiered structure in the first place. Nevertheless, answering these questions is far from being a trivial matter: once the complexity of Donnellan's distinction is understood, it is clear that accommodating it is a challenging objective for any theory of referring. Thus, it may be methodologically advantageous to proceed with the three aspects of Donnellan's distinction kept constantly in mind, as indeed I do in this study. Of course, the theory must account for numerous other issues as well. There is much more to using a referring expression than simply choosing between the referential and the attributive.

3.4   Summary of Chapter 3

Donnellan's distinction cuts across two linguistic parameters, which give rise to two independent criteria for deciding whether a particular use of a definite description is referential or attributive. The first one is the *denotational criterion*, based on the role played by the descriptive content of the referring expression in determining truth conditions. The second one is the *mental-state criterion*, based on the notion of "having a particular object in mind." It is generally assumed that any use of a definite description that is referential according to one criterion should also be so classified according to the other (similarly for attributive usage). But this is not the case.

Moreover, the mental-state criterion itself is explicated in terms of two distinct ideas. According to the first (the *epistemic*), an agent has a particular object in mind only when he knows who or what that object is. According to the second (the *modal*), to have a particular object in mind is to use a representation of it (either in thought or in speech) as a rigid designator. Both ideas are employed in attempts to articulate a formal semantics for reports of *de re* beliefs; consequently, both are intertwined in interpretations of the mental-state criterion. Thus, this criterion has two separate aspects, the epistemic and the modal. If we add the denotation criterion we obtain the result that Donnellan's distinction has three independent aspects. A summary of these appears in Figure 3.1.

To show how the three aspects are interrelated, they are first represented within three computational components: the *database*, the *planner*, and the *utterance generator*.

An abstract data structure called an *individuating set* contains an exhaustive list of presentation modes, all believed to be denoting the very same object. Whether or not an agent knows who or what a certain object is (the epistemic aspect) depends on features of the relevant individuating set. This is represented in the database.

When a speaker plans to make a hearer recognize what he is talking about, he can have two distinct referring intentions: he may select a presentation mode from the relevant individuating set, intending this *particular* mode to be recognized by the hearer, or he may intend to refer to an object determined by an individuating set without concerning himself unduly with the question of which presentation mode is actually used by the hearer (as long as the hearer gets the referent right). The latter illustrates an intention to use a referring expression as a rigid designator, i.e., an intention to express a singular proposition. Forming such intentions and devising ways to carry them out constitute a process that belongs in the planner, which is where the modal aspect of Donnellan's distinction is represented.

Once the speaker knows what specific presentation mode (if any) should be part of the proposition he is attempting to express, he must generate a referring expression. Whether or not a definite description must denote one and only one object for the speech act to succeed depends on the relation between that description and the particular presentation mode the speaker considers important. Thus, the denotation criterion is represented in the utterance generator.

Figure 3.2 summarizes the correlation between Donnellan's distinction, on the one hand, and the computational model, on the other.

In the paradigmatic examples of the attributive use, the speaker has no knowledge of the referent; he selects a particular mode of presentation from the relevant individuating set and chooses a definite description that expresses that presentation mode. In the paradigmatic examples of referential usage, the speaker knows who or what the referent is, and he does not take any *particular* mode of presentation to be of importance. In such a case, identification of the referent can be accomplished, to a large extent, independently of the descriptive content of the referring expression. Hence, strict denotation is frequently not necessary.

The three-tiered structure suggested by the foregoing analysis of Donnellan's distinction serves as an outline for the computational model that is developed further in the following chapters.

4
Referring intentions and goals

4.1   Communication intentions

Suppose I ask a guest of mine to take out the garbage. In making
this request, I may have a whole range of intentions and goals that
have motivated my utterance. For example, I may have intended to
make my visitor feel at home, to avoid doing something I hate, to get
the house cleaned, and so on. However, not all of these objectives
are relevant to our discussion. What we are after are *communication*
intentions and goals — that is, goals that are intended to be *recognized*
or, more precisely, to be achieved (at least in part) through
their recognition. For example, deception is not a communication
goal because it is not (and could not be) intended to be recognized.
A speaker may very well intend the hearer to recognize the speaker's
attempt to eliminate boredom, but the elimination of boredom is
still not a communication goal because its mere recognition would
hardly contribute to making things more interesting. In contrast,
my goal of obtaining some information from you is indeed a communication goal because the most efficient plan to achieve it would
include letting you know what it is. Here not only do I intend that
you recognize my need for this information, but I also intend that
your recognition play a role in inducing you to provide me with it.
Such goals, along with the intentions to satisfy them, are the communication goals and intentions that are of interest to us.

This view of communication intentions originates with Grice's
analysis of the concept of meaning (1957). But much research in
computational linguistics, though obviously influenced by Grice, has
nevertheless stressed the role of intention and goal recognition in

discourse, quite independently of a theory of meaning. Allen's dissertation (1978) and his subsequent work with Perrault (1978; 1980), for example, emphasize the importance of goal recognition for inferring the speaker's plans. So do Grosz and Sidner (1986), as well as Sidner herself in her own work (1983; 1985). These authors show how the recognition of what the speaker is "up to" contributes to coherence and comprehensibility of the discourse (see also Perrault *et al.* 1978), and is essential for the hearer's generation of an appropriate response. However, not all goals that are intended to be recognized are alike.

Sometimes the recognition of a goal suffices for its satisfaction. For example, if my objective is to congratulate you, I can succeed if (and in this particular case, only if) you recognize my intention to do so. Once you have recognized my intention, you are thereby congratulated. I call such goals, whereby recognition is sufficient for success, the *literal goal* of the speech act. In addition, there are *discourse purposes*, which are the goals underlying both the choice to engage in discourse in the first place (rather than in a nonlinguistic activity) and the choice of a particular propositional content to be expressed (Grosz and Sidner 1986). In the case of congratulating, the literal goal and the discourse purpose are one and the same — but this is the exception rather than the rule. For example, in the case of the guest who is asked to take out the garbage, the literal goal of the request is essentially to make the guest *realize* what he is asked to do. The discourse purpose is to make him actually *do* it. Note that, unlike the case of literal goals, recognition of the discourse purpose, albeit vital for the success of the speech act, is not enough for the objective to be achieved. The guest may very well recognize that my purpose is to induce him to take out the garbage, but, alas, this in itself does not guarantee his cooperation. So the recognition of literal goals is sufficient for its success (sometimes it is also necessary), while the recognition of discourse purposes, as distinct from literal goals, is neither sufficient (it does not guarantee cooperation) nor necessary (my guest may take the garbage out without realizing that he is complying with my wishes). Rather, given certain assumptions about the disposition of discourse participants, it is *rational* to expect that the hearer's recognition of a discourse purpose will enhance the speaker's chances of achieving his goal.

The discourse purpose should characterize the *point* of the institution of referring and, consequently, determine under what conditions an act of referring can be called a success. In this sense, the discourse purpose of referring is analogous to Searle's illocutionary point. However, melding Grosz and Sidner's notion of discourse purpose with Searle's notion of the point or purpose of a speech act masks a subtle difference between the two concepts. In Grosz and Sidner's theory, discourse purposes are *perlocutionary* (Austin 1962): they are defined in terms of effects on the *hearer's* beliefs and actions. Searle, on the other hand, insists that the terminology of "point" or "purpose" is not meant to imply that every illocutionary act has a definitionally associated perlocutionary intent (Searle 1979c, 3). But the difference between the discourse purposes and illocutionary points should not concern us too much. Grosz and Sidner's focus on perlocutionary effects is a natural consequence of their computational approach and is quite typical of the research in their field. Searle's eschewal of any general interpretation of illocutionary points as perlocutionary effects is consistent with his rejection of Grice's theory of meaning (Searle 1969, sec. 2.6). Searle, of course, does not deny that some speech acts do have perlocutionary intentions associated with them (for example, requests), and I take referring to be one of them. If we regard it intuitively, the point of referring is to make the hearer identify an object — a perlocutionary effect *par excellence*.[1]

Literal goal and discourse purpose are obviously not independent of each other: my expectation that my guest will actually carry out the garbage depends partially on my expectation that he will understand what I have said. This is indeed the basis for our use of language as a means for attaining some of our objectives, and is the foundation for a plan-based theory of speech acts. For example, the distinctions between surface speech acts and illocutionary acts (Allen and Perrault 1980), and between utterance-level and discourse-level intentions (Grosz and Sidner 1986), are, in my opinion, particular computational realizations of the distinction between literal goals and discourse purposes. Since I accept the plan-based approach and consider referring to be a speech act, I must specify the literal goals and discourse purposes that typically motivate the use of referring expressions. Needless to say, the literal goal and the discourse purpose must be characterized in a way that is useful for the referring model. That is, they must be spelled out in a vocabulary that makes computational sense.

---

[1]It is not surprising that Cohen (1984) views referring as a request for identification.

70

4.2   The literal goal of referring

Let us begin with Grice's theory of communication intentions. The motivation for Grice's philosophical project is an attempt to analyze semantic concepts in terms of propositional attitudes. In a nutshell, Grice begins by distinguishing between natural and nonnatural meaning (as well as between natural and nonnatural signs). Roughly defined, natural meaning is the meaning of *symptoms*: smoke is a natural sign of fire, spots on the skin are a natural sign of measles, and when we say that smoke in the house means that there is fire somewhere, or that spots on the patient's skin mean that he has measles, the sense of "mean" here is a *natural* one.

In contrast, when we say that sentences have meaning and that agents can mean something by uttering them, the concept of "meaning" here is a *nonnatural* one: the utterance "the patient has measles" means that the patient has measles, but the utterance, unlike the spots, is surely not a symptom of the disease.

The conceptual dependency in Grice's theory between what utterances mean (what Grice calls *timeless meaning of an utterance type*) and what speakers mean when they use these utterances (*utterer's occasion meaning*) is roughly as follows. The statement

(4.1) Expression E means P

is to be understood in terms of the statement

(4.2) In uttering expression E, speaker S means that P,

where the analysis of (4.2) is to be founded on the analysis of the statement

(4.3) S, in performing act A, means *something*.

Now, the keystone of Grice's analysis of meaning *something* — in fact, the foundation of his entire approach — consists of three intentions that are supposed to be both necessary and sufficient for a speaker to mean anything (Grice 1957):

Int$_1$: S intends to produce an effect in hearer H.
Int$_2$: S intends H to recognize his intention Int$_1$.
Int$_3$: S intends that intention Int$_1$ be satisfied by
means of H's recognition of intention Int$_2$.

In other words, if S is to mean anything at all, he must intend to produce an effect in H *by means of H's recognition of this intention.* The profound insight contained in Grice's paper is the discovery of this defining feature of communication. It is the observation that communication necessarily involves intentions whose very recognition suffices to satisfy them.

As a theory of meaning, Grice's original account was burdened by a number of difficulties. Confronted by a series of counterexamples, he was compelled to modify his three intentions substantially (Grice 1969). However, my interest here is not in a theory of meaning. Whether Grice's account is, or could be made to be, a correct analysis of the concept of meaning is debatable, but quite apart from that, his original insight about the nature of communication intentions and goals remains valid. My point of departure, therefore, is Grice's concluding remarks in his 1969 essay:

> I see some grounds for hoping that, by paying serious attention to the relation between nonnatural and natural meaning, one might be able not only to reach a simplified account of utterer's occasion-meaning, but also to show that *any human institution, the function of which is to provide artificial substitutes for natural signs, must embody, as its key-concept, a concept possessing approximately the features which I ascribe to the concept of utterer's occasion-meaning.* (1969, 177. Italics mine.)

Now, whether or not referring is a special case of utterer's occasion meaning, clearly the prime function of the linguistic institution of referring is to provide an artificial substitute for natural signs. The whole point of referring is that one does not need to carry around samples of the things one wants to talk about. So, if Grice is right, referring intentions must include communication intentions with a structure corresponding rather closely to the Gricean picture. Actually, it can be argued that the institution of referring is more essentially a *communication* institution than its relatives, the illocutionary acts. Communication requires at least two agents, i.e., our ubiquitous speaker and hearer; in this respect Grice's theory of meaning has been criticized for requiring the presence of an audience for a person to mean anything. Surely, it is argued, a person could correctly be said to have meant something without addressing anyone in particular (for example, when making entries in a diary or scribbling notes while trying to prove a mathematical theorem). Under such circumstances, an agent may mean something without intending to produce an effect in anyone through recognition of his intention. How damaging this argument is to Grice's theory is unclear. In any case, such an assessment is not crucial to our purpose because, unlike asserting, promising, congratulating and the like, referring *does* require an audience. I can congratulate myself for being such a nice fellow, promise myself to go on a diet next week, tell myself that the situation in Israel is terrible, and so on. But there seems to be little point in *referring*, unless I do it for someone else. Of course, when I mutter to myself "The situation in Israel is terrible," I am, in a sense, referring to the situation in Israel, but this type of "referring" is substantially different from performing the same act for a hearer. To see why, consider what the intuitive point of referring is: to make the hearer identify what is being talked about by supplying him with adequate information. This is what I do when I tell *you* that the situation in Israel is terrible. But none of that is required when I talk to myself, since I already know what I am thinking about. Thus, it seems that referring is essentially a communication act in a way that illocutionary acts are not and, if this is so, one would expect a key referring intention to correspond approximately to Grice's original analysis. What we need to find, therefore, is the kind of referring intention whose fulfillment requires no more than its recognition. This intention would provide the *literal goal* of the referring act.

Once we adopt the descriptive approach to reference, such an intention is not hard to find. Consider what an intuitive account of referring looks like from a descriptive standpoint. A speaker has a mental representation denoting an object; by using a noun phrase that is intended to be interpreted as a linguistic representation of the object, the speaker intends to invoke in the hearer a mental representation denoting that very same object. But it should be noted that such an intention has precisely the Gricean quality we are looking for. Once the hearer recognizes the intention that he have a mental representation denoting the same object that the speaker has in mind, the hearer *does* have such a representation. For example, if I recognize your intention to convey to me a representation of whatever object you are talking about, then I *do* have a representation of that object in the presentation mode: *the object the speaker is talking about*. In other words, *the mere recognition of the intention to represent an object suffices to produce a presentation mode of that object.* A central referring intention, therefore, is the intention to invoke a representation of a particular object in the hearer by means of his recognition of this intention. The goal of satisfying this intention is the literal goal of referring.

We can also describe the literal goal of referring in terms of features of noun phrases. As Grice points out

> Characteristically, an utterer intends an audience to recognize ...some "crucial" feature F [of the utterance], and to think of F ...as correlated in a certain way with some response which the utterer intends the audience to produce. (ibid., 163)

If the property of being a referring expression is taken to be a feature of some noun phrases, and if this feature is correlated with the invocation of a mental representation in the hearer's mind of whatever object the speaker is talking about, then we can say that the literal goal of referring is to have the hearer recognize that an utterance of a noun phrase is to be interpreted as a referring expression. Of course, noun phrases that are used as referring expressions have other features relevant to the act of referring. For example, when used as a referring expression, the noun phrase "the gray whale" has a feature that is conventionally correlated with the act of invoking in the hearer a representation of a gray whale. Thus, the literal goal of referring is not merely to invoke the representation of *the particular object the speaker wishes to talk about*, but to invoke a representation of that object with properties that correspond to certain features of the noun phrase.

In Chapter 3, I defined an *individuating set* as an exhaustive list of presentation modes, all believed by the agent to denote the same object. Let us distinguish between two kinds of individuating sets: the *quasi-permanent* type and the *local* type. Quasi-permanent individuating sets are those more or less permanent representations of objects that we carry around in our mental database. They can be formed and modified independently of any discourse situation and, in general, can be viewed as the data structures that allow us to *think* of things. *Local* individuating sets, on the other hand, are those that are constructed, modified, merged with other individuating sets, or discarded during an actual discourse. They are a subset of the class of discourse entities (Webber 1983; Kamp 1984); figure prominently in participants' representations of the discourse focusing-structure (Grosz 1978b; 1979; Grosz and Sidner 1986); and, by and large, reflect which objects are being discussed. The distinction between quasi-permanent and local individuating sets is not necessarily sharp, and there are obviously many links between the two types: a local individuating set may turn into a quasi-permanent one when the conversation ends, and access to a quasi-permanent set may be required while a local one is being processed. Nevertheless, the distinction is useful very much in the same sense as the distinction between long-term and short-term memories.

Given the concept of a local individuating set as a data structure representing a particular object during discourse, we can restate the literal goal of referring as follows. If we assume a speaker's intention to refer to an object by using a noun phrase, the literal goal of his referring act is to make the hearer generate a local individuating set that determines that object by virtue of the hearer's recognition that the noun phrase is to be interpreted as a referring expression. In computational terms, this means that when it is recognized that the noun phrase is to be interpreted as a referring expression, the hearer generates a local individuating set containing a single presentation mode, namely,

(4.4) The one and only x such that x is the object the
speaker wants to say something about.

Of course, the hearer may have some beliefs about the object that the speaker has in mind. For example, if the noun phrase is "the gray whale," the hearer may have good reason to believe that the object about which the speaker wants to say something is a gray whale. But as we have seen, this may or may not indeed be the case. Note, therefore, that the descriptive content of referring expressions is not at all necessary for the initial individuation of the referent. The literal goal of referring can be achieved even if the descriptive content denotes nothing at all, is applied incorrectly, or is lacking altogether.

4.3   The discourse purpose of referring

Success in achieving the literal goal of referring is hardly enough. "And then we'll go out, Piglet, and sing my song to Eeyore," says Pooh. "Which song, Pooh?" asks Piglet. "The one we're going to sing to Eeyore," explains Pooh (Milne [1928]1965, 3). Pooh has certainly succeeded in achieving his literal goal, but Piglet is still puzzled. He is yet to *identify* the song Pooh is talking about.

Referent identification is the discourse purpose of referring. But the concept of identification itself is so vague and ambiguous that it is of little help to a computational approach. Let us begin, therefore, with two important distinctions.

First, the speaker's sense of "identify" is quite different from that of the hearer. A speaker is said to identify an object *for* or *to* a hearer, while the hearer is said to identify that object if the referring act is successful. Searle (1969), paying scant attention to the hearer's sense, bases his account of reference as a speech act on the speaker's sense of referent identification. He is, after all, interested first and foremost in showing how language use is a structured, rule-governed behavior, and he wants to show what it takes for a speech act to be performed *felicitously*, i.e., according to the rules. He is less interested in what makes a speech act a *success*, namely, what allows it to achieve its intended effects. As regards a computational model within the plan-based approach, on the other hand, effects on the hearer's mental state are really what counts. If no intended effects are formulated, there is little point in planning. Thus, in what follows I shall concentrate on the hearer's sense, taking the speaker's sense simply to be his plan to achieve the hearer's identification of the referent. Of course, Searle's notion of language as a rule-governed behavior still holds: conformity to the institutional rules of referring would constitute an important step in this plan.

Second, identification, as the discourse purpose of the referring act, should be carefully distinguished from identification in the sense of *knowing who* someone is. The former may be considered a *pragmatic* notion of identification. The latter is an *epistemic* one. Although the pragmatic notion of identification is also connected with knowledge (in the sense of knowing who the speaker is talking about), the two are quite distinct. To illustrate the difference, consider again the fingerprint example in which the detective, referring to Smith's murderer, says "The man whose fingerprints these are, whoever he is, is insane." Neither speaker nor hearer in this case knows who Smith's murderer is, and they cannot "identify" him if identification is interpreted epistemically. From a pragmatic point of view, however, there is a clear dichotomy: if the hearer makes the connection between "the man whose fingerprints these are" and "Smith's murderer," he has identified the person the speaker is talking about. Otherwise he has not.

The pragmatic and the epistemic senses of identification are obviously closely related conceptually, and the distinction between them is not as sharp as my example might suggest. Nevertheless, the distinction is important. As we have seen (Section 2.3.5), part of the argument against a descriptive theory of referring is that the notion of identification, on which such a descriptive account is founded, cannot be applied uniformly to both "referential" and "attributive" uses of definite descriptions. In the referential use, it is argued, there is an object to be identified. In the attributive, on the other hand, there is none. But the sense of "identification" in this argument is clearly epistemic. It pertains to the question of whether speaker and hearer know, in some manner, *who* the person the speaker is talking about is (e.g., who murdered Smith). However, the sense of "identification" that a descriptive theorist regards as being common to *all* successful uses of referring expressions (be they "referential" or "attributive") should be a pragmatic one. It should indicate when the hearer's grasp of what the speaker is talking about is adequate, *relative to the speaker's goals*. In planning terms: if, in the course of the speaker's attempt to achieve his objectives, it becomes clear that, as a precondition for further steps in the plan, he must achieve certain changes in the hearer's state of mind, and if the speaker believes that, by a successful act of referring, he can effect such changes, then these changes define the pragmatic notion of referent identification, i.e., the discourse purpose of referring. In other words, the hearer's sense of the pragmatic notion of referent identification is to be defined in terms of the appropriate changes in hearer's beliefs regarding a particular object that the speaker has in mind. These changes are "appropriate" relative to the goals of the speaker. Whether the hearer should ultimately come to know *who* the referent is does not necessarily have to be part of these goals (although sometimes it may be).

Not having to deal with the complicated concept of *knowing who* is certainly a relief, but we are hardly in the clear as yet. The pragmatic notion of identification seems as elusive as the epistemic one. Consider the following examples:

(4.5) Look at *this fellow* move! He must be doing at least a five-minute mile!

(4.6) Do you remember *the little playwright* who used to hang out with us in the sixties? He has just won the Pulitzer prize.

(4.7) Tell me what other plays were written by *Shakespeare*.

(4.8) (a) *Your friend* has just won $10,000.

(b) *My friend* has just won $10,000.

(c) *A friend of mine* has just won $10,000.

When we try to formulate the conditions under which a hearer can be said to identify the referents correctly in these examples, we find that in each case there is a different standard. In Sentence (4.5), the hearer is asked to identify the runner visually, but visual identification of Shakespeare is clearly not required in Sentence (4.7), although the hearer is still expected to identify the referent in some other way. In Sentence (4.6), locating the playwright in one's field of vision is also not called for, but the requirements for correct identification are surely different from Shakespeare's case. In the latter situation, the hearer needs to associate the name with a store of shared cultural knowledge. In the case of the talented playwright, a connection between the description and, perhaps, a memory image is essential.

Not only do methods of identification differ from utterance to utterance, but there are also differences in expected *degrees* of identification (analogous, perhaps, to variations in degrees of illocutionary force). In Sentence (4.8 a), the speaker would usually expect the hearer to know (or inquire) which friend the speaker is talking about. In uttering (4.8 c), on the other hand, the speaker usually signals that the hearer need not know which friend the speaker means. All that the hearer is expected to do is to note the existence of a particular individual, a friend of the speaker, who is lucky enough to have won such a large sum of money. The identification requirements in (4.8 b) may be similar to either (4.8 a) or (4.8 c), depending on contextual factors and on the purpose of the conversation.

Obviously, there is not just one "correct" method of referent identification. Still, we can look for a way to express the differences as variations in applying a single mechanism. If the reason for referent identification is the need to establish mutual agreement as to which object is being talked about, then a necessary precondition for successful referring is that the hearer understand the ground rules for reaching such an agreement. In general, such ground rules follow from the propositional content of the illocutionary act itself, general knowledge about the discourse (in particular, the speaker's goals), and principles of rational behavior. For example, according to any theory of action, if the speaker asks the hearer to pick up an object, it would have to follow that the hearer can comply with the request only if he can perceive the object he is about to manipulate. This fact implies a rather specific mode of identification: locating the object in one's immediate vicinity. Different ways to identify the referent are similarly derived in other circumstances. What is important for our model at this stage is this: if we accept the descriptive approach, we are committed to expressing or formalizing the rules for pragmatic identification *in terms of presentation modes*. In other words, the assumption is that a necessary and sufficient condition for a hearer to identify who or what the speaker is talking about is that the hearer come to think of the referent in terms of one or more appropriate presentation modes. For now, let us not trouble ourselves as to what an "appropriate" presentation mode is. The important point is that pragmatic identification is regarded as *entirely* a matter of having a representation whose descriptive content denotes the referent and which is appropriate in a sense to be explained. Of course, this does not mean that the appropriate presentation mode required for pragmatic identification can always be verbalized as a definite description. When I want you to locate an object in your vicinity, I want you to see it (or touch it, etc.). Now, perception is as good a source of presentation modes as any, but obviously, I do not necessarily expect you to translate what you see into words.

How can we begin to represent such a view in our model? If the hearer is cooperative, his pragmatic identification of the referent commences once the literal goal has been achieved. At this point, the hearer thinks of the referent in terms of a single presentation mode that is guaranteed to denote whatever the speaker has in mind. What happens next depends on circumstances, but it would be wrong to assume that there is always a unique representation upon which alone the hearer's identification succeeds or fails. For example, suppose that during a discussion of German theater I mention Bertolt Brecht to you. I believe that you have an individuating set of presentation modes associated with the name "Bertolt Brecht" that allows you to understand who it is I am talking about. But, although I hope that a significant segment of your individuating set would be rather similar to mine, there is usually no *particular* presentation mode that must be there, nor, of course, do I expect your individuating set to be identical to the one I have. What I expect, rather, is that your individuating set satisfy certain *constraints*: it should include, for example, a sufficient number of individuating facts concerning important plays that Brecht wrote, but the list does not have to correspond exactly to my list (nor does it have to be exhaustive).

Thus, instead of representing pragmatic identification as a relation between a hearer and a presentation mode, it is better to represent it as a relation between a hearer and a pair of formal entities: an *individuating set* and a set of *identification constraints*. If the literal goal of referring is to make the hearer generate an individuating set that contains a presentation mode of the referent, then the discourse purpose of referring is first, to make the hearer understand what identification constraints are operative, and second, to make him apply these constraints to the newly generated individuating set. Possible identification constraints may include the following:

- A requirement that the relevant individuating set should contain a *perceptual* presentation mode, to be acquired now or later.

- A requirement that the hearer should be able to merge the newly generated local individuating set with a preexisting, quasi-permanent one (additional identification constraints may be required so as to ensure that the latter set will be adequate for current purposes — see below).

- A requirement that the hearer be able to connect the new local individuating set with an existing *local* one. In particular, this includes such cases as "An old girlfriend of mine got married yesterday. *The lucky man* met her only three weeks ago."[2]

- An indication that identification is not expected *yet*, but that the hearer should "stay tuned": "Although *the lucky bastard* does not deserve it, John got a raise last week."

- A requirement that the relevant individuating set contain one or more presentation modes that are *privileged* with respect to the goals of the speaker. Suppose Art asks Ben:

---

[2] I intentionally refrain from using the term "anaphora" here. Although anaphora resolution is essential for pragmatic identification, it belongs to the *internal* perspective (see Section 1.1 above) and is a much more general phenomenon. The two should be kept apart, at least conceptually. The same goes for cataphora (Halliday and Hasan 1976), i.e., "backward anaphora," as shown in the next example of an identification constraint.

"Do you think *Ronald Reagan* will send the marines to invade Nicaragua?" Ben may have a very rich individuating set for Reagan. He may know, say, each and every detail of Reagan's Hollywood career. But if this individuating set does not contain a presentation mode such as *president of the United States* or *commander in chief* (at the time of the utterance), pragmatic identification has not been accomplished.

- The null identification constraint, under which success of the literal goal is already sufficient for pragmatic identification. "*An old friend of mine* once told me that ..." is an example. Since the speaker merely indicates the existence of an old friend whose actual identity is irrelevant, no further identification is necessary once the literal goal has been achieved.

This view of pragmatic identification in terms of individuating sets and constraints upon them is but a tentative suggestion at this stage. From a theoretical standpoint, such a view depends on an aforementioned central descriptive thesis — namely that, except in rare cases, individuating representation is both necessary and sufficient for a belief to be *de re*. A defense of this thesis will have to wait until Chapter 6. From a computational standpoint, this approach to pragmatic identification awaits careful specification and formalization of identification constraints and their derivation and satisfaction by a hearer — not an easy task by any means. But an important advantage of this view can already be pointed out: it enables us to eliminate the *standard-name assumption*.

As already mentioned, all natural-language systems I am aware of assume that every object in the domain has a standard name that is known to everyone. In these systems, referent identification is accomplished when (and only when) the system associates the referring expression that is being processed with the right standard name. This is undoubtedly quite useful if the system is expected to handle only a small number of objects in a very limited way; as a general principle, however, the standard-name assumption is obviously too strong. It is unreasonable to assume that every object that can be talked about has a universally known standard name. A doctor and a nurse, for example, can discuss a patient's left ear without bothering to give it a standard name. Similarly, we all know that the number 2^{64} has a standard name, but few of us know what it is. This does not prevent us from referring to this number — as, in fact, I just did.

Moreover, within the framework of the logic of knowledge and belief, the standard-name assumption has a rather nasty consequence, namely, that agents can never be wrong about the identity of objects they talk about. For example, under the standard-name assumption, it would have been impossible for Oedipus not to know that his mother was his wife. Since he could identify both, he must have had a standard name for each. The two names denoted the same thing in all possible worlds, including, of course, all possible worlds compatible with what Oedipus knew. Hence, Oedipus could not fail to know that his wife and his mother were one and the same. But surely an agent can be confused about the identity of an object while being perfectly capable of identifying it pragmatically. Representing pragmatic identification in terms of individuating sets and identification constraints solves this problem and, in general, eliminates the need for the standard-name assumption (although it does not *exclude* standard names). The question, of course, is whether the interpretation of pragmatic identification in terms of identification constraints can really be made to work computationally. This remains to be seen.

To sum up, here are the goals that motivate an act of referring: (1) the literal goal is to activate in the hearer's mind, by means of the hearer's recognition of this goal, a presentation mode denoting the referent; (2) the discourse purpose of referring is pragmatic identification. This latter goal is achieved, if the hearer is cooperative, in two steps: first, the hearer derives the appropriate identification constraints; he then attempts to identify the referent by applying those constraints to the set containing the initial presentation mode.

4.4   Summary of Chapter 4

The intentions or goals of a speaker that are relevant to the study of communication are those whose recognition plays a part in their satisfaction. But there are two types of such intentions or goals. First, there is the intention whose recognition guarantees its satisfaction (e.g., the intention to congratulate); second, there is the goal whose recognition constitutes a part of the plan to achieve it, but the recognition is not sufficient in itself to ensure success (e.g., the goal of making a hearer answer a question). The former constitutes the *literal goal* of utterances, while the latter represents the conversation's *discourse purposes.*

In a communication situation, a speaker typically attempts to achieve his discourse purpose by achieving the literal goal. This is what makes language useful for attaining some of our objectives, and is the foundation of the plan-based approach to a theory of speech acts. Since we take referring to be a speech act and accept the plan-based approach, we need to specify the literal goal and discourse purpose that typically provide the rationale for the performance of a referring act.

Literal goals are satisfied once they are recognized. To find the literal goal of referring, therefore, we must isolate a referring intention that would require no more for success than its recognition. Once we adopt the descriptive approach to reference, this is not hard to do. If, according to the descriptive approach, mental representations that denote an object are an essential part of the ability to think of that object, and if invoking such a representation in the hearer's mind is an essential part of referring, we then have what we want — namely, that the recognition of an intention to invoke in the hearer a representation of an object suffices to produce such a representation. Once the hearer recognizes that the speaker wants him to have a representation of the object the speaker has in mind, the hearer does indeed possesses such a representation, namely, *the object the speaker has in mind*. The literal goal of referring, therefore, is the goal of producing a representation in the hearer's mind by means of the hearer's recognition of this goal. Said in a different way, the literal goal of referring is to have the hearer interpret a noun phrase as a referring expression. The two formulations are equivalent: to interpret a noun phrase as a referring expression is to recognize that the speaker intends that the hearer should have a representation of an object.

Satisfying the literal goal is only the first step. The hearer must yet *identify* the referent. We should, however, make two important distinctions. First, we should distinguish between identification as something the speaker does *for* the hearer and identification as something the hearer is expected to do. Second, we should distinguish between identification in terms of the hearer's *knowing who* the referent is (epistemic identification) and identification in terms of the hearer's understanding who the speaker is talking about (pragmatic identification).

What is important to us is the hearer's sense of pragmatic identification. Making the hearer identify the referent pragmatically is the discourse purpose of referring, but there is no single canonical way of defining success. Criteria for pragmatic identification that are acceptable in one context would be inappropriate in another. Nevertheless, we can try to find a single model in which all the criteria are reflected. Here too the descriptive approach provides a clue.

Within the descriptive approach, the rules for pragmatic identification must be specified in terms of presentation modes. To identify an object is to possess the "appropriate" presentation mode. Moreover, as we do not have a single criterion for pragmatic identification, we usually do not have a single presentation mode in accordance with which identification succeeds or fails. Rather, we have *identification constraints* on the kind of representation the hearer should possess. This suggests that pragmatic identification can be depicted as a relation between a hearer and a pair of formal entities: an *individuating set* and a set of *identification constraints*. The discourse purpose of referring, therefore, is to first make the hearer derive the appropriate identification constraints, then have him identify the referent by applying these constraints to the set containing the presentation mode generated by the satisfaction of the literal goal.

5
Conversationally relevant descriptions

Any descriptive theory of referring as a speech act must address, among other things, the following two questions: (1) what is the difference between an intention to express a singular proposition and an intention to express a general, "Russellian," one? (2) why does a speaker choose one rather than the other?

To place these questions in their proper perspective again, let us return to the argument against the descriptive approach. In a nutshell, there are four related claims. The first is really a cluster of linguistic observations: some referring expressions do not have any descriptive content conventionally associated with them and even if such content is present, it is usually not rich enough to individuate an object; moreover, even if the requisite richness exists, the individuated object may not be the one the speaker actually has in mind. This is the first claim.

The second claim is a theoretical abstraction of the first: in all cases in which descriptive content plays a limited role (if any) in determining reference, the proposition expressed by the speaker is singular — namely, it contains the referent itself as a constituent, rather than any representation of it.[1]

---

[1] Since the descriptive content can indicate a relational property, a proposition expressed by a simple subject predicate sentence can be singular without having the referent as a constituent. For example, the proposition expressed by "the square root of 9 is odd" contains the integer 9 as a constituent (and is therefore formally singular), but its referent is the number 3 — which is not a constituent at all. For the sake of simplicity, however, I shall continue to assume that a proposition is singular if and only if it contains its referent (i.e., the object it is about) as a constituent.

The third claim is that, as far as referring is concerned, the act of expressing a singular proposition is fundamentally different from the act of expressing a nonsingular proposition in which a representation plays the crucial role in determining what the proposition is about. Indeed, the new theorist of reference would insist that "real" referring takes place only when a singular proposition is expressed.

The fourth claim is putatively supported by the previous three. It is the thesis that the mind has a rather limited role in determining reference. When we use referring expressions, the new theorist argues, what we think and talk about is less a function of representations inside the mind than a function of causal chains outside it.

I accept the first and second claims. That is, I do not dispute the observations that constitute the first claim. Given the way the literal goal and discourse purpose of referring are formulated, these observations should not be surprising. The descriptive content of *referring expressions*, if it exists at all, indeed has a limited role in securing reference. Moreover, if a speaker does not intend any particular mode of presentation to be recognized by the hearer, the proposition expressed by the former must be singular. If descriptive content is not intended to be recognized, it cannot be meant.

At the same time, I reject the third and fourth claims. That is, I believe the capacity for referring to be grounded in the existence of individuating mental representations (clustered in individuating sets) and, in addition, I consider the general mechanism of referring to be the same regardless of whether singular or nonsingular propositions are expressed. In both cases, the speaker intends to invoke in the hearer an individuating set under certain identification constraints. Yet I cannot just leave things at that. If there are genuine differences between expressing a singular proposition and expressing a nonsingular one, the model I propose should be capable of representing these differences. The task at hand, then, is to explain the disparate roles that descriptive content fulfills in referring acts.

5.1 Speaker's reference and indirect speech acts

As we have seen, a speaker may sometimes be successful in his speech act, even though the referring expression he uses fails to denote the object he wishes to say something about. Thus, a speaker may make, say, a true statement about something, even though the definite description he uses applies to a different object entirely or worse yet, to nothing at all. On other occasions, however, if the speech act is to be about anything, some object must uniquely fit the description used. It is this pair of linguistic phenomena that gave rise to the *denotation criterion*, which in turn provided one way of distinguishing referential from attributive uses of definite descriptions.

How should we explain what it is that the denotation criterion characterizes? What sort of intentions and goals does a speaker have in each case? Why is it that in one case the description used is dispensable, while in the other case it is crucial? Both Kripke (1977) and Searle (1979b) have proposed some answers to these questions, using as their point of departure the Gricean distinction between what sentences mean and what speakers mean in uttering these sentences. Yet both Kripke and Searle leave important aspects of referring intentions unaccounted for.

Kripke distinguishes between semantic reference and speaker's reference. The semantic referent of an expression is the object denoted or designated by that expression in accordance with the conventions of the language. Speaker's referent, on the other hand, is the object the speaker wishes to talk about. As speaker's meaning can differ from sentence meaning, Kripke argues, so can speaker's referent be distinct from the semantic referent (indeed, the latter two notions, according to Kripke, are just special cases of speaker's meaning and sentence meaning, respectively). Suppose Art and Ben see Charles in the distance and mistake him for their old friend David P. Shnorkel. "What is David P. Shnorkel doing?" asks Art. "David P. Shnorkel is raking the leaves," answers Ben. Whenever Art and Ben use the name "David P. Shnorkel," they have the *general* intention to refer to David P. Shnorkel. On this particular occasion, however, they both also have a *specific* intention to refer to the man raking the leaves (i.e., Charles). Now, Kripke argues, the *general* intention gives us the semantic referent, while the *specific* intention provides the speaker's referent. The two intentions diverge, but, since the context is sufficient to indicate who is being discussed, all is well. When reference can succeed despite the failure of denotation, the general and specific intentions are distinct. But when successful denotation is required, the specific intention and the general intention are one and the same, namely, to indicate the semantic referent as the object the speaker is talking about.

Searle's point of departure is also the distinction between what expressions mean and what speakers mean in uttering these expressions. Instead of the semantic-versus-speaker's-*referent* dichotomy, however, he uses his own distinction between direct and indirect speech acts (Searle 1979a). According to Searle, one way in which sentence meaning can differ from speaker's meaning is when a primary speech act is performed indirectly by means of a secondary one. For example, I might ask a man to get off my foot by asserting "You are standing on my foot." My primary speech act is a request I made indirectly by performing a secondary speech act, i.e., an assertion. Now the act of referring, Searle argues, is always accomplished by invoking a representation of an object under one *aspect* or another, where an aspect of an object is a fact that individuates it (very much like the way presentation modes are understood in this study). But, Searle continues, just as a primary speech act can be performed by means of a secondary one, so can a primary aspect of the referent be invoked by means of another aspect. In other words, a speaker's act of referring to an object as satisfying the primary aspect can be performed by virtue of an act of referring in which a secondary aspect is mentioned. For example, I may say "Her husband is kind to her," whereas what I really mean is that the man she is being seen with is kind to her. Reference succeeds even though the secondary aspect may fail to denote the right object simply because the primary aspect is recognized as such by the hearer and is sufficient for indicating who the speaker is talking about. Cases in which the referring expression *must* denote the referent are simply those in which the aspect actually expressed by the hearer's utterance is the primary one — that is, no indirect referring act is being performed and the speaker's meaning and sentence meaning are identical.

Both Kripke's and Searle's accounts are explanations of Donnellan's distinction within a theory of language use. As far as the *denotational aspect* of the distinction is concerned, there is much that I agree with in both accounts. At the same time, I do not think that they capture one important aspect of the way referring expressions are used. To see what the problem is, let us consider the following three variations of Donnellan's example:

Referential case: Ralph attends the trial of Jones, who is charged with having murdered Smith. Ralph is inclined to believe that Jones is guilty. Being familiar with Jones's medical history and having observed his strange behavior over an extended period, Ralph also believes that Jones is insane. He expresses his belief by saying

(5.1) Smith's murderer is insane.

Attributive case: Ralph is investigating Smith's murder. He is sure that whoever murdered Smith in such a brutal way must be insane; expressing his belief, he says

(5.2) Smith's murderer, whoever he is, must be insane.

Fingerprint case: This is similar to the attributive case except that, after discovering clear fingerprints on the murder weapon, the detective says

(5.3) The man whose fingerprints these are must be insane.

Although the speaker utters (5.3), what he *means* is the proposition expressed by (5.2).

Let us see first how Searle's account applies to the referential case. The secondary aspect is clear enough: *Smith's murderer*. But what is the primary aspect? Searle argues that

> one says "Smith's murderer" but means also: that man over there, Jones, the one accused of the crime, the person now being cross-examined by the district attorney, the one who is behaving so strangely, and so on. *But notice that ... though the expression actually used may be false of the object referred to and thus the object does not satisfy the aspect under which it is referred to, there must always be some other aspect under which the speaker could have referred to the object and which is satisfied by the object. Furthermore, this aspect is such that if nothing satisfies it the statement cannot be true*. (Searle 1979b, 144. Italics in original.)

The basic premise of Searle's argument lies squarely within the descriptive approach and, in my opinion, it is essentially correct. It boils down to the following thesis: referring to an object presupposes the ability to think of it, which in turn requires a presentation mode that uniquely individuates that object (this thesis is discussed below in Chapter 6). However, there is a question I would like to pose here. Is there a particular aspect (or collection of aspects) in the referential case *that the hearer is expected to recognize as the one that really counts?* In other words, is there a primary aspect (in

89

Searle's sense) under which the speaker intends the hearer to think of the referent? I believe the answer must be in the negative. There is no particular aspect or presentation mode that, if the hearer failed to grasp it, he would misunderstand the speaker.

Let us consider the situation in terms of individuating sets. When Ralph initiates the referring act, he has an individuating set for Jones that includes the presentation mode *the murderer of Smith*; when the referring act is completed, the hearer has an individuating set for Jones that contains the presentation mode *the person Ralph is talking about*. Searle's point is that, although several presentation modes in Ralph's set may fail to denote anything, at least *some* of them must be correct; otherwise Ralph could not have referred to Jones at all. This, I believe, must be right. But which of Ralph's representations of Jones must be in the *hearer's* individuating set if the referring act is to be successful? It seems to me that none of Ralph's representations of Jones are really required. As a matter of fact, it is not difficult to concoct a case in which Ralph's and the hearer's respective individuating sets differ radically without hindering Ralph's ability to refer successfully. In other words, in the referential case the speaker does not mind much under which of the aspects on Searle's list (if any) the hearer thinks of Jones, as long as the hearer, under appropriate identification constraints, recognizes Jones as the subject of conversation. This is very different from the fingerprint case, in which there is a particular way the speaker intends the hearer to think of the referent and a primary aspect is easily discernible. Thus, Searle's account does not distinguish between a case in which a primary aspect is intended to be recognized and one in which such recognition is not essential for comprehension.

Kripke's account reveals the same weakness, albeit for different reasons. His notion of the specific intention to refer to an object on a particular occasion does not imply any intention to refer under a particular aspect or presentation mode. While this seems to be the situation in the referential case, the specific referring intention in the fingerprint case is more complex. In the latter, not only is the hearer expected to identify the speaker's referent, but he is expected to do so in a *particular* way. Kripke, like Searle, misses the important distinction in referring intentions between the referential case and the fingerprint case.

Moreover, this shortcoming in both Searle's and Kripke's accounts leaves their explanation of the attributive case incomplete. In the latter case, according to Kripke, the specific referring intention is simply identical to the general one, namely, an intention to refer to the semantic referent. But the speaker's referring intentions in the attributive case are very similar to those in the fingerprint case. In both, the speaker intends the hearer to recognize the referent under the presentation mode *the murderer of Smith*; in the one case, however, the semantic and the speaker's referents are distinct, while in the other they are identical. Searle, on the other hand, takes the attributive case to be one in which the primary aspect is the one actually expressed and, consequently, there is no gap between the speaker's meaning and sentence meaning (as far as the referring expression is concerned). But the speaker's referring intentions in the fingerprint case are very different from those in the referential case, even though in both the description actually used expresses only a secondary aspect. We still have to account for the fact that sometimes there is a particular aspect that is intended to be recognized, whether or not it is in fact represented in the utterance.

At this point, it should be obvious what the problem is. The fundamental question to be asked is not whether a speaker's meaning is the same as sentence meaning, but rather what kind of referring intentions are at work. Such intentions fall into two types: (1) referring without being overly concerned as to the presentation mode under which the referent is identified by the hearer, and (2) intending the hearer to think of the referent *in a particular way*. The problem of explaining the different roles of descriptive content in referring acts should therefore be rephrased as follows: why is it sometimes important for a speaker *how* the hearer identifies the referent?

5.2   Functional and conversational relevance

The primary function of definite descriptions (as referring expressions) is to identify an object for the hearer. They must enable the hearer to recognize what object is being talked about. A descriptive theorist (e.g., Strawson 1959) would insist that a necessary condition for identification in conversation is that the hearer learn an individuating fact about the referent. But surely this is hardly sufficient in itself to secure reference. As Searle (1969) points out, not all individuating facts are equally useful for identification. Compare the following examples:

(5.4)   The flight whose number is the square root of 585,225 from the home of the 1975 NBA champions to the city that is 186 miles north of New York is ready for takeoff.

(5.5) Flight No. 765 from Oakland to Boston is ready for
    takeoff.

It is clear why the latter description is useful for identification,
whereas the former is not. Not too many people remember that
the Oakland Warriors won the National Basketball Association title
in 1975, fewer yet take the trouble to memorize mileage charts, and
hardly any passenger would bother to calculate the square root of a
six-digit number. Thus, for a definite description to be useful for referent identification, a speaker must take into account not only what
individuating facts are true of the referent, but also what the hearer
knows or, at least, is willing to find out.

Sometimes, however, two descriptions — both equally useful for
identifying the intended referent — still cannot be used interchangeably in a given conversation. The description employed, in addition
to being useful for identification, has to be *relevant.* Consider the
following example. As part of his effort to recruit more young people
into the police force, the mayor of New York proclaims in a public
speech that

(5.6) New York needs more policemen.

Instead of "New York" he might have used "The Big Apple," or "The
city by the Hudson," or some such description, but

(5.7) The city with the world's largest Jewish community
    needs more policemen

won't do, even though the latter description might be useful enough
in identifying New York for the audience. It is simply irrelevant
in this context. On the other hand, the same description that is
employed in (5.7) may be quite relevant in another context. For
example, suppose the mayor is giving a speech during a reception in
honor of Israel's prime minister. In that context, the statement

(5.8) The city with the world's largest Jewish community
    welcomes Israel's prime minister

makes perfect sense. The difference, of course, is in the relevance of
the description to the statement in (5.8), contrasted with its irrelevance to the one in (5.7).

Thus, there are two senses in which a definite description might
be regarded as relevant. First, a description serves the purpose of

letting the hearer know what the speaker is talking about. Taking into account what the hearer knows about the world, the description (in conjunction with the context of the utterance) should delineate identification constraints that the hearer is able to satisfy. A description that has utility in this sense may be called a *functionally relevant* description. Second, as Examples (5.7) or (5.8) indicate, a description might exhibit a type of relevance or irrelevance that is not merely related to its usefulness for identification. Such a description might be regarded as *conversationally relevant* (or conversationally *irrelevant*, as the case may be).[2]

Every instance of a definite description as a referring expression has to be functionally relevant, since it must enable the hearer to identify the subject of the conversation. However, if identification is the *only* intended function of the description, any other functionally relevant description would do just as well (provided that it is not conversationally *irrelevant*). For example, suppose Art wants Ben to bring him a certain book from the library. Art must refer to the book in a way that enables Ben to identify the book in question, but which description he uses is unimportant. He can refer to the book by its name, its color and shape, its content, its location, or by some other adequate description. Any characteristic that can efficiently identify the book for Ben will do. Moreover, once it is established that the description has to be only functionally relevant, Ben is free to use the context in any way he finds helpful in determining the intended referent. Indeed, he can identify what Art is referring to by using contextual information that Art may not be aware of himself or even have any knowledge about. For example, if a child tells a doctor who has just diagnosed his color blindness: "I want the red book," the doctor, using the medical information as yet unknown to the speaker, may identify the referent (a green book). As long as the description is only functionally relevant, the hearer can simply *ignore* it, in whole or in part, if he has grounds for believing that he can figure out what the speaker has in mind independently of the description employed.

In other cases, the description is expected to do more than just identify the intended referent for the hearer. Consider the following examples:

---

[2] A speaker may intend to convey a conversationally relevant description without actually uttering it (e.g., in the fingerprint example). In such cases, what we have are not *descriptions* but conversationally relevant *presentation modes*. In the following pages I ignore this distinction.

(5.9) This happy man must have been drinking champagne.

(5.10) The man who murdered Smith so brutally has to be insane.

(5.11) The winner of the race will get $10,000.

In these examples, the description is used to imply something that is not part of what the speaker says. In Example (5.9), it is implied that the man's happiness is due to his drinking. In (5.10), it is implied that the main reason for the belief that the murderer is insane is the very fact that he committed such a brutal homicide. The implication in (5.11) is that the only reason the winner received $10,000 is his victory in a particular race. In all these cases, there is a certain relationship between a specific characteristic of the referent mentioned in the description and whatever is said about that referent. In such cases, the choice of the description is important as the latter is both functionally and conversationally relevant. Other descriptions, even if equally useful for identification, would not be as successful in conveying the intended implication. For example:

(5.12) This man from North Carolina must have been drinking champagne.

(5.13) The man whose fingerprints these are has to be insane.

Suppose a particular race is fixed, the winner is going to be Sam, and I know that to be the case. Compare (5.11) with

(5.14) Sam will get $10,000.

The intended implications *can*, of course, be conveyed by Sentences (5.12), (5.13), and (5.14), if the context is rich enough to reveal the unmentioned conversationally relevant description (i.e., if the context indicates that (1) the man from North Carolina is happy in a special way, (2) the man whose fingerprints these are is Smith's murderer, and (3) Sam is going to win the race). But note the difference between these cases and those in which only identification is required. In the latter, the hearer is allowed to elicit any clue from the context that might enable him to identify the referent. The speaker himself may not be aware of such a clue. In the case illustrated by Examples (5.12–5.14), however, it is not enough that the hearer merely identify the referent. He must identify it under a certain mode of presentation that the speaker intends the hearer to recognize, or else the intended implication cannot be understood. Such a mode of presentation is what the conversationally relevant description expresses. Sentences (5.12–5.14) need a highly constrained context to convey their implication, while Sentences (5.9–5.11) do not, simply because the conversationally relevant description of the referent is explicitly indicated in the latter, but not in the former.[3]

Of course, not only definite descriptions but *any* referring expression should be functionally relevant. Moreover, a conversationally relevant description may be implied even when the referring expression actually used lacks any conventional descriptive content. A speaker may *say* "Shakespeare wrote the best play about jealousy," and the proper name "Shakespeare" indeed lacks any conventionally associated descriptive content. Nevertheless, a conversationally relevant description of Shakespeare — namely, "the author of *Othello*" — may be required in order to understand what the speaker is talking about.

Schematically, therefore, I distinguish two kinds of referring intentions, which influence a speaker's choice of referring expressions in three general ways:

Functional referring: If the conversation does not require any conversationally relevant description, any adequately identifying description will do (provided that it is not conversationally irrelevant). Let us call this the case of *functional referring*. In functional referring, the proposition the speaker expresses is singular, and the speaker's meaning and sentence meaning may or may not be the same depending on what kind of referring expression is employed. If a description is used (for example, in the referential case), the speaker's meaning and sentence meaning are mutually distinct, since the meaning of the utterance includes the descriptive content of the referring expression, while the proposition expressed by the speaker does not. If a proper name is used, then, as far as the act of referring is concerned, the speaker's meaning and sentence meaning are identical, as proper names do not have descriptive content conventionally associated with them. In other words, when the sentence "David P. Shnorkel is raking the leaves" is uttered in the aforementioned cir-

---

[3]Thus, Examples (5.12–5.14) illustrate a case in which the description *used* is only functionally relevant, whereas some other unmentioned presentation mode of the object is *conversationally* relevant.

cumstances, the content of the *utterance* is the singular proposition that the speaker intends to express.

Conversational referring: If a certain description of the referent is conversationally relevant, the speaker must make sure the hearer will recognize that. In choosing a referring expression, however, the speaker has two options:

1. The speaker may choose to express the conversationally relevant description explicitly. Let us call this the case of *explicit conversational referring*. In such cases, the speaker's meaning and the sentence meaning are one and the same — at least as far as the act of referring is concerned — and the proposition expressed is not singular. Paradigmatically attributive uses are like this.

2. The speaker may use a referring expression that is only functionally relevant, but he can do so only if the context is sufficient to indicate the conversationally relevant description. If the hearer fails to recognize this description or is unable to determine in what manner the description is relevant, his comprehension of the utterance remains incomplete. This is *implicit conversational referring*, which is illustrated by the fingerprint case. In implicit conversational referring, a speaker's meaning and sentence meaning are always distinct and the proposition expressed is not singular.

A summary of these options can be found in Figure 5.1.[4]

With this analysis, we can express the difference between the referential case and the fingerprint case, on the one hand, and between the latter and the attributive case, on the other. However, we still have not answered the question that initiated this discussion: *why* does it sometimes matter how the hearer identifies the referent? What role, in other words, do conversationally relevant descriptions play in the speech act as a whole? A preliminary answer, based on Grice's theory of implicature, is offered in the next section.

---

[4]The distinctions depicted in Figure 5.1 involve a fair amount of idealization. For example, a speaker may use a definite description containing several predicates, some of which are merely functional, while the others are conversationally relevant.

5.3 Descriptions as implicatures

A conversation, as Grice views it, is a verbal exchange among agents who, at any given moment, share some mutually accepted objective. If it is assumed that the agents are rational, they are expected to follow what Grice calls the *cooperative principle*:

> **Cooperative Principle:** Make your conversational contribution such as is required, at the stage at which it occurs, by the accepted purpose or direction of the talk exchange in which you are engaged. (Grice 1975, 67)

To *implicate* something, according to Grice, is to imply, suggest, or mean something without expressing it explicitly. Grice's theory of conversational implicature shows how, given certain assumptions regarding the structure of conversation, a speaker is able to convey what he does not say explicitly.

Grice's theory of conversational implicature can be seen as comprising two elements: (1) a list of *conversational maxims* and (2) an *inference mechanism* for inferring the implicature.

	Functional referring (Identification only)	Conversational referring Explicit (CRD[a] uttered)	Implicit (CRD[a] implied)
Speaker's meaning	Singular propositions	General propositions	General propositions
Sentence meaning	General or singular[b]	General propositions	General or singular[b]
Gap[c]	Possible[d]	No	Always

[a] Conversationally relevant description.
[b] Depending on the referring expression used.
[c] Between speaker's meaning and sentence meaning (as far as referring is concerned).
[d] If a definite description is used.

Figure 5.1: Functional and conversational referring

The conversational maxims state general instructions on how to conduct a conversation in a cooperative manner. These directions for specific fulfillment of the cooperative principle are divided into four groups, as shown in Figure 5.2.

The inference mechanism utilizes the maxims to show how a hearer can be expected to understand what the speaker implicates. Consider, for example, this short dialogue:

> **Art:** What do you think of the movie *The Year of the Dragon* Ben?
>
> **Ben:** I made the mistake of going to see it, but no force on earth could make me discuss it any further.
>
> **Art:** That bad, eh?

On the face of it, Ben seems not as cooperative as he should be, since he does not *say* what he thinks of the movie. Nevertheless, Ben counts on Art's ability to reason as follows:

> Ben seems to have violated the first maxim of quantity, yet I have no reason to believe that he does not wish to cooperate with me. This apparent contradiction can be resolved if Ben thinks the movie is so bad that there is no point in even discussing it. Furthermore, Ben knows (and knows that I know that he knows) that I can arrive at such a conclusion. He has done nothing to stop me from so interpreting his utterance (for example, he has not indicated in any

Quantity	Relation
Make your contribution as informative as is required.	Be relevant.
Do not make your contribution more informative than is required.	
Quality	**Manner**
Do not say what you believe to be false.	Avoid obscurity.
Do not say that for which you lack adequate evidence.	Avoid ambiguity.
	Be brief.
	Be orderly.

Figure 5.2: Grice's conversational maxims

way that he does not wish to discuss the movie because he is angry with me). Therefore, he intends
to make me think that, in his opinion, the movie is
worthless. So this is what he has implicated.

Note that Art's reply serves as a confirmation that he indeed understood the implicature.

This example illustrates the general mechanism whereby conversational implicatures are understood (cf. Grice 1975, 70). A hearer
begins by observing a speaker's apparent violation of one or more
conversational maxims. The hearer then attempts to resolve the difficulty by generating hypotheses about the speaker's intentions that
explain his seemingly uncooperative behavior. The hypothesis that
the hearer takes to be, in some sense, the "most obvious" represents
the intended implicature.[5]

In the remainder of this chapter, I make use of Grice's theory
in an attempt to characterize the role of conversationally relevant
descriptions in discourse. The main point is simple enough: conversationally relevant descriptions function as part of implicatures of a
particular type. The problem is to specify what this type is.

Why should we think that an implicature always exists when a
conversationally relevant description is used? The reason for this has
to do with the fact that discourse is something more than a simple
sum of the isolated sentences that constitute its parts. Judging from
many examples I have used so far, one might conclude that my model
for human communication is the Chinese fortune cookie; that typical
conversations consist of long stretches of silence, punctuated by such
enigmatic expressions as "Shakespeare was born in Stratford-upon-
Avon," or "9 is necessarily odd." Such examples are occasionally
useful for making a point succinctly, but, at the same time, I am sure
they drive some linguists to tears. They are right in their indignation,
of course: this is not what linguistic behavior is all about. Discourse
consists of a sequence of utterances that are linked in ways that *make
sense*. That is, there are usually *reasons* a speaker says what he says
in the order and manner in which he says it and, in general, a hearer

---

[5] Recognizing a hypothesis as "the most obvious" is surely insufficient. The
hearer should believe that the hypothesis he formulated is *mutually believed* to
be the obvious one. That is, not only should the hearer take this hypothesis to
be the most obvious, but he should also believe that the *speaker* thinks so, that
the speaker believes that he, the hearer, thinks so, and so on. The role of mutual
belief (and knowledge) in referring will be discussed later on.

must have a clue as to what these reasons are (this is why plan recognition is so important for plan-based theories of speech acts). Of course, the hearer cannot hope to know or even guess *all* the reasons that made the speaker participate in the discourse, but he can — indeed *must* — recognize some of them. As already mentioned (Chapter 4), many researchers have pointed out how the recognition of what the speaker is "up to" contributes to the coherence and comprehensibility of the discourse.

Now, the unstated reasons that must be recognized for discourse coherence are *by definition* implicated, since they must be inferred in order to preserve the assumption that a speaker is being cooperative. This is precisely what an implicature is. Moreover, turning to conversationally relevant descriptions, we should observe that, by their very nature, they cannot be just functionally relevant. That is, the assumption that they are intended merely as tools for identification is not enough to make the discourse coherent. This, after all, is precisely what distinguishes functionally relevant descriptions from conversationally relevant ones. Hence, additional assumptions are required to make sense of the way the speaker employs the latter descriptions. These assumptions themselves must be implicated.

Thus, when he uses a conversationally relevant description, a speaker implicates something. The content of implicatures that accompany such descriptions depends on circumstances, but they all share a rather specific form. My method in uncovering this form is this: adopting the hearer's perspective, I begin by postulating that, if the referring expression used by the speaker is merely functionally relevant, he must be viewed as uncooperative. Then I outline a sequence of deductions that eliminate the apparent conflict between what the speaker says and the assumption of his cooperation.

5.3.1 *Recognizing conversational relevance*

The general mechanism for recognizing a conversationally relevant description follows the familiar Gricean path. A hearer begins by assuming that the referring expression is only functionally relevant, and then gets into difficulties. An obvious strategy is illustrated by Example (5.8) above. At first glance, it appears that the mayor violated the third maxim of manner ("Be brief"): he used a long and cumbersome description ("the city with the largest Jewish community"), although a much shorter and functionally superior one was available ("New York"). However, a hearer can easily make sense of the mayor's behavior by assuming that the referring expression is not merely a tool for identification. That is, it must be conversationally relevant.

Another strategy for letting a hearer recognize a conversationally relevant description is illustrated by "Smith's murderer" (interpreted "attributively"). In this example, the assumption that the description is only functionally relevant would lead to an inexplicable violation of the second maxim of quality. It is obvious that no one really knows yet who murdered Smith. Thus, if the description is only functionally relevant, the hearer would be puzzled as to how the speaker could form an opinion about the sanity of a person whose identity is unknown to him.

5.3.2 Speaker's assertion

As already mentioned, when a conversationally relevant description is used (or implied), the proposition the speaker is trying to express is not singular, and lends itself to Russellian analysis. Thus, if a speaker asserts a statement of the form

(5.15) D is F,

where D is a conversationally relevant description, the proposition expessed by the speaker is this: something that uniquely has the property of being D also has the property of being F. That is,

(5.16) $(\exists x)(D(x) \,\&\, (\forall y)(D(y) \to x = y) \,\&\, F(x))$.

Note that (5.16) is equivalent to the conjunction of two propositions. The first is the *uniqueness* condition, which states that one and only one thing has the property of being D. That is,

(5.17) (**Uniqueness**) $(\exists x)(D(x) \,\&\, (\forall y)(D(y) \to x = y))$,

while the second is the universal generalization, according to which any object that has the property of being D also has the property of being F:

(5.18) (**Universality**) $(\forall z)(D(z) \to F(z))$.

Both the uniqueness and the universality conditions have to be satisfied if what the speaker means is to be true. But it does not follow from this that the speaker *asserts* these conditions. Both Strawson ([1950]1971) and, following him, Searle (1969, 157ff.) have argued in their criticism of Russell's theory of descriptions that the uniqueness condition, though presupposed, is not *asserted*. For example, when a speaker says that the queen of England is ill, he is not simultaneously *asserting* that there is one and only one queen of England. This is surely true of the uniqueness condition, but I think that, when a conversationally relevant description is used, the *universality* condition is indeed asserted or, at least, strongly implied. In a sense, what the speaker attempts to convey is that *any* object satisfying the description has the property F, which is why it is so natural to insert "whoever he is" in the paradigmatic examples of attributive uses of definite descriptions. By saying "Smith's murderer, whoever he is, is insane" the speaker obviously means that for *any* person, if he is Smith's murderer, he is insane, which has exactly the same form as (5.18). Note that the convention for using definite descriptions to express universal statements already exists in the language ("The whale is a mammal" — i.e., for any x, if x is a whale, then x is a mammal). Moreover, very frequently, when a conversationally relevant description is used, the speaker would maintain that the universality condition is true even if uniqueness fails. Suppose it turns out that not one but two culprits are responsible for Smith's sorry state. If our speaker asserted that Smith's murderer, whoever he is, is insane, he is very likely to say now that *both* are insane, rather than withdraw his original judgment altogether. All in all, it seems to me very plausible to assume that, when conversationally relevant descriptions are used, the universal claim is not only one of the truth conditions (together with uniqueness), but part of what is asserted as well.

5.3.3 Extensional and intensional justification

A rational speaker who observes the Gricean maxims is expected, among other things, to obey the second maxim of quality. That is, he is expected to have "adequate evidence" for what he asserts. What counts as adequate evidence obviously depends on the context: we have different standards for assertions in a scientific article than we do for those made in a gossipy chat. Nevertheless, in all verbal exchanges a speaker is expected to provide reasonable justification for what he says. He must be able to answer such questions as "How do you know?" "Why do you think so?" and so on. If he cannot, the assumption as to his cooperation cannot be maintained.

   If a universal statement such as (5.18) is part of what a speaker asserts, he must be able to justify it. The hearer may not know exactly what the speaker's evidence is for believing this generalization but the hearer can reason about the *type* of evidence or justification the speaker is expected to have. In particular, I want to draw a distinction between *extensional* and *intensional* justification of universal statements. This distinction will help us see what sort of justification a speaker can offer for a statement such as (5.18) when a conversationally relevant description is used.

The distinction between extensional and intensional justification of universal statements is based on a familiar distinction in the philosophy of science between accidental and lawlike generalizations (see Walters 1967 for a survey). Not all universal generalizations are scientific laws. For example, the following statement, although true, is not a law of nature:

(5.19) All mountains on earth are less than 30,000 feet high.

On the other hand, this next statement is:

(5.20) All basketballs are attracted to the center of the earth.

What is the difference? Well, there are several, but two related ones have specific relevance for us. First, only the latter generalization supports counterfactual statement. If a mountain on earth were to be examined a billion years from now, would it still be less than 30,000 feet tall? We don't know. Changes in the earth's surface occur constantly; Mount Everest, for instance, needs a mere 972 additional feet to render (5.19) false. On the other hand, if a player were to make a jump shot a billion years from now, the basktball would still find its way to the ground. A law of nature does not lose its validity over time.

Second, there is a crucial difference in the manner in which statements (5.19) and (5.20) are *justified*. The generalization about mountains on earth is supported by observation: all mountains on earth have been measured and found to be under 30,000 feet in hight. I do not know *why* this is so. As far as I am concerned this is just one more incidental fact about the world I live in. The generalization about basketballs, on the other hand, is derived from a more general principle that explains why such material objects as basketballs behave the way they do. Such a derivation is an essential part of an explanation as to why (5.20) is true. It also contributes to the cohesiveness of our experience: what science provides us with, among other things, is the reassuring knowledge that natural phenomena do not just happen, but rather conform to a general scheme that provides the basis for both explanation and prediction. Thus, our confidence in the truth of (5.20) is not merely the result of examining a large sample of basketballs. We also have a theory that explains why they do not just happen to descend whenever dropped, but, in a sense, *must* do so.

Given these two differences between accidental and lawlike statements, let *extensional* and *intensional* justifications of universal generalizations be defined as follows. An extensional justification of a generalization such as "all *As* are *F*'" would rely on the fact that all, most, or at least a good sample of the things possessing the property *A* have been examined and found to have property *F*. In such a case, there would not be any attempt to explain why this is so, only a claim that, as things stand, all *As* do in fact have the property *F*.

An intensional justification of a universal generalization, on the other hand, would attempt to show that anything with the property of being *A must* also have the property of being *F* by virtue of a more general principle or theory from which the generalization can be derived.[6]

The distinction I have just described is obviously not restricted to science, nor am I interested in elucidating various scientific methods of corroboration (I am in deep enough water already). Rather, I want to apply this distinction to the kind of justification a speaker, in light of Grice's second maxim of quality, is expected to have for what he says. In a sense, what I am after is a "folk theory" of justification, not the foundation of knowledge. Thus, the extensional/intensional dichotomy between types of justification lies outside the question of whether the evidence for a statement is good or bad, as an intensional justification can be either silly or brilliant. Moreover, the distinction applies to all sorts of judgments, not merely theoretical ones. The bigoted justification for holding stereotypical beliefs would presumably be extensional ("Look, I don't know why they are all such dirty cowards, but I have met enough of them to know that they are!"). On the other hand, when the notorious fundamentalist preacher Jimmy Swaggart states that all adulterers are sinners, he does not want us to believe that he has examined all (most, or a large sampling of) adulterers and found that they happen to be sinners. If

---

[6]Statistical correlations belong to the extensional realm, causal explanations to the intensional counterpart.

someone who is not an adulterer now were to become one, he would obviously have to be a sinner as well — for an elementary reason. According to Swaggart's world view, adulterers *must* be sinners simply because the Bible says so, and whatever the Bible says is true. The same distinction applies to the most mundane generalizations that can arise in discourse. "All the nursery schools in our area are simply unacceptable," our friend tells us. We all assume that the justification for what he says is extensional (i.e., he has checked out each and every one), but then he adds: "they are all Montessori schools," and an intensional justification is revealed.

Clearly, extensional and intensional justifications are not mutually exclusive. Nor do they exhaust the types of justifications one can use. Thus, justification of the most fundamental principles of any theory (scientific or otherwise), although clearly not extensional, would not be intensional either, since by definition they are not derivable from any other principles (they would still support counterfactuals, though). However, apart from such fundamental axioms, the justification of any universal generalization, if it is not extensional, must be intensional.

Now let us return to the universality condition asserted by a speaker when he uses a conversationally relevant description. As mentioned earlier, the hearer may not know why the speaker believes the generalization; yet from the hearer's point of view it stands to reason that because of the uniqueness condition, the speaker's justification must be *intensional*. If the uniqueness condition is presupposed, an extensional justification of a universal generalization amounts to no more than this: there is evidence that the referent happens to possess the property F. But, if this is all the speaker has in mind, it would be very misleading to give the impression that a universal generalization is meant. To see why, consider a case in which I tell you that all my books are published by Cambridge University Press. If subsequently you find out that I have published only one book, you would surely be puzzled by my apparent misuse of the plural; formally, however, my statement was technically true. In other words, if the uniqueness condition is presupposed, it makes little sense to assert a universal generalization unless the speaker believes that the generalization *must* be true whether the uniqueness condition itself is true or not. Thus, if a speaker has intensional justification for what he says, the uniqueness condition no longer interferes with universality. If I tell you that I have just signed a lifetime contract with Cambridge University Press, and that therefore all my books *must* be published by them, the fact that I have written only one book so far does not matter any more. In view of the contract, if I *were* to write others, they *would* be published by Cambridge.

For the speech act to be coherent, therefore, the speaker must have an *intensional* justification for (5.18). This is why frequently, when a conversationally relevant description is used (for example, in the paradigmatically "attributive" uses of definite descriptions), it is natural to replace the auxiliary verb with an appropriately tensed occurrence of "must." For example,

(5.21) The inventor of the sewing machine, whoever he or she was, $\frac{was}{must\ have\ been}$ very smart.

(5.22) If my political analysis is correct, the Democratic candidate in 1992 will $\frac{be}{have\ to\ be}$ a conservative.

(5.23) The thief who stole your diamond ring $\frac{knew}{must\ have\ known}$ how valuable it was.

My hypothesis, therefore, is that conversationally relevant descriptions are used to assert universal generalizations for which the speaker has intensional justification. Therefore, when a speaker says "D is F" and D is conversationally relevant, a first approximation of what is usually being implicated is this:

(5.24) Any D must be F.

When the modal auxiliary is actually added, the speaker simply makes (part of) the implicature explicit.

5.3.4   The meaning of "must"

As it stands, the implicature expressed by (5.24) is hopelessly vague. The problem is with the modal verb "must." How is it to be interpreted? Compare, the following examples:

(5.25) The bird *must* have entered through the attic.

(5.26) Whether I like it or not, I *must* pay my taxes.

(5.27) The Butcher of Lyons *must* pay for his crimes.

If I do not pay my taxes, I shall be punished. This is why I feel I must do it. But if the bird did not enter through the attic, or if the Butcher of Lyons does not pay for his crimes, neither bird nor beast will be punished for *that*. Moreover, if the bird did not enter through the attic, the speaker uttering (5.25) would simply be wrong. But whether or not the Butcher of Lyons ever pays for his crimes, the speaker uttering (5.27) would be right nevertheless. Thus, in each case, the intended interpretation of the modal verb is radically different.

Is the word "must" multiply ambiguous then? Not necessarily. As Angelika Kratzer argues (1977; 1979; 1981), the force of modal verbs such as "must" is relative to an implied contextual element. The examples in (5.25–5.27) are elliptical pronouncements whose full meaning can be expressed by the following:

(5.28) In view of what we know, the bird must have entered through the attic.

(5.29) In view of what the law is, I must pay my taxes, whether I like it or not.

(5.30) In view of our moral convictions, the Butcher of Lyons must pay for his crimes.

The interpretation of "must" in each example is indeed different; yet, Kratzer argues, there is a core of meaning that is common to all. This core is specified as a *function* that can be precisely formulated within the framework of possible-world semantics. In schematic terms, Kratzer's suggestion is that the meaning of "must" is given by the function *must-in-view-of*, which accepts two arguments. One is the proposition within the scope of the modal verb (e.g., *The bird came through the attic* in [5.25]). Values for the other argument are phrases such as "what is known," "what the law is," and "our moral convictions." Thus, for example, Sentence (5.28) is interpreted as

(5.31) **Must-In-View-Of**(What is known, *The bird entered through the attic*)

The sentence is true in possible world w just in case the proposition expressed by "The bird entered through the attic" logically follows from what we know in w (Kratzer 1977, 346).[7]

---

[7] Phrases such as "what is known," "our moral convictions," and "what the

Kratzer's suggestion can be utilized in elucidating the implicature conveyed by a conversationally relevant description. Let f stand for such phrases as "what is known," "what the law is," etc. Applying Kratzer's analysis to (5.24) we obtain

(5.32) In view of f, any D must be F

or more accurately:

(5.33) Must-In-View-Of(f, *any D is F*).

(5.33), then, is the implicature conveyed by a typical use of a conversationally relevant description. How "in view of f" is to be interpreted is up to the hearer to find out, but we may assume that possible values for f come from a list that is scanned by the hearer until a particular item on the list provides a satisfactory interpretation. Such a list may contain the following (see Kratzer 1981, 44–45, for possible-world interpretation):

- *Factual*: In view of facts of such-and-such kinds...(including institutional facts such as what the law is).

- *Epistemic*: In view of what is known...(or, alternatively, what is believed, assumed, hypothesized, and so on).

- *Stereotypical*: In view of the normal course of events...

- *Deontic*: In view of what is the right thing to do...

- *Teleological*: In view of our objectives ...(or, alternatively, our wishes, our intentions, and so on).

---

facts are" are represented by Kratzer as functions from possible worlds to sets of propositions. For example, "what is known" is represented as a function f, which assigns sets of propositions to possible worlds such that, for each possible world w, $f(w)$ contains all the propositions that are known in that world. According to Kratzer's first suggestion, for any function f from worlds to sets of propositions, and for every proposition P, "it must be the case that P in view of f" is true in w just in case $f(w)$ entails P. As Kratzer notes, this is only the first step in elucidating the meaning of modal verbs; it works only when $f(w)$ is guaranteed to be consistent (as is indeed the case when f is "what is known"). When $f(w)$ can be inconsistent (e.g., when f is *what the law is*), problems arise that Kratzer solves by using the concept of the set of all consistent subsets.

While the list may turn out to be much longer, there is no reason to assume that it will be infinite.

The assumption that a conversationally relevant description is used to implicate a modal operator provides a formal reason explaining why, in paradigmatically attributive uses, if nothing fits the description, the speech act as a whole must fail. If (5.33) is part of what the speaker means in these cases, the description is within the scope of a modal operator — hence, within an intensional context in which substitution is not guaranteed to be a valid form of inference. Suppose Ralph asserts that, in view of what we know about the normal human propensity for violence, Smith's murderer, whoever he is, must be insane; suppose also that Ralph believes Smith's murderer to be Jane's uncle. Substituting "Jane's uncle" for "Smith's murderer" yields the wrong result: it is *not* the case that, in view of what we know about the normal human propensity for violence, Jane's uncle, whoever he is, must be insane. Since *in general* substitution is precluded in intensional contexts, failure of the description (i.e., no one murdered Smith) means that Ralph's speech act must fail too. The fact that he may know quite well who he thought the culprit to be does not matter.

By way of summary, here are the steps a hearer might go through in calculating the implicature that is typically intended when a conversationally relevant description is used:

1. Recognizing a conversationally relevant description.

2. Identifying the universal generalization.

3. Postulating an intensional justification.

4. Locating an appropriate set of propositions relative to which the modal operator is interpreted.

These are typical steps that are initiated when a conversationally relevant description is actually uttered (the case of explicit conversational reference). If this type of description is only implied, the reasoning process begins in the same way; however, when the hearer reaches Step 4, he is not able to find the appropriate function that would allow him to postulate reasonable intensional justification. In the fingerprint case, for example, the hearer can find nothing in view of which all persons whose fingerprints are found on the murder weapon must be insane. There is simply no correlation between leaving a fingerprint and insanity. Backtracking, the hearer recognizes that the referring expression employed is only functionally relevant after all and that a conversationally relevant description is implied by the context. The hearer must then search for such a description in order to provide a coherent interpretation of the discourse.

Of course, this mechanism is actually much more flexible than I make it out to be, and a speaker can use it to satisfy various other goals. For example, a definite description can be used to provide information (Appelt 1985b), to highlight shared knowledge, or simply to avoid mechanical repetition of a proper name. The following quotation illustrates how a conversationally relevant description can achieve all these goals simultaneously:

> In the Democratic primaries, Mr. Jackson, who is considered a long shot for the Vice-Presidential nomination, received more than seven million votes. *The 46-year-old Chicago clergyman* has not said whether he wants the second spot on the Democratic ticket. (*New York Times*, June 28, 1988. Italics mine.)

Since the name "Jackson" is already available as the best functionally relevant referring expression, it should be obvious to the reader that the description "the 46-year-old Chicago clergyman" is conversationally relevant. But when the reader goes through the steps outlined above, he reaches a dead end. There is nothing in view of which it *must* be the case that *any* 46-year-old Chicago clergyman has not said whether he wants the second spot on the Democratic ticket. Thus, the implicature that usually accompanies a conversationally relevant description is ruled out. Nor is there an obvious *implicit* description that serves to convey a similar implicature. The reader is then forced to search for other explanations; one obvious possibility is that the author wants to inform the reader (or remind him) that Jackson is a 46-year-old clergyman from Chicago. Later on we shall see how this shift can be represented in a computational model.

5.3.5 Nonassertives and indefinite descriptions

So far I have assumed that the conversationally relevant description is used within the context of an assertion and I have relied, in my derivation of the implicature, on the fact that a speaker is expected to have adequate evidence for what he asserts. In other speech acts, however, evidence and justification play a completely different role, if any. For example, a speaker who asks a question is not expected to have "evidence" for it. Still, the use of conversationally relevant descriptions is clearly not restricted to assertions. Consider the following:

(5.34) After the verdict is pronounced, the mayor to the district attorney: Congratulations on nailing *the most fearsome criminal in recent history*.

(5.35) While the serving plate is passed around, a guest tells the host: I am not very hungry. Could I please have *the smallest steak*?

(5.36) A young cop tells his superior, as the chase begins: One thing I can promise you: I won't let *Smith's murderer* get away!

A detailed description as to how my account could be extended to cover these cases would take us too far afield. In general, however, the same analysis can apply to nonassertives as well. Coherence is no less important in a discourse containing requests, warnings, promises, etc., than in one containing assertives. The hearer must understand the reasons underlying a congratulation, a request, or a promise. The role of conversationally relevant descriptions in such speech acts is similar to their roles in assertives, with similar implicatures. As rough approximations, the implicatures involved in the three foregoing examples are expressed by the following statements, respectively:

- In view of the danger that criminals pose to society, nailing the most fearsome criminal in recent history is an act for which I must congratulate you.

- In view of my wish to stay both slim and polite, I must have the smallest steak.

- In view of my moral convictions, I should try my utmost to bring Smith's murderer to justice.

Finally, a note on indefinite descriptions. In this study, I take referring expressions to be uses of noun phrases intended to indicate that a particular object is being talked about. Hence, indefinite descriptions can obviously serve as referring expressions, and the distinction between functional and conversational relevance should apply to them as well. The use of an indefinite description as a referring expression normally signals to the hearer that the identity of the referent is not important (e.g., "*A policeman* gave me a speeding ticket"). Some indefinite descriptions, however, are clearly employed with the intention that the hearer identify whom the speaker has in mind. For example,

(5.37) *A person I know* did not take out the garbage as he promised.

Here identification is obviously required, but it does not matter at all under what presentation mode the referent is identified. The indefinite description is therefore only functionally relevant. In contrast, consider the following:

(5.38) *A cardiovascuclar specialist* told me that I exercise too much.

Although the identity of the physician is not important, the fact that he is a specialist surely is. The indefinite description is therefore *conversationally* relevant.

Deborah Dahl discusses interesting cases in which an indefinite description is both *specific* (i.e., used with the intention that the hearer know the identity of the referent) and *attributive* (that is, conversationally relevant). Here is one of her examples:

(5.39) Dr. Smith told me that exercise helps. Since I heard it from *a doctor*, I'm inclined to believe it. (Dahl 1984)

Clearly, an accurate interpretation of "a doctor" would connect the referent with Dr. Smith. At the same time, the use of the indefinite description highlights a property of Smith that is conversationally relevant. Note that the indefinite description is used to implicate a universal generalization — namely that, in view of what doctors are presumed to know, any doctor who gives you advice, should (other things being equal) be listened to. This is very similar in structure to the implicature that is typically associated with conversationally relevant *definite* descriptions.

As is the case with definite descriptions, such uses of indefinite descriptions can accomplish other purposes besides (or instead of) implicating a universal generalization. For example,

> Mr. Truman was thought to be a weak leader who could not carry out his strong predecessor's program. His election prospects were bleak. The pundits were against him and *a highly successful northeastern governor* was poised to sweep into the White House. (*New York Times*, May 26, 1988. Italics mine.)[8]

The calculation of the implicature conveyed by the indefinite description is left as an exercise for the reader.

5.4   Summary of Chapter 5

Any descriptive theory of referring as a speech act must address, among other things, two questions: (1) what is the difference between an intention to express a singular proposition and an intention to express a general, "Russellian," one? (2) why does a speaker choose one rather than the other? These questions are forced upon us if we consider four related claims put forth by critics of the descriptive program:

1. Descriptive content may play a very limited role, if any at all, in determining the referent.

2. When it does, the proposition expressed is singular.

3. "Real" referring occurs only when a singular proposition is expressed.

4. Reference is less a function of descriptive content in the mind than of causal chains outside it.

As I indicated initially, I accept the the first and second claims, while rejecting the third and fourth. However, if there is a genuine difference between expressing a singular proposition and expressing a general, "Russellian," one, a computational model should explain what this difference is, as well as which referring intentions govern the choice of one rather than the other.

The different roles performed by descriptive content in speech acts correspond to the denotation criterion, which in turn provides

---

[8]In this article, the author argues that recent polls showing Michael Dukakis leading George Bush in the race for the Presidency do not mean much. Note that, in May 1988, Dukakis was the governor of Massachusetts, a northeastern state.

one way of distinguishing referential from attributive uses of definite descriptions. Both Kripke and Searle have suggested an explanation for the phenomena characterized by the denotation criterion, and, in addition, have adopted the Gricean distinction between speaker's meaning and sentence meaning as a point of departure. Yet both of them leave important aspects of referring unaccounted for. Searle's account does not distinguish between the case in which the speaker intends a particular *aspect* of the referent to be recognized and the case in which he does not. Similarly, Kripke's does not distinguish between the case in which a speaker's meaning includes a presentation mode of the referent and the case where it does not. The source of their difficulty is the nature of the question asked. Instead of asking when a speaker's meaning and sentence meaning can diverge, we should ask what kind of referring intentions are at work. Such intentions fall into two types: (1) referring without being overly concerned regarding the presentation mode under which the referent is identified by the hearer, and (2) intending that the hearer think of the referent in a particular way. Hence, if we know why it sometimes matters to a speaker *how* the hearer identifies the referent, we can explain the different roles fulfilled by descriptive content in speech acts.

The primary function of definite descriptions is to help the hearer identify the referent, but sometimes two descriptions, both equally suitable for identification, still cannot be used interchangeably in a given discourse. Besides identification, such descriptions are employed to satisfy other goals. Those descriptions whose purpose is identification only are *functionally relevant*. The other kind is *conversationally relevant*. Since a conversationally relevant description can be either mentioned explicitly or implied by the context, there are three general ways in which referring intentions can influence a speaker's choice of referring expressions. They are summarized in Figure 5.1.

Conversationally relevant descriptions are typically used as part of a Gricean implicature. The content of such an implicature varies with the circumstances of discourse, but they all share a rather specific structure. If the statement uttered is "D is F," where "D" is conversationally relevant, then the hearer typically conveys the following implicature:

In view of f, any D must be F.

The interpretation of "must" within the framework of possible-world semantics is borrowed from Kratzer's work. The steps implemented by the hearer in calculating this implicature are schematically as follows:

1. Recognizing a conversationally relevant description.

2. Identifying the universal generalization.

3. Postulating a modal operator (such as "must") to preserve the coherence of the discourse.

4. Locating an appropriate set of propositions (the value of the function f), relative to which the modal operator is interpreted.

Indefinite descriptions and descriptions in nonassertive speech acts can be analyzed similarly.

6
Thoughts and objects

Up to now our focus has been on *speech*, in particular on the speech act of referring. But our ability to refer to an object by speaking about it is dependent upon our ability to *think* of it. At the heart of any explanation of referring, there must be an explanation of the way thoughts are related to objects. This is the problem of *de re* propositional attitudes: what does it take for a thought to be *about* an object?

The cornerstone of the descriptive program is its response to this question, which goes something like this: a thought is about an object by virtue of an individuating representation that is part of the thought and that denotes the object. The exact nature of this individuating representation changes from one descriptive theory to another. For Frege it is an objective *sense* that exists in a third realm that is neither physical nor mental; for Russell it is a propositional function; for Carnap it is an individual concept; and for Strawson it is an identifying description. But all those notions share the feature that characterizes the descriptive program: for reference to succeed, each of these notions must be associated with a property that is instantiated by one and only one object. That object is what the thought is about.

Without a coherent version of a descriptive theory of *de re* propositional attitudes, the model of referring as a speech act that I have developed so far would be groundless. I believe I can offer an account of *de re* thought that is well within the descriptive program; yet, as far as I can judge, is immune to the criticism that is said to have brought the descriptive program down once and for all.

Let us begin with the strongest and most straightforward formulation of the descriptive approach to *de re* thought. Consider Ralph's belief that Wiley is a spy. Taking the descriptive approach at face value, we can say that Ralph has a belief *about* Wiley that he is a spy *if and only if*, for some property ϕ, Wiley is the one and only person to have this property and Ralph believes that the person uniquely instantiating the property ϕ is a spy.

Figure 6.1 shows a generalized version of this view, which I shall call the Fregean view of *de re* thought. It should be emphasized that, in this formulation, ϕ contains nothing but general terms. It contains no names or indexical elements, and is very much like the Fregean *sense* of a referring expression, or like Carnap's *individual concept*. What makes the Fregean view quintessentially descriptive is the requirement that the existence of ϕ as a representation connecting Ralph's belief with Wiley be taken as *both necessary and sufficient* for Ralph to have a belief about Wiley. Consequently, there are two lines of argument countering the descriptive theory: first, that an individuating representation denoting the object is not *necessary* for a *de re* belief; second, that it is not *sufficient*.

6.1 The essential indexical

Already mentioned in Chapter 2 was a version of the argument that an individuating representation is not necessary for a *de re* belief to be held. If a referential use of a definite description is correlated with conveyance of a *de re* belief, and if in such a use the descriptive content of the referring expression is not part of what the speaker *means*, why should it be part of what he *believes*? By now, however, it should be obvious why this line of thought does not show anything. The tacit assumption is that whatever is true about propositions as the content of utterances is also true of propositions as the content of beliefs. But there is no reason to assume that this is indeed so. For although one can easily *mean* a particular object without necessarily meaning any particular representation of it (as is the case in functional referring), it is difficult to see how one can *believe* some-

---

Ralph has a belief about o that it is F if and only if:

$(\exists \phi)$ $[(\exists x)(\phi(x)$ & $(\forall y)(\phi(y) \rightarrow y = x)$ & $x = o)$ &
$\textbf{BEL}_{\textbf{ralph}}(\exists z)(\phi(z)$ & $(\forall w)(\phi(w) \rightarrow w = z)$ & $F(z)))]$

Figure 6.1: The Fregean view of *de re* thought

thing about an object without being able to individuate the latter in one's mind. Thus, singular propositions may constitute the content of what the speaker means, but not, as we have already seen, the content of his beliefs.

But the argument against a descriptive theory of *de re* thought goes deeper, as Donnellan himself was quick to point out. In "Proper names and identifying descriptions" (Donnellan 1970), he offers an example in which a speaker expresses a belief that is obviously *de re*, yet apparently lacks any descriptive content denoting the referent. Suppose Ralph is seated before a screen of uniform color, large enough to fill Ralph's field of vision entirely. Two squares of identical size and shape are painted on the screen, one directly above the other. Asked to name the squares, Ralph decides to call the top one Alpha, the bottom one Beta. It seems that the only way Ralph can use descriptions to distinguish the squares is by stating their relative positions. However, unbeknownst to Ralph, he has been fitted with specially constructed spectacles that invert his field of vision. Thus, the square he sees as being on top is really on the bottom, and vice versa. Surely, Ralph may have *de re* beliefs about, say, Alpha. But it seems that Ralph has no individuating representation that denotes Alpha. Ralph *thinks* that the description "the top square" denotes Alpha, but he is of course, wrong; the top one is in fact Beta. Nevertheless, Ralph has no difficulty in having beliefs about Alpha. Hence, the descriptive analysis of *de re* belief must be wrong and individuating representation is not necessary for *de re* beliefs. Let us call this the *two-squares* argument.

Perry (1979) has offered another argument that seems to undermine the descriptive model even further, i.e., that some *de re* beliefs seem *in principle* to be devoid of individuating representation. The argument is as follows: beliefs are supposed to explain behavior, in the sense that a change in behavior is very often attributed to a change in belief. Now imagine yourself following a trail of sugar on a supermarket floor, pushing your cart down the aisle on one side of a high shelf rack and back up the aisle on the other side, seeking the shopper with the torn sack to tell him he is making a mess. With each trip around the rack the trail grows thicker, yet you seem unable to catch up. Finally it dawns upon you: *you* are the shopper with the torn sack of sugar. At this point you stop and, hoping nobody has noticed your embarrassment, adjust the offending sack carefully in your cart.

What happened? You believed all along that the shopper with

the torn sack of sugar was making a mess; then you suddenly came to believe that *you* were the one making a mess. The change in your behavior indicates this change of belief. But the content of the belief expressed by the sentence "I am making a mess" cannot contain any individuating representation. For suppose that it did — suppose that you were the mayor of El Cerrito and that the content of your belief was "The mayor of El Cerrito is making a mess." Still, someone who knew you might have been walking behind you all along, thinking "The mayor of El Cerrito is making a mess," and it just cannot be the case that the two of you were thinking the same thing. After all, *he* was trying to catch up with you, whereas *you* stopped to adjust your sack. So the content of your respective beliefs could not have been identical. This seems to be true relative to any individual concept that denotes you, and therefore your own *de re* belief, which you have expressed by saying "I am making a mess," cannot be accounted for in strictly descriptive terms.

How can a descriptive theorist answer these two objections? Let's begin with the two-squares argument. Recall that Russell's theory of reference makes a distinction between knowledge by description and knowledge by acquaintance (Russell [1910]1953). We know an object *o* by description if *o* is the one and only so-and-so, and we know that the so-and-so exists. We are *acquainted* with *o* if *o* can be presented to us without being *represented*. Thus, according to Russell, physical objects can be known only by description, but such things as the self, pain, numbers, one's thoughts or visual experience can be known by acquaintance. We do not need a *representation* of ourselves in order to be aware of ourselves, nor is such a representation necessary for our pains, thoughts, and sensory experience. But for us to be aware of, say, a chair, it must be somehow represented — for example, as a two-dimensional image on the retina. Now, according to Russell's theory, the description by which we know an object *o* quite often contains reference to object *b* with which we are acquainted. In other words, the individuating representation used for a *de re* belief about *o* may indicate a *relational* property that individuates an object only relative to some other object with which we are acquainted.

Once we realize that concepts can individuate objects relative to other objects with which we are acquainted, there are a lot of individuating representations available to Ralph in the two-squares argument. For example, Loar (1976) and Schiffer (1978) maintain that one has knowledge by acquaintance of one's self and the current time (what "now" denotes). As Loar observes, the objects of our beliefs are often individuated for us by virtue of the unique relationship between them and us. Thus, an individual concept that denotes the Alpha square for Ralph is: *the square I* (Ralph) *am now looking at.* Other options are also available, depending on the sort of entities one takes to be known by acquaintance. For example, Searle (1983) has offered an analysis of the intentionality of perception within the descriptive program and, although he does not use the Russellian terminology, it is clear that, in his account, visual experiences are the sort of entities that are obviously presented to us without being *r*epresented. A concept that would denote the square for Ralph in Searle's account is *the square before the person who has this visual experience such that the presence and features of the square are causing this visual experience* (cf. Searle 1983, 37ff.). Thus, while Schiffer and Loar individuate the square relative to Ralph himself, Searle individuates it relative to Ralph's visual experience.

I prefer the Schiffer–Loar approach, in which knowledge by acquaintance of the self plays a central role in the individuation of objects. Not only is it simpler and formally cleaner, but it is also closer to Russell's original treatment of the problem. The same idea can be found in Strawson's work on reference (1959, 15–30). But this answer to the two-squares argument seems merely to push the problem down one level without solving anything; when we turn to Perry's *de re* belief ("I am making a mess"), the Schiffer–Loar suggestion cannot work without circularity. For an individual concept that denotes Perry only in relation to Perry himself is worthless; it would be like trying to refer by using expressions such as "his wife's husband," or "the man to the right of the woman who is to the left of that man." This obviously cannot work.

The way to meet Perry's challenge is simply to show that it is not a challenge at all. Perry is right in saying that no individual concept can be found as the one determining the referent of "I" in "I am making a mess." *But no such individual concept is needed!* In Section 2.4, I presented an argument explaining why presentation modes are needed in any theory of reference. But that argument is restricted to physical, public objects; it does not apply to entities with which we are acquainted. In other words, the singular proposition

(6.1) MakingMess(*perry*)

can be the complete content of Perry's belief. Unlike the case of Ralph and Wiley in Section 2.4, Perry *cannot* at one and the same time both believe and not believe himself to be making a mess. Of course, Perry can believe himself to be making a mess under one description, yet not hold this belief under another. But he cannot both believe and not believe that he *himself* is making a mess. Leaving cases of schizophrenia aside, a person cannot think simultaneously "I am making a mess" and "I am not making a mess." The reason is simple: while Wiley is always presented to Ralph under one mode of presentation or another (and thus Ralph may not recognize him as the object of his earlier belief), Perry has knowledge by acquaintance of himself: he does not need a mode of presentation under which he is represented to himself.

Does this explanation save the descriptive program? A critic of the latter may argue that it does not. If we accept a solution based on Russell's notion of knowledge by acquaintance, we would have to admit that descriptive content is sometimes not necessary for a belief to be *de re* and that, furthermore, singular propositions can sometimes be the content of beliefs. But, our critic may continue, these are precisely the points in dispute and to concede them is simply to abandon the descriptive program altogether.

Such a critic, however, would fail to understand the real difference between the descriptive program and its alternative. The issue is not whether singular propositions exist or can be the content of beliefs. As I argued in Chapter 2, Russell is as much part of the descriptive program as Frege, Strawson, and Searle. The central issue with regards to *de re* thought is rather this: propositional attitudes can be directed at objects whose existence and features are independent of those attitudes. How is this possible? The descriptive theorist maintains that this is established by virtue of descriptive content. The opposition adds an *external* factor, e.g., a causal relation between agent and object. Both sides must acknowledge, however, that the dispute is over the relation between mental states and *physical, public* objects. Our critic argues that, since the content of one's belief about one's self or one's visual experience is a singular proposition, the descriptive program must be in error. But to so argue is to miss the point entirely. The relation between one's belief and the self cannot be the model for understanding how reference works. Entities such as visual experiences and the self have a special ontological and epistemological status that enables the descriptive theorist to consider them as constituents of the content of beliefs. Accepting the special status of such entities is not a rejection of the descriptive program, nor does it in any way involve a commitment to external reference-fixing mechanisms of the sort insisted upon by the new theory of reference.

Incorporating the Russellian approach into the descriptive analysis of *de re* thought, we derive a modification of the Fregean view. The result is presented in Figure 6.2. Note that, in the Russellian view, "ϕ" no longer must contain general terms exclusively. It may indicate a relational property that individuates an object only relative to another. Still, the latter object must either be known by acquaintance or depend for its own individuation on another object of which we have such knowledge.

Incidentally, the Russellian position avoids the difficulties raised by Putnam's *Twin Earth* argument. In a well-known article (Putnam 1975), he has argued that descriptive content in the mind is insufficient for determining reference. The argument is founded on the logical possibility of a massive duplication whereby two agents whose brains are in identical states nevertheless each think of a different object. Thus, let us suppose that in a distant galaxy, there is someone *exactly* like me (down to the subatomic level), living in a world exactly like ours. When I think "my mother is coming for a visit," my *doppelgänger* also thinks "my mother is coming for a visit." We are both in exactly the same mental state, but I am thinking about *my* mother, while he is thinking about *his*.

Ralph has a *de re* belief about o that it is F if and only if:

1. Ralph has knowledge by acquaintance of o and believes that o is F, **OR**

2. Ralph has knowledge by description of o and believes that o is F,

where knowledge by description of o is expressed by the following conjunction:

$$(\exists \phi) \quad [(\exists x)(\phi(x) \ \& \ (\forall y)(\phi(y) \to y = x) \ \& \ x = o) \ \&$$
$$\textbf{BEL}_{\textbf{ralph}}(\exists z)(\phi(z) \ \& \ (\forall w)(\phi(w) \to w = z) \ \& \ F(z)))]$$

Figure 6.2: The Russellian view of *de re* thought

Putnam's argument indeed raises interesting questions about the so-called "software of the brain" and the meaning of linguistic expressions, but it does not touch upon the descriptive position. Since, in the Russellian view of *de re* thought, individuation may be relative to the self, it is clear what the difference between me and my *doppelgänger* is. When I think about my mother, the content of my thought includes me as a constituent, not him. When he thinks about his mother, the content of his thought includes him, not me. In short, once individuation is made relative to the self, massive duplication is no longer a threat to the descriptive program, as was observed quite some time ago by Strawson (1959, 20–21).

6.2 The pragmatics of belief reports

In the preceding section, I examined the claim that an individuating representation is not necessary for a belief to be *de re*. I turn now to the argument that it is not *sufficient*.

As we have seen in Chapter 3, a criterion for a *de re* belief is the ability to report it by either using existential generalization or substituting other referring expressions for the one that actually corresponds to what the believer has in mind. Suppose Ralph believes that Wiley, his neighbor, is a spy. In reporting Ralph's belief, it would be correct to say, for example,

(**6.2**) As regards Wiley, Ralph thinks that he is a spy.

Or, applying existential generalization,

(**6.3**) There is someone Ralph believes to be a spy.

Or, in a conversation with Wiley, substituting "you" for "Wiley,"

(**6.4**) Ralph believes that *you* are a spy.

This is a clear indication that Ralph's belief is indeed *de re*.

There is a host of problems connected with reports such as (6.2–6.4), not all of which are relevant to our discussion. To begin with, we have the initial problems that arise from intensional contexts. In the sentence

(**6.5**) Ralph believes that his neighbor is a spy

the expression "his neighbor" is not necessarily being used to refer to anything, since the sentence may be true even if whoever Ralph takes to be his neighbor is actually a pure figment of his imagination. The Fregean view is that, within such an intensional context, the denotation of the description "his neighbor" is not the neighbor but rather the *sense* of that expression. But this raises other problems. For example: (a) If expressions in intensional contexts denote their senses, how should we interpret such sentences as (6.2), in which both "Wiley" and the pronoun "he" apparently denote the same thing? (b) What kind of entities are quantified over by the existential quantifier in (6.3): objects, or senses of expressions? (c) Is it reasonable to postulate that when the speaker says "you" in (6.4), he is referring not to Wiley, but to the sense of "you"? What could this sense be?

Such questions have long kept logicians busy. Some of them have even been led to the conclusion that, because of these difficulties, *quantifying-in* statements (such as 6.3) do not make sense. I find such a conclusion silly, reminiscent of the equally silly positivistic adage that declares unverifiable statements to be meaningless. But there is no doubt that the logical questions raised by intensional contexts, quantifying-in statements, and *de re* reports of propositional attitudes are indeed important and exceedingly complicated. To forestall any false expectations, let me state at the outset that I have nothing to say in this study about these matters. I am not concerned with the logical form of such sentences as (6.2–6.4). Rather, I take it for granted that sentences of that type are well formed, make sense, and are capable of being true or false. The problem at hand is to specify the conditions under which they are true. Obviously, one of the truth conditions for these sentences is that Ralph's neighbor exists. Given the discussion in the last section, Ralph should also have knowledge by description of Wiley. But is this all that is required?

According to the descriptive position developed so far, it is. Variations of the following argument, which I shall call *the case of the military attaché*, are usually offered in confutation of the descriptive view. Suppose Ralph believes that all military attachés are spies, that each American embassy has a military attaché, and that there is an American embassy in El Salvador. The following sentence, therefore, is true:

(6.6) Ralph believes that the American military attaché in El Salvador is a spy.

However, Ralph has no idea who the military attaché is, what his name is, or anything else about him. As a matter of fact, he hardly knows where El Salvador is. Now, suppose the military attaché there is Wiley. Ralph indeed has an individuating representation denoting Wiley, as required by the descriptive program, but (so goes the argument) it would be *false* to assert (6.2), (6.3), or (6.4) just on the basis of Ralph's vague and general suspicions that have nothing to do with Wiley in particular. Consequently, it is argued, Ralph's belief — although containing a concept that denotes Wiley — does not concern Wiley at all. It is a belief *that*, not a belief *about*: *de dicto*, but not *de re*. Hence, an individuating representation is not sufficient for a belief to be *de re*, and so the descriptive position must be wrong as it stands.

When Kaplan was still a descriptive theorist, he accepted this argument and tried to modify the descriptive position accordingly ([1968]1975). What was missing from the descriptive account, he argued, was a systematization of intuition according to which an agent must both be related causally to *and* have a rich conception of an object if a belief about that object is to be characterized as *de re*. Assume that (6.6) represents the content of Ralph's belief accurately, and that the definite description indeed denotes Wiley. According to Kaplan, Sentence (6.3) (as well as Sentences [6.2] and [6.4]) would be true if, in addition, the following conditions are satisfied:

1. The definite description is *of* Wiley, i.e., there is an appropriate kind of causal chain from Wiley to the occurrence of the description in Ralph's thought.

2. The definite description is part of a *vivid* mental name, i.e., of a conglomeration of images, names, and partial descriptions of Wiley that is rich enough in descriptive content to allow us to say that Ralph knows Wiley or is familiar with him.

Kaplan's account can be criticized on several grounds. To begin with, the inclusion of causality as a necessary ingredient for the truth of *de re* reports precludes any *de re* beliefs about objects in the future. Kaplan recognizes this consequence and endorses it but, as Sosa observed (1970), the *de dicto/de re* distinction applies to beliefs about the future as much as it does to the present or past. Sosa offers the following examples:

(a) I believe there is to be a seditious meeting [i.e., at least one].

(b) There is to be a meeting that, I believe, will be seditious [i.e., the one on August 5].

Another difficulty in Kaplan's account has to do with the notion of vividness. As Kaplan himself admits, vividness may depends on the agent's special interests, but he assumes that an increase in detail always enhences vividness. This seems wrong to me. Like the concept of *knowing who*, it is not so much the quantity of information that makes a mental image vivid in Kaplan's sense, but its appropriateness relative to specific purposes. Take, for example, the case of Stinky, the Berkeley rapist (as far as I know, still unidentified to date). When one of his victims said that she believed the man who attacked her was Stinky the rapist, the mental image in her mind associated with Stinky was, I am sure, too vivid to bear. However, she still did not know who he was in the relevant sense, and the mental image she had of him was unfortunately not vivid enough for the purpose of identifying him. She surely has a *de re* belief about him, but it would still be quite misleading, to say the least, to tell Stinky: "This woman believes that *you* are Stinky the rapist."

I think Kaplan was right about the significance of causality and richness of information for our intuitions concerning *de re* reports, but I think he was wrong in insisting that these notions are relevant to the *truth conditions* of such reports. Note that the argument against the descriptive position works only if, in the case of the military attaché, Sentences (6.2–6.4) are *false*. Accepting the conclusion that those sentences are indeed false, but intent on preserving a descriptive perspective, Kaplan tried to place more restrictions on the truth conditions of such sentences. In contrast, I am going to argue that, in the case of the military attaché, Sentences (6.2–6.4) are true, albeit highly *misleading*.

As far as I know, Sosa (1970) was the first author to hint at such a direction. In his attempt to provide truth conditions for *de re* reports of beliefs, he considered at one point a formulation virtually identical to the Fregean version. When an argument similar to the case of the military attaché is invoked, Sosa says (1970, 887):

> Nevertheless, I have myself been tempted to accept something like the [Fregean view of *de re* propositional attitudes], and to meet the objection by in-

voking a distinction between what is true, and what
it is appropriate and not misleading to say.

After some consideration, Sosa gave up this view for reasons that
he could have ignored if he had had Grice's theory of conversational
implicature available. (He was clearly searching for such a theory to
explain different ways in which a true statement can be "misleading,"
i.e., implicate a falsity.) Nevertheless, I think Sosa was on the right
track. That pragmatic considerations are relevant for acceptance
or rejection of *de re* reports should already have been suggested by
the context dependence of vividness. The following examples furnish
more justification for this view:

(6.7) As regards his mother, Oedipus believes that she is
dead.

(6.8) As regards his wife, Oedipus believes that she is
beautiful.

(6.9) As regards his mother, Oedipus believes that she is
beautiful.

(6.10) As regards his wife, Oedipus believes that she is dead.

Given the plot line of the Greek tragedy, (6.7) and (6.8) are surely
true. I find (6.9) acceptable (though somewhat misleading), while
Sentence (6.10) is completely off target. But note that all four are
de re reports of beliefs; the referring expressions "his wife" and "his
mother" occur in purely extensional contexts. As far as logic is
concerned, the application of Leibniz's Law in extensional contexts
should be unlimited: whatever is true of Oedipus' mother should
also be true of his wife. Nevertheless, (6.10) remains unacceptable.

I propose adopting Sosa's original position. My reply to the
new theorist, therefore, is that, in the case of the military attaché,
Sentences (6.2–6.4) are *true*. The problem is to specify the reasons
why we are so reluctant to accept them as such.

6.2.1   A conflict of interest

In reporting someone else's belief or any other propositional attitude,
a speaker has two goals that may be in conflict. First, the speaker
attempts to represent the content of the belief as accurately as possible. Second, the speaker attempts to make the hearer identify the

object of the belief (i.e., the referent) to the extent appropriate for the purposes of the conversation. Sometimes the referring expression that is most suitable for identification purposes is also the best for representing the way the agent whose belief is being reported thinks of the referent. But, if a conflict arises, the goal to be preferred is determined by the specific nature of the conversation. At one end of the spectrum, we have the case in which no identification of an object is necessary — simply because the speaker does not believe the object exists. For example:

(6.11) Poor John, he is so delirious, he thinks that *the first intergalactic spaceship* has just landed in People's Park.

At the other end of the spectrum, there is the type of conversation in which *only* identification matters. For example,

(6.12) Watch out! Ralph wants to kill *you*.

Barring special circumstances, it is unlikely that the hearer is very much interested in the exact mode of presentation under which Ralph wants him dead.

De re reports of beliefs (and other propositional attitudes) are a device for informing the hearer that accuracy of *representation* (of the belief) is being sacrificed in favor of easier *identification* (of the referent). Other devices may include the use of pronouns and demonstratives. But even if it is clear that the speaker has decided *not* to represent the complete content of the belief he is reporting, he is nevertheless expected to follow — among other maxims and submaxims of conversation — certain rules that act as filters for possible choices of a referring expression. These rules, all of which derive from the requirement that the speaker should not implicate something that is not true, may include the following:

Consistency: In reporting an agent's belief that t is F, you may not substitute another referring expression t_1 for t, if the agent believes that t_1 is *not* F.

Functionality: You may refrain from accurate representation of the reported belief *only* to improve chances of identification. It would be misleading to choose a referring expression that neither represents what the believer has in mind nor offers any advantages for identification over one that does.

An illustration of a violation of the *consistency rule* is the Oedipus example. Oedipus clearly believes his mother to be dead, and in reporting his belief we may use referring expressions other than "his mother." However, since Oedipus clearly believes that his wife is *not* dead we cannot use "his wife" in this manner.

The Functionality Rule explains why some substitutions in belief reports work, while others do not. Some critics of the descriptive position were puzzled by the fact that a pronoun can be used in reports of beliefs, even when the believer has no idea who the referent is (Burge 1977). Here is a dialogue from the television series *Vegas*:

(6.13) A: Mrs. Payne wants to see you.

B: But she doesn't know me from the Lone Ranger!

A: She asked me for the best private eye in town.

Masterpiece Theater it is not, but I think that this example illustrates the point. On the other hand, it is clear that not just any old referring expression denoting **B** (the private eye) can be employed in this context. Had the private eye been, say, also the author of *Playing Blackjack to Win*, it would have been misleading to tell him that Mrs. Payne wants to see the author of the book. The use of the pronoun "you" in (6.13) is justified because it is functionally superior. The use of "the author of *Playing Blackjack to Win*" is excluded because, given the circumstances, it is neither the best functionally relevant description available nor an accurate representation of Mrs Payne's wish, in violation of the rule. Such a description, of course, could have been necessary for identification under different circumstances. For example, suppose that Mrs. Payne's secretary calls the publisher of the book and tells him:

(6.14) Mrs. Payne wants to get in touch with the author of *Playing Blackjack to Win*. Could I get his phone number from you?

A description that would surely have been awkward in the dialogue of (6.13), is perfectly acceptable here.

6.2.2 The shortest spy revisited

Another pragmatic rule that a speaker should observe when making a *de re* report is the following:

> **Relevance:** In reporting a belief that t is F , you may substitute another referring expression t_1 for t. But it should be mutually assumed that an accurate representation of the original belief is as relevant to the conversation as the inaccurate one. Other things being equal, had there been no conflict between representation and identification, an accurate report of the belief would have done just as well.

Thus, in Example (6.13), the first speaker is not initially accurate in reporting the content of Mrs. Payne's wish, since he does not supply the mode of presentation under which Mrs. Payne wants to see the private eye. He is able to do that, however, knowing full well that a report containing the missing presentation mode is as relevant to the discourse as the sentence he actually uttered. On the other hand, when a speaker tells Wiley, the military attaché in El Salvador, "Ralph believes that you are a spy!" he is violating the Relevance Rule. Wiley is entitled to assume that the presentation mode under which he is believed to be a spy is relevant to the conversation, while in fact it is not. As Ralph is not about to blow Wiley's cover, his vague and genral beliefs about military attachés around the world should not concern Wiley at all.

The most difficult cases for the descriptive position can also be explained as violations of the Relevance Rule. As noted in Chapter 3, on the basis of the obviously true statement

(6.15) Ralph believes that Smith's murderer is Smith's murderer,

it seems impossible to conclude that

(6.16) There is a person about whom Ralph believes that he murdered Smith.

Yet, according to the descriptive position, this is exactly what we should conclude (assuming that someone indeed murdered Smith). Similarly, as Kaplan observes ([1968]1975), given the fact that Ralph believes that no two spies are of exactly the same height and that all analytic statements are true, it follows that (6.17) is a true description of Ralph's belief:

(6.17) Ralph believes that the shortest spy is a spy.

But even though the shortest spy exists, it would be totally false, Kaplan continues, to assert

(6.18) There is a person Ralph believes to be a spy.

After all, Kaplan quips, if (6.18) is true, the FBI should be interested, but "we would not expect the interest of that organization to be piqued by Ralph's conviction that no two spies share a size" ([1968]1975, 168).

Whether Sentences (6.16) and (6.18) are false or not, it is obvious that, in view of the *relevance rule*, they are highly misleading. If I call the FBI and articulate these sentences, there is a clear implication on my part that they should be interested in the *complete* content of Ralph's belief. Since, of course, they want to identify both the murderer and the spy, they hope that the content of Ralph's beliefs may help them do so. However, the true content of Ralph's beliefs is not helpful in that way at all; had I represented these beliefs in full, their complete irrelevance would have been evident.

Many people who are sympathetic to the descriptive position wince when they are asked even to consider the possibility that Sentences (6.16) and (6.18) are true, albeit highly misleading (Sosa, as noted, is a rare exception). Nevertheless, I consider these sentences to be indeed true. They are the limiting cases of the descriptive approach, and limiting cases, after all, are frequently strange. We could of course avoid such cases altogether by saying, for example, that the descriptive position of *de re* belief is correct *unless* the belief is a tautology and individuation is to a large extent a matter of logic ("the first...," "the shortest...," and so on). Such ad hoc qualifications, however, only cloud the picture. Note that odd cases are accepted elsewhere if their acceptability is anchored in a well-motivated principle. For example, it is surely true that the empty set is a subset of any set. Why? Simply because a set A is a subset of a set B if and only if each member of A is also a member of B. Since the empty set has no members, the condition for considering it a subset of any other set is vacuously satisfied. Such a view has advantages for set theory, but some of its consequences are bizarre nonetheless. For example, what looks like a patently false statement,

(6.19) All my sisters got married at age twelve and within six
months gave birth to a Persian rug.

is nevertheless true, since I have no sisters. By the same token, Sentences (6.16) and (6.18) should be interpreted as vacuously true, and our reluctance to accept them is due to pragmatic reasons. They are true simply because individuating representation — that is, *intentional content in the mind* — is all that we need (and all that we have) to enable us to think about objects in the world around us.

This concludes my discussion of some of the pragmatic rules governing the possible resolutions of conflicts between the representation of beliefs and the identification of objects. Of course, like other maxims and submaxims of conversation, these rules (and others like them) can be violated in various circumstances to generate implicatures, essentially along the lines of the conversationally relevant descriptions that were discussed in the preceding chapter.

6.2.3 Causality and vividness

If my defense of the descriptive position has been correct so far, Kaplan's requirements to the effect that a *de re* belief must both be causally related to its object and contain a "vivid" mental name should not be considered part of the truth conditions of *de re* reports. Still, one feels that the intuition reflected in Kaplan's account must be essentially correct: causality and vividness do play a role in the acceptability or unacceptability of such reports. I indeed think the intuition is correct, but that it has to do with the *justification* of beliefs, not with their truth or falsity.

Take, for example, Ralph's belief that his neighbor is a spy. Ralph can defend his belief only if, among other things, he has some justification for his belief that his neighbor exists. Now, as regards beliefs about physical objects, evidence for their existence is typically *causally grounded*. In other words, such evidence ultimately rests on perceptual beliefs in which confirmation of the existence of the perceived object is simply the effect it has on the sensory organs. This does not mean, of course, that all evidence is causally grounded in this manner, but the causal element in the justification of empirical beliefs is still expected to be the rule, rather than the exception. For example, Ralph can feel fully justified in believing that, say, there is a spy who is shorter than all the rest, even though there is no causal interaction between Ralph and that person. In this case, however, Ralph's beliefs about the shortest spy are either trivial (e.g., that he or she is a spy, can breathe, etc.), or likely to be completely unjustified. When one of Ralph's beliefs is reported in a *de re* form, we assume that Ralph is rational and can justify his beliefs, and that the relevance rule is being observed. Thus, we assume that Ralph has evidence for a nontrivial belief that is relevant to the discourse. Since Ralph's belief is empirical, a causal interaction between Ralph and the object of his belief is presupposed by default.

The requirement that an agent "know enough" about the object of his belief for the belief to be *de re* (the "vividness" condition) appears to be motivated by the following argument:

1. The ability to substitute one referring expression for another in a belief report indicates that this belief is *de re*.

2. The more an agent knows about an object, the more acceptable it is to substitute one referring expression for another in reporting the agent's beliefs concerning that object.

3. **Hence:** The agent's "knowing enough" about an object is necessary for a *de re* report of the agent's belief to be true.

This argument, however, confuses substitutivity as a logical property of occurrences of terms with legitimacy of substitution as a result of pragmatic and epistemological factors. Consider first why the first premise is true. The answer is self-evident. The ability to substitute freely indicates that the context is extensional; *by definition* such a context indicates a *de re* report, which in turn indicates that the belief reported is *de re*. This is why we began investigating *de re* reports of belief in the first place.

Now let us consider the second premise. Suppose that following the Democratic convention in the summer of 1988, Ralph had come to the conclusion that Michael S. Dukakis was going to win the presidential election. We certainly could have reported his belief then as follows:

(6.20) Ralph believes that the Democratic candidate will win the American presidential election.

The reason substitution works here has nothing do with *de re* reports, but rather with the assumption that Ralph, like everybody else who followed the news, already knew that Dukakis was the Democratic candidate in 1988. Note that the same substitution would have worked even if Dukakis had never existed and his entire candidacy had been a complete media fabrication. In that case, of course, no *de re* beliefs about Dukakis would have been possible, but we would still have been able to use (6.20) in reporting Ralph's belief. In other words, unlike the logical notion of substitution, substitution in the sense of the second premise is *not* an all or nothing affair. Rather, it is a function of the likelihood that a particular presentation mode of the referent is included in the agent's conception of the object his belief is about. Therefore, the more the agent knows about the object, the more likely it is that the report of his belief will remain accurate after substitution. But this has nothing to do with the question of whether or not the agent's belief is *de re*.

6.2.4 Individuating sets and the descriptive view

Schiffer (1978, 203–204) presents the following example as an argument against the descriptive view of *de re* thought. Assume that the following facts are true:

1. Sister Angelica of the Holy Names Convent holds the world's record for eating the most spaghetti at a single sitting.

2. Ralph mistakenly believes himself to be the holder of that record.

3. Hence, since Ralph believes that he had sex with his wife, he also believes that the holder of that record had sex with her.

If the descriptive account of *de re* thought presented so far is correct, we would have to conclude that Sister Angelica is believed by Ralph to have had sexual relations with Ralph's wife. For, on the basis of the facts, it is the case that (1) one and only one person is the record holder; (2) Ralph believes that the recordholder had sexual relations with Ralph's wife; and (3) the recordholder is Sister Angelica. These are precisely the conditions that, according to both the Fregean and the Russellian views, are jointly sufficient for Ralph's belief to be about the nun. The conclusion is inescapable. Yet Schiffer insists (and who can argue with him?), even the most stubborn descriptive theorist would have to admit that this conclusion is absurd.

As a result of this example, Schiffer has modified his theory of reference substantially and, in my opinion, has effectively given up its descriptive character. This, however, is quite unnecessary. I propose a rather simple solution embodying the concept of an *individuating set*. It is a mistake to treat individuating representations in isolation, letting each determine an object on its own, independently of all the others. What determines the object of the belief is not a single presentation mode, but the entire individuating set of which that mode is a member.

Ideally, all presentation modes in a given individuating set denote one and the same object. But the world is not perfect. Sometimes mistakes are made and an individuating set is "contaminated." This is in fact what happened to Ralph. He has an extremely rich individuating set that determines his own self, but a presentation mode denoting Sister Angelica crept into this set by mistake.

It is not an easy matter to decide when, despite a certain amount of confusion, an individuating set nevertheless continues to determine an object and when it does not determine anything at all. If each presentation mode in one of my individuating sets denotes a different object, this set determines nothing and I am just confused. However, it is obvious that an individuating set may still determine an object regardless of some mistakes that may have been made in one or more of the presentation modes contained in that set. This reveals the basic flaw in the case of Sister Angelica. Although she is indeed the holder of the record for pasta consumption, and although Ralph believes that the recordholder has had sex with Ralph's wife, the object of Ralph's belief is not Angelica because, in Ralph's mind, the presentation mode *holder of the record* belongs to an individuating set that unquestionably *determines Ralph*, not Sister Angelica. This presentation mode, it is true, happens to denote Angelica, but there can be no doubt that the overwhelming remainder of that individuating set denotes Ralph; hence, it is him that his belief is about.[1]

Sometimes, however, a certain presentation mode can fulfill a role in a *de re* thought similar to the role of conversationally relevant descriptions in speech acts. In referring, as we have seen, we can distinguish two types of referring intentions. First, a speaker may intend to refer to an object determined by an individuating set without simultaneously intending that any particular presentation mode from the set be part of the proposition he wishes to express. Second, a speaker may select a presentation mode from the relevant individuating set, intending that this particular mode be part of the proposition understood by the hearer. A similar distinction exists in

---

[1] Ralph can have beliefs about himself independently of any modes of presentation, of course. After all, he has knowledge by acquaintance of his own self. However, he also has an individuating set that determines him and he can have beliefs that contain presentation modes from this set.

thought: an agent may have a belief about an object that is determined by the relevant individuating set as a whole, or he may have a belief that somehow depends on a *particular* presentation mode in the set. This is a manifestation of what I have called the *modal intuition*, in which we distinguish between considering an object *in itself* and considering an object *qua* object possessing a certain property. Here is an example of the latter. After reading the article "Speaker's Reference and Semantic Reference" (Kripke 1977), I formed the following belief:

> **(6.21)** Kripke is right in claiming that Donnellan's distinction does not refute Russell's theory of descriptions.

Suppose that through a rather bizarre misunderstanding, it was not Kripke at all who wrote this article, but, say, Gödel. The presentation mode *author of "Speaker's Reference and Semantic Reference"* (SR&SR, for short) is but one element in a rather extensive individuating set that I have representing Kripke. Yet, it is obvious that my belief is not about Kripke per se, but about whoever wrote this article. Thus, upon learning about the mistake, I would revise my belief as follows:

> **(6.22)** *The author of SR&SR* is right in claiming that Donnellan's distinction does not refute Russell's theory of descriptions.

The belief conveyed by (6.21), therefore, is one I hold about Kripke *qua* the author of SR&SR. This contrasts with the case of Sister Angelica, in which, the object of Ralph's belief is determined by the individuating set as a whole. Upon learning of his mistake, Ralph would simply remove the presentation mode *holder of the record* from the individuating set that determines him. The difference between us can be summarized as follows. Before our respective mistakes are found out, I have an individuating set that contains the presentation mode *author of SR&SR*, and that determines Kripke, who is the object of my belief. Similarly, Ralph has an individuating set that contains the presentation mode *holder of the record*, and that determines Ralph, who is the object of *his* belief. After the mistakes have been exposed, we both shift our respective erroneous presentation modes into newly created individuating sets: Ralph's new set determines Sister Angelica whereas my new set determines the author of the article. The difference between Ralph and me, however, is that the object of my belief has changed, while the object of his has not. His belief is still about himself; mine is no longer about Kripke but about Gödel.

Now we see how the Russellian view can be changed to accommodate Schiffer's counterexample without giving up the main thrust of the descriptive approach. Figure 6.3 provides my final version of what is required for an agent to have a belief about a particular object. Surely this is only a preliminary account. We still do not have an adequate theory of knowledge by acquaintance. Furthermore, the notion of having a belief about someone *qua* having a certain property needs elucidation. Nor do we have satisfactory answers to many questions about individuating sets. (For example, how "wrong" can an individuating set be without losing the object it determines? Are some elements in an individuating set more important than others?) Nevertheless, I think the view outlined in Figure 6.3 is viable and attractive enough to serve as a foundation for a computational model.

6.3 Summary of Chapter 6

At the heart of any explanation of referring, there must be a view about the way thoughts are related to objects. The descriptive posi-

---

Ralph has a *de re* belief about o that it is F if and only if:

1. Ralph has knowledge by acquaintance of o and believes that o is F, **OR**

2. There is a presentation mode ϕ such that Ralph believes that ϕ is F, and either

   - o is the one and only object with the property of being ϕ and Ralph believes that ϕ, *qua* being the ϕ, is F, **OR**

   - There is an individuating set A (for Ralph) such that ϕ belongs to A, and A determines o.

Figure 6.3: A descriptive theory of *de re* thought

tion is that a thought is *de re* by virtue of an individuating representation that is part of the thought and denotes the object. Critics of the descriptive program have argued that this is wrong; in general, their arguments follow two possible paths: (1) that an individuating representation is not necessary for a belief to be *de re*; (2) that it is not sufficient.

Donnellan and Perry have argued that individuating representations are not necessary for a belief to be about a particular thing. Donnellan, in his two-squares argument, describes a case in which one can clearly have a belief about a certain shape on a screen without having any identifying description that actually denotes that shape. Perry seems to undermine the descriptive position even further by showing convincingly that beliefs about one's self cannot be accounted for in descriptive terms.

A descriptive response to these arguments is to accept Perry's argument and use it to answer Donnellan. In essence, a Russellian view is adopted. According to Russell, we can have either knowledge by acquaintance or knowledge by description of an object, and the description by which we know a certain object may contain reference to another object with which we are acquainted. Perry's argument is valid because one is acquainted with one's self, and there is no need for a presentation mode under which one has beliefs about one's self. However, once we realize that representations can individuate objects relative to other objects with which we are acquainted, there are a lot of individuating representations available to account for Donnellan's example.

Arguments attempting to show that an individuating representation is not sufficient for a belief to be *de re* consist of examples in which an agent may indeed have an individuating representation of an object — but it would nevertheless be false to report his belief in a *de re* form. This type of argument works only if such *de re* reports are in fact false. I contend that such reports are not false but rather misleading, in the sense that they *implicate* (in Grice's sense) a falsity. The reason they are misleading has to do with the function of *de re* reports in conversation.

In reporting another person's belief, the speaker has two goals that may be in conflict. First, the speaker attempts to represent the content of the belief as accurately as possible. Second, the speaker attempts to make the hearer identify the object of the belief (i.e., the referent) to the extent appropriate for the purposes of the conversation. Sometimes the referring expression that is most suitable for identification purposes is also the best for representing the way the agent whose belief is being reported thinks of the referent. If a conflict arises, however, the preferred goal is determined by the specific nature of the conversation. At one end of the spectrum, we have the cases in which no identification of an object is necessary simply because the speaker does not believe that the object exists. At the other end of the spectrum, there are the types of conversation in which *only* identification matters. *De re* reports of beliefs are a device for signaling to the hearer that completeness of *representation* (of the belief) is sacrificed for the benefit of easier *identification* (of the referent). But even if it is clear that the speaker has chosen *not* to represent the complete content of the belief reported by him, he is still expected to follow certain rules that act as filters for possible choices of a referring expression. These rules, all of which derive from the requirement that the speaker should not implicate something that is not true, may include the following:

> **Consistency:** In reporting an agent's belief that t is F, you may not substitute another referring expression t_1 for t, if the agent believes that t_1 is *not* F.
>
> **Functionality:** You may refrain from accurate representation of the reported belief *only* to improve the chances of identification. A choice of a referring expression that neither represents what the believer has in mind nor offers any identification advantages over one that does would be misleading.
>
> **Relevance:** In reporting a belief that t is F, you may substitute another referring expression t_1 for t. But it should be mutually assumed that an accurate representation of the original belief is as relevant to the conversation as the inaccurate one. Other things being equal, had there been no conflict between representation and identification, an accurate report of the belief would have done just as well.

In the examples that are offered as refutations of the descriptive approach, the *de re* reports of beliefs are true but misleading because they involve blatant violations of such pragmatic rules.

The Russellian view of *de re* thought must still be modified, however. It is a mistake to always treat individuating representations in isolation, letting each determine an object, independently of all other such representations. What determines the object of a belief is not a single presentation mode, but the entire individuating set of which that mode is a member. Nevertheless, a particular presentation mode can sometimes play a role in a *de re* thought similar to the one performed by conversationally relevant descriptions in speech acts. This is the case in which the *de re* belief is about a certain object *qua* having a certain property. These two possibilities must be accounted for within a descriptive theory of *de re* thought. A sketch illustrating such a theory is presented in Figure 6.3.

7
Computational models

So far I have argued for a particular view of reference. Assuming that this view is well motivated, how should a designer of a natural-language system proceed if the position I have outlined is assumed to be correct?

This study is not intended to be a blueprint for the construction of a particular computer program. Nevertheless, several general principles that should underlie such a system can easily be discerned. In this chapter, I examine how some of these principles can be embedded in a computational model.

7.1   General principles

My starting point is that the speech act of referring is a transaction between a speaker and a hearer in which the speaker begins with one mental representation and the hearer ends up with another. That is, the speaker has a mental representation denoting what he believes to be a particular object, and he intends the hearer to come to have a mental representation denoting the same object, at least in part through the use of a noun phrase that is intended to be a linguistic representation of that object. This, according to the descriptive view that I am advocating, is a necessary condition for an act of referring to be performed

Reference, according to this view, is by virtue of *denotation* — the crucial relation between mental representations and objects. In a computer system, these mental representations themselves can be represented in various ways, but no matter what model we choose to simulate mental representations, it must obey the Russellian principle: if objects cannot be individuated by means of general terms alone, they must be individuated by their unique relations to things with which the agent is acquainted. That is, a mental representation may indicate a relational property that individuates one particular object only relative to another, which in turn is individuated relative to a third, and so on. But the chain cannot go on forever. The final link would involve something which is no longer *represented* but rather *presented*. Thus, a possible strategy would be to define a set of entities with which an agent is acquainted, and to insist that all mental representations must ultimately be reduced to representations containing only elements from this set and general terms. Obvious candidates for membership in this set of entities with which all agents are acquainted are the self and the present, i.e., what is indicated by "I" and "now."

Mental representations, in turn, are grouped into *individuating sets*. From a computational point of view an individuating set can be seen simply as an abstract data type: it is a list of representations with a collection of operations defined on it. Such operations may include **MERGE** (with another individuating set), **PUSH** (onto a stack), and so on. Thus, the main feature of my proposed approach is that it takes individuating sets, rather than isolated presentation modes, as essential to a referring model. There are three reasons for this.

First, the concept of an individuating set solves a major problem for a descriptive account of *de re* thought. As we have seen in Chapter 6, there are cases where the presentation mode chosen for the expression of a particular belief cannot be the sole factor in determining what the belief is about. This task must be left to the whole of the relevant individuating set of which the presentation mode is an element.

Second, by interpreting the act of pragmatic identification as the act of applying appropriate constraints to individuating sets, it is possible to create a unified account of identification as the discourse purpose of referring. Thus, there is no need to confound pragmatics and epistemology while insisting that "real" referring takes place only when it is known who or what the referent is. Moreover, it enables us to show how a hearer can identify the object that is being discussed without necessarily possessing a standard name for it.

Third, and most significantly, the need for individuating sets has to do with the *modal* intuition (see Chapter 3). According to the modal intuition, an agent can think of or refer to an object in two distinct ways: either *qua* having a certain property, or *in itself*. This dichotomy manifests itself both in thought and in speech, as we have seen, and the concept of an individuating set provides a very convenient way of representing it entirely within a descriptive framework: either a particular presentation mode is selected out of the relevant individuating set and is taken as crucial for the identity of the referent, or no such presentation mode is chosen and the referent is determined by the individuating set as a whole. Viewing the modal intuition in this way solves a host of related problems for the descriptive approach. To begin with, it shows what the intention to express a singular proposition amounts to. This, in turn, reconciles a descriptive model of mind with rigid designators (such as proper names and demonstratives) which lack any descriptive content conventionally associated with them. Moreover, by making the individuating set the fundamental unit that determines what a belief or a statement is about, we see how referring can succeed even if the actual definite description used is not rich enough in content to denote the particular object or indeed is entirely wrong.

Using the concept of an individuating set as an abstract data type, we can refine the necessary conditions for referring to include its *literal goal* and *discourse purpose*, in accordance with the discussion in Chapter 4:

> **Referring:** When a speaker performs the speech act of referring, he has in mind an individuating set which he believes determines a particular object, and he uses a noun phrase with the following intentions:
>
> 1. **Literal goal:** that as a result of the hearer's recognition of the noun phrase as a referring expression, the hearer will generate a local individuating set that will determine this very same object.
> 2. **Discourse purpose:** that the hearer will apply various operations to the newly created individuating set so that it will meet the appropriate identification constraints.[1]

This, in a nutshell, is what I take to be the foundation for a computational model of referring. In what follows I will outline two preliminary attempts to construct such a model. The first involves a concrete implementation: it is a program called **BERTRAND** that

---

[1] Note that identification of the referent *qua* having a particular property is a special case of the satisfaction of identification constraints.

implements individuating sets. The second is more theoretical in nature. Based on the work reported in (Appelt and Kronfeld 1987), it offers a computational model of referring within the framework of a general theory of speech acts and rationality.

7.2 A Prolog experimental system

BERTRAND is an experimental program in Prolog that I wrote to provide a context for implementing and examining some central aspects of a computational treatment of referring expressions. A simple dialogue program, **BERTRAND** is modeled after **TALK** (Pereira and Shieber 1987). It parses each sentence while building a representation of its logical form. Then it converts the logical form to a Horn clause (if this is possible) and, depending on whether the sentence is a statement or a question, either adds the clause to the Prolog database or interprets it as a query and retrieves the answer. The following is a typical **TALK** dialogue:

```
Talk> John loves every child.
    Asserted 'love(john,X) :- child(X).'²
Talk> Mary is a child.
    Asserted 'child(mary).'
Talk> Does John love Mary?
    yes.
```

BERTRAND, however, concentrates on questions that require a referring expression as an answer, in particular, questions of the form "Who is X?" where an appropriate answer must be a proper name or a definite description. The reason for concentrating on such questions is that they provide concrete cases where various notions related to referring play an important role. In order to generate appropriate replies to such questions in real discourse, a speaker must (a) identify the referent of "X," (b) decide which presentation mode denoting X is relevant as an appropriate answer, and (c) choose a referring expression that successfully expresses this presentation mode. This type of question, therefore, provides a non-trivial test case for a model of referring, while at the same time serving as an example of linguistic cooperation which is specific enough to be tractable. The idea was to discover how far **BERTRAND** can be pushed toward

---

²The symbol ":-" is read "if," and capitalized letters represent universally quantified variables. Thus, love(john,X) :- child(X) means: "for all x, John loves x if x is a child."

providing appropriate answers without imposing ad hoc restrictions, and given a rather limited grammar.

BERTRAND does not go very far. At this stage, it is merely an academic exercise. But despite its limitations, it can serve as a skeletal frame capable of supporting further refinements to be built up around it at a later stage. What follows is a brief description of BERTRAND's main features, and the theoretical justification for them.

When BERTRAND encounters a referring expression, it associates the logical form of the expression with a new internal symbol x_i. For example, if the referring expression is "John," the unit clause designate(xi,john) is added to the database. If the referring expression is "the man" or "a man," then either def(xi,X^man(X)) or indef(xi,X^man(X)) is added, respectively. (Following Pereira and Shieber, I use the caret ["^"] to encode lambda expressions. Roughly, X^man(X) means "the x such that x is a man.") The new internal symbol henceforth takes the place of the referring expression in the process of building the logical form of the sentence. This marks a significant difference between BERTRAND and TALK. For example, after parsing the sentence "John loves a woman from Paris," TALK would produce the following logical form:

```
exists(X, woman(X) & from(X,paris) & loves(john,X))
```

BERTRAND, on the other hand, processes the sentence by first asserting the following unit clauses in its database:

```
designate(xi,john)
designate(xj,paris)
indef(xk,X^(woman(X) & from(X,xj)))
```

The logical form of the sentence is then taken to be simply

```
loves(xi,xk)
```

The principle justification for this mechanism is that it provides a means for implementing the Russellian principle. For example, the referring expression "The man from the city by the bay" is transformed into

```
man(X) & from(X,xi),
```

where xi is the internal symbol associated with

```
city(Y) & by(Y,xj),
```

and xj is associated with

bay(Z).

BERTRAND, of course, has no idea what entity "the bay" stands for, but one can imagine a system that maintains a knowledge base of objects independently of a particular conversation (that is, it has quasi-permanent individuating sets, not only local ones). Such a system would coordinate perceptual data with linguistic information, and would associate internal symbols with presentation modes rather than with the logical form of referring expressions. In such a system the unit clause bay(Z) would be replaced by a more complex structure containing other internal symbols, and the process of reduction would continue until we get a formula that makes reference only to things with which the system is "acquainted" — for example, raw perceptual data, or the time according to an internal clock. It is important to emphasize the difference between presentation modes and the logical form of referring expressions, which is crucial, as regards a model of referring. A presentation mode should contain enough information to individuate an object; if it does not, something is wrong. By contrast, neither referring expressions nor their logical form are usually expected to have enough content to individuate an object.

BERTRAND can do no better than treat the logical form of a referring expression as if it were a presentation mode. Individuating sets, in this scheme, are really sets of logical forms. Such sets are defined by an equivalence relation that holds among internal symbols. Two internal symbols belong to the same individuating set if, according to the information interpreted so far, the two referring expressions associated with them are used to refer to the same object.

In constructing individuating sets, BERTRAND uses a combination of a *logical* and a *pragmatic* strategy. The first strategy exploits various logical properties of the relation *belonging to the same individuating set*. Specifically, BERTRAND can conclude that two internal symbols, x_1 and x_2, belong to the same individuating set in one of the following ways:

1. Directly — i.e., when the referring expressions "R_1" and "R_2" are associated with x_1 and x_2 respectively, and the statement "R_1 is R_2" (or "R_2 is R_1") has been asserted.

2. Recursively using transitivity — i.e., when, for an internal

symbol x_3, it can be shown that x_1 and x_3, as well as x_3 and x_2, belong to the same individuating set.

3. Recursively using substitution — i.e., when the descriptions associated with x_1 and x_2 are identical, except that the first contains an internal symbol x_i exactly where the second contains an internal symbol x_j, and x_i and x_j belong to the same individuating set.

There are two major problems with the logical strategy just outlined. First, the substitution principle entails that the relation of belonging to the same individuating set always holds between two identical tokens of a referring expression. This is obviously too strong an assumption for any realistic discourse. As pointed out by Grosz (1979), the same description (e.g., "the screw") may be used within the same discourse to identify two different objects at different times. In addition, the logical strategy fails to capture cases in which it is implied (although never actually asserted) that two distinct referring expressions are used to refer to the same thing. For example,

(7.1) I met *Marvin Maxwell* yesterday. *The man* is utterly insane!

These difficulties are part of the very complex problem of anaphora resolution, which **BERTRAND** was never intended to handle. However, some effort was made to compensate for weaknesses of the logical strategy. The method **BERTRAND** uses is based on the notion of a "focus stack."

The concept of a focus stack as a computational tool for modeling discourse was developed by Grosz (1977; 1978a; 1979), and Grosz and Sidner (1986) incorporate it into a general model of discourse. According to Grosz and Sidner, a crucial component of discourse structure is the *attentional state*, which is a representation of the participants' focus of attention as their discourse unfolds. The attentional state is modeled as a stack of *focus spaces*, each of which is associated with a discourse segment. Each focus space records the objects (as well as properties, relations, etc.) that are in focus in each particular segment of the conversation. **BERTRAND**, of course, cannot recognize discourse segments and tacitly assumes that each conversation consists of a single focus space. Instead of a stack of focus spaces, then, it maintains a dynamic stack of individuating sets representing those objects that are in focus at each stage of the conversation.

The focus stack is used to solve some of the problems that the logical strategy cannot handle. To see how this is done we need the concept of *subsumption*. We will say that one description *subsumes* another when from the assumption that an object satisfies the first it follows that it also satisfies the second. For example, the description "the green metal box" subsumes the description "the metal box." Moreover, since to have a name is to satisfy the description "the person called such-and-such," proper names, too, can subsume one another. For example, the name "John Foster Dulles" subsumes the name "John" (or more precisely, the description "the man called 'John Foster Dulles'" subsumes the description "the man called 'John'"). This notion of subsumption can be extended to hold between individuating sets and internal symbols. An individuating set I is said to subsume an internal symbol x_i when I, taken as a conjunction of (logical forms of) referring expressions, subsumes the referring expression associated with x_i. For example, let I be the individuating set containing (the logical forms of) the descriptions: "the green, expensive box" and "the heavy metal box," and let x_i be associated with the description "the green metal box." Then I subsumes x_i since whatever is a green, expensive, heavy, metal box cannot fail to be a green metal box.[3]

We now return to the problems involved in maintaining individuating sets. Whenever a new referring expression is processed, **BERTRAND** must decide whether the corresponding internal symbol should be included in some preexisting individuating set. First, the logical strategy is applied (although the substitution rule must be used with caution to avoid the conclusion that two identical tokens of a description are necessarily used to refer to the same object). If the logical strategy fails, then each individuating set in the focus

---

[3] Grosz's work on focusing leaves open the question of whether elements of the focus space are *representations* of objects or are the objects *themselves*. Grosz and Sidner (1986) argue that the focus structure "is a property of the discourse itself, not of the discourse participants" (p. 179). Grosz (1979), on the other hand, emphasizes that "not only do speaker and hearer concentrate on particular entities, but they do it using particular perspectives on those entities" (p. 1), and she notes that "the only kind of object an interpreter can focus on are structures in its memory" (p. 2, n. 1). This, I think, is an interesting example of the hesitation in AI between a descriptive model and its alternative. Within the framework of Situation Theory (Barwise and Perry 1983), focus spaces, very much like propositions, should contain the objects themselves as elements. Within the descriptive view developed in this study, the focus structure should contain the individuating sets that are active during each stage of the discourse. Needless to say, the design of **BERTRAND** follows the descriptive approach.

stack is examined in order. The new internal symbol is added to the the first individuating set in the stack that subsumes this symbol. If none is found, then the internal symbol is pushed onto the stack, as representing a new individuating set. This strategy provides a way to overcome the aforementioned problems. First, two tokens of the *same* referring expression are considered as referring to the same object only if both are subsumed by the same individuating set in the focus stack. Second, two *distinct* referring expressions may still be considered as referring to the same object even when the logical strategy fails to show this, provided that both are subsumed by the same individuating set in the focus stack.

Given **BERTRAND**'s way of handling individuating sets, an answer to a question of the form "Who is X" is constructed in three steps:

1. Using the strategies outlined above, **BERTRAND** searches for an individuating set I that includes the internal symbol associated with the logical form of X.

2. **BERTRAND** then selects an "appropriate" internal symbol x_j from I (for example, if X is a proper name, **BERTRAND** will attempt to return a description).

3. Once an internal symbol is selected, **BERTRAND** converts the logical form associated with it into a referring expression and returns the expression as the answer.

Figure 7.1 (p. 151) shows a typical dialogue with **BERTRAND**. Prompted lines are input, and indented ones are the computer responses. System acknowledgments after statements are omitted.

7.3 Formalizing referring effects

BERTRAND represents a concrete attempt to implement certain aspects of individuating sets. The second approach to modeling the speech act of referring is more theoretical in nature. It focuses on one essential aspect of referring, namely, that it is a planned activity intended to achieve particular goals. As mentioned in Chapter 1, this aspect entails that a computational model of referring should show how the use of a referring expression is systematically related to changes in both the speaker's and the hearer's mental states. A central concept in this endeavor is that of *mutual belief* (or *mutual* *knowledge*), and in the next section I discuss how this notion applies to referring.

7.3.1   Mutual individuation

As we have seen in Chapter 4, a speaker means something, according to Grice's original analysis (1957), if and only if he intends to produce an effect in the hearer by means of the hearer's recognition of this intention. Several authors have shown that this analysis is insufficient (Strawson 1971; Searle 1971; Schiffer 1972), and in order to solve the problem, Schiffer uses the concept of mutual knowledge. S and H are said to mutually know that P when each and every condition in the following infinite list is true:

(1a) S knows that P.
(1b) H knows that P.
(2a) S knows that H knows that P.
(2b) H knows that S knows that P.
(3a) S knows that H knows that S knows that P.
(3b) H knows that S knows that H knows that P,
and so on.

A similar sequence defines mutual belief. What is required for a correct analysis of meaning, Schiffer argues, is, roughly, that both speaker and hearer mutually know (or believe) that the speaker has produced his utterance with the aforementioned Gricean intentions.

Schiffer's argument is implicitly accepted by Cohen and Levesque (1985; 1987; 1988). This means, for example, that in formalizing the effects of a speech act, it would not be enough to state that the act of producing an utterance causes certain effects to follow. Rather, the statement should be that, for such effects to follow, the hearer must think that it is *mutually believed* by speaker and hearer that such an utterance was produced. Similarly, in encoding the Gricean intentions, it would not be enough to state that the hearer believes that in uttering a sentence the speaker has certain intentions in mind. Rather, the hearer must also believe that it is *mutually believed* by both speaker and hearer that the speaker has these intentions. I take these requirements to be correct and will simply adopt Cohen and Levesque's formalization of mutual belief. However, there is a particular instance of mutual knowledge or belief that has to do specifically with the act of referring. I shall call it *mutual individuation*.

To see what mutual individuation is, it is best to contrast it with the type of mutual knowledge discussed by Clark and Marshall (1981). In this article, Clark and Marshall examine a simple and straightforward case of referring and then show that the identity of the referent must not only be known to all participants, but *mutually* known, in Schiffer's technical sense of the term. To see why, consider an example which they use.

Suppose that there is a Marx brothers film festival at the Roxy this week, with a different film showing each night. Now assume that on Wednesday night the movie is going to be *Monkey Business*, and that on Wednesday morning Ann asks Bob, "Have you ever seen the movie showing at the Roxy tonight?"

Ann is using the description "the movie showing at the Roxy tonight" to refer to *Monkey Business*. What sort of beliefs must she have in order to assure herself that her referring act has a good

```
Bert> The woman from Paris loves the
man from the city by the bay.
Bert> The friend of the employee owns
a dog.
Bert> The dog is Fido
Bert> Smith loves the woman from
Paris.
Bert> John is the man from Oakland
Bert> Oakland is the city by the bay.
Bert> The woman from Paris is Mary.
Bert> Who is the man?
     The man from the city by the bay.
Bert> Who loves Mary?
     Smith.
Bert> Who loves John?
     Mary.
Bert> Who owns Fido?
     The friend of the employee.
Bert> Who is John?
     The man from the city by the bay.
```

Figure 7.1: A dialogue with **BERTRAND**

chance of being successful? At a bare minimum, Clark and Marshall argue, Ann herself must know, or at least believe, that the movie at the Roxy that night is *Monkey Business*. Adopting Clark and Marshall's notation, let t and R stand for the description "the movie showing at the Roxy tonight" and the name "Monkey Business" respectively. Then under the circumstances described, at least the following must be true:

> **Ann$_1$:** Ann believes that t is R.[4]

This, however, is obviously not enough. Ann needs to believe not only that the movie tonight is *Monkey Business*, but that Bob believes it as well, or else he would not be able to answer the question. So in addition to **Ann$_1$**, it must be the case that

> **Ann$_2$:** Ann believes that Bob believes that t is R.

But this is not quite enough either, as Clark and Marshall demonstrate:

> On Wednesday morning Ann and Bob read the early edition of the newspaper, and they discuss the fact that it says that *A Day at the Races* is showing that night at the Roxy. When the late edition arrives, Bob reads the movie section, notes that the film has been corrected to *Monkey Business*, and circles it with his red pen. Later, Ann picks up the late edition, notes the correction, and recognizes Bob's circle around it. She also realizes that Bob has no way of knowing that she has seen the late edition. Later that day Ann sees Bob and asks, "Have you ever seen the movie showing at the Roxy tonight?" (Clark and Marshall 1981, 13)

Both Ann and Bob believe that the movie showing tonight is *Monkey Business*, and Ann is aware of this. Hence both conditions **Ann$_1$** and **Ann$_2$** are satisfied. But Bob thinks that Ann is still under the impression that the movie showing tonight is *A Day at the Races*, and thus, when she asks him the question, he thinks she is still talking about that movie. To ensure successful reference, then, the following should also be true:

---

[4] Clark and Marshall use knowledge instead of belief in their example, but the difference is immaterial here.

Ann₃: Ann believes that Bob believes that Ann believes that t is R.

Further examples demonstrate that the process never ends, and that no finite nesting of beliefs will do. A similar argument shows that for Bob to convince himself that he has understood Ann's referent correctly, he must believe that t is R, that Ann believes it, that Ann believes that he believes it, and so on. Hence, for Ann's referring act to be successful, Ann and Bob must mutually believe that t is R.

It turns out that mutual belief is too strong a concept for referring in general. We do not always aim to avoid mistakes at all cost; sometimes we can use them to our advantage. Take the case where Ann knows that *Monkey Business* has been substituted for *A Day at the Races*, but Bob does not yet know this. If Ann wants to talk about *Monkey Business*, she needs to tell Bob about the change. But if she wants to talk about *A Day at the Races*, she may very well use the description "the movie showing at the Roxy tonight." She knows, of course, that that movie is not *A Day at the Races*. Yet she also knows that Bob thinks that it is, and that he thinks that both he and Ann mutually believe this. Ann, therefore, can use Bob's mistake in her planning, and hence **Ann₁** is not necessary for successful reference. Moreover, as is shown (using a different example) by Perrault and Cohen (1981), it is possible to construct circumstances in which, for any n, the statements **Ann₁** through **Annₙ** are false and yet Ann's referring act is still successful. This is what Perrault and Cohen call *mutual agreement*, which is a weaker notion that includes mutual belief as a special case.[5]

Clark and Marshall's argument is not affected by these considerations. Their example shows that referring requires the verification of an infinite number of conditions, and their goal is to explain how finite beings with limited resources like us can do this. The fact that **Ann₁** through **Annₙ** can be false does indicate, however, that Clark and Marshall's particular version of mutuality (either of knowledge or of belief) cannot be generalized to *all* referring acts. Moreover, even if we substitute mutual agreement for mutual belief, there is still a problem. To see why, consider the nature of the proposition that is supposed to be mutually believed by Ann and Bob. In setting up their example, Clark and Marshall state (ibid., 11) that

---

[5] *S* and *H mutually agree* that *P* if for some n, the initial n statements in the infinite sequence that defines mutual belief are false, and the rest are true. When $n = 0$, mutual agreement is the same as mutual belief.

> our interest is in Ann's use of the definite referring
> expression *the movie showing at the Roxy tonight*,
> term *t*, by which Ann intends to refer to *Monkey
> Business*, referent *R*.

This creates the impression that when it is asserted, say, that Ann
believes that *t* is *R*, Ann has a *description* on the one hand (term
t), and an *object* on the other (referent *R*). But when Ann believes
that the movie showing at the Roxy tonight is *Monkey Business*,
she does not have *the movie* in her head. Rather, she has various
representations of it, and the same is true of Bob. One of Ann's
representations is *the movie showing at the Roxy tonight*, and another
is something like *the Marx brothers movie called "Monkey Business."*
But when Ann reasons about Bob's belief she may not know how
the movie is represented in *his* mind. Suppose, for example, that in
Bob's copy of the paper, the name of the movie is obliterated, but
a detailed description of the plot is provided. Bob, having seen the
movie, easily recognizes it, although he cannot remember the name.
When Ann asks, "Have you seen the movie showing at the Roxy
tonight?" Bob, knowing exactly which movie she is talking about,
simply answers, "Yes." Reference is obviously secured, but note the
difference in Ann's and Bob's respective beliefs. What Ann believes
is that the movie showing at the Roxy tonight is *Monkey Business*,
and what Bob believes is that the movie showing at the Roxy tonight
is the one where the four Marx brothers stow away on a luxury liner,
each pretending to be Maurice Chevalier in order to get off. But if
Ann and Bob each believe a different proposition, how can they be
said to *mutually* believe anything?

What Clark and Marshall have in mind, I think, is an intuitive
attribution of *de re* belief to speaker and hearer. Ann and Bob do
not mutually believe *that t* is *R*. Rather, *about R* they mutually
believe that it is *t*. That is, Ann has a belief about *Monkey Business*
that it is the movie showing at the Roxy tonight, and she thinks that
Ralph has the same belief about this movie, and she thinks Ralph
thinks she has the same belief about it, and so on. As mentioned
in Chapter 6, the intuitions underlying our ability to attribute *de re*
beliefs in this way have to do with the fact that both Ann and Bob
are supposed to know *which* movie is showing at the Roxy tonight.
But as we have seen earlier (Chapter 4), this epistemological sense of
referent identification is in general not at all necessary for successful
referring. For example, suppose that both Ann and Bob know that

there is a Marx brothers festival at the Roxy this week, but they do not know which movie is on tonight. Now suppose Ann tells Bob: "The babysitter is available this evening, and I feel like seeing Groucho again. Shall we go see the movie showing at the Roxy tonight?" Both in this example and in Clark and Marshall's the fundamental mechanism of reference is the same. But in the latter example, Clark and Marshall's reconstruction of mutual knowledge (or belief) does not work.

Let me, then, suggest an alternative. The mutual belief that is crucial for referring in general is not what is mutually believed about the *referent*. Rather, it is what the speaker and hearer mutually believe about *each other*. What is common to *all* referring acts is that *both speaker and hearer need to mutually believe that they are focusing on the same object*. At each stage, one of them (or even both) may not know *which* is the object they are focusing on, but they must mutually believe that there is indeed a unique object that is the common subject of their thoughts. This is not simply an assertion that in successful referring both speaker and hearer must be thinking of the same thing. The claim is that they must *mutually believe* that they do so. This is what I call *mutual individuation*.

Mutual individuation is obviously needed in Clark and Marshall's example. But it is also needed *whenever* a referring expression is uttered, even if the identity of the referent is entirely unknown. Consider one of Perrault and Cohen's examples (1981, 227):

(7.2) What is *the departure time of the next train to Montreal?*

Obviously there is no mutual belief (or agreement) in this example about what the departure time of the next train to Montreal is. Had there been, the question would have been pointless. In this sense, the use of the referring expression here is radically different from Ann's "the movie showing at the Roxy tonight" in Clark and Marshall's example. But note that in (7.2), reference to the departure time depends on reference to Montreal, and although there need not be any particular proposition of the form *Montreal is the F* that speaker and hearer *mutually* believe to be true, surely the entire speech act is successful only if there is a mutual belief that when the name "Montreal" is used, both speaker and hearer have the same city in mind. Moreover, given the context (an information booth at a train station), the phrase "the next train to..." can be interpreted as a function that maps Montreal onto a unique train, and the phrase "the departure time of..." can be similarly interpreted as a function that maps trains onto their unique departure time. Hence, if after the utterance the speaker and hearer mutually believe that they have the same city in mind, and if both mutually believe that each knows the meaning of the phrase "the next train to..." and "the departure time of...," then they must also mutually believe that they have the same departure time in mind. The difference is that one of them does not know what that departure time is, and the other does, or at least is able to look it up. As with Clark and Marshall's example, mutual individuation is necessary, whether the identity of the referent is known or not.[6]

With the concepts of mutual belief and mutual individuation established, we can now turn to a model that treats the speech act of referring within the framework of a general theory of speech acts and rationality.

7.3.2 Speech acts and rationality

One approach to modeling speech acts as a planned activity is based on two related ideas: (a) mental representations can be modeled by logical formulas, and (b) the process of planning to achieve a goal can be seen as a search for a derivation proceeding from axioms representing the world as it is, to theorems that represent a world in which the goal is satisfied. The method, roughly, is to look for a formal system that is rich enough to capture central concepts of communication. Once such a formal system is available, there are two things that need to be done. First, the goal structure that typically motivates a speech act, and the likely effects of such an act on the hearer's mental state, must be formalized. Second, the relation between goals and effects must be spelled out. That is, it must be shown why, given these effects, it is *rational* for the speaker to expect that his goals will be satisfied.

The connection between the achievement of communication goals and the assumption of rationality is not a new idea, of course. Grice's principle of conversational cooperation (1975) provides a theoretical framework in which discourse is seen as a means toward an end, and

---

[6] Even in cases where individuation does not depend on any other object (e.g., talking about the shortest spy), speaker and hearer still need to mutually believe that they are focusing on the same thing. After all, it is not enough that both speaker and hearer know that "the shortest spy" denotes the shortest spy; they must *mutually* know it.

the project of grounding conversational maxims in general rationality constraints is developed further by Kasher (1976; 1982; 1987). Recently, Cohen and Levesque (1985; 1987; 1988) have developed a detailed formal theory in which illocutionary acts are characterized in terms of what the speaker and the hearer mutually believe about each other's mental states as the result of a speech act. Moreover, Cohen and Levesque are able to show why utterances are expected to be successful given reasonable assumptions about the rationality of discourse participants. Their approach provides an excellent framework within which principles of referring can be formalized.

The foundation of Cohen and Levesque's theory of rational communication is a formal system which models (idealized versions of) beliefs, goals, and actions. All that is needed for our purposes is the notation for five of the concepts in their logical apparatus:

$\mathbf{BEL_a}(P)$: Agent A believes that P.

$\mathbf{GOAL_a}(P)$: Agent A has the goal of making P true.

$\mathbf{BMB_a^b}(P)$: Agent A believes that A and B mutually believe that P. This is the unilateral mutual belief from A's perspective — that is, the infinite conjunction of:

> $\mathbf{BEL_a}(P),$
> $\mathbf{BEL_a BEL_b}(P),$
> $\mathbf{BEL_a BEL_b BEL_a}(P),$
> and so on.

$\mathbf{DONE_a}(E)$: E is an action-event that has *just* happened, and whose only agent is A.

$\mathbf{AFTER}(a, P)$: P is true in all courses of events that follow an occurrence of act a.[7]

---

[7] Cohen and Levesque first introduce $\mathbf{AFTER}$ as a primitive, branching-time concept (1985). In later work they use $\mathbf{HAPPENS}(a)$ (action a happens next) as a linear-time primitive (1987). The semantics of Cohen and Levesque's logic is based on possible-world interpretation. Each possible world consists of a sequence of primitive events that indicates what has happened and what will happen in that world. As usual, accessibility relations among possible worlds characterize the operators representing propositional attitudes. For a complete specification of the syntax and semantics of this logic, see (Cohen and Levesque 1987, sec. 3).

We will also need a partial characterization of rational action and cooperation in terms of *sincerity, helpfulness,* and *competence.* Although Cohen and Levesque provide formal definitions for these concepts, it would be convenient to treat them here as *derivation rules,* as follows:

Sincerity: From $\mathbf{GOAL_a BEL_b}(P)$ infer $\mathbf{BEL_a}(P)$, provided that A is *sincere* (with respect to P). That is, if you assume that A is sincere, then from A's attempt to make B believe that P you may conclude that A believes P himself.

Helpfulness: From $\mathbf{BEL_b GOAL_a GOAL_b}(P)$ infer $\mathbf{GOAL_b}(P)$, provided that B is *helpful* (with respect to P). That is, if you assume that B is helpful, then from B's believing that A is trying to make him do something, you may conclude that B will indeed try to do it.

Competence: From $\mathbf{BEL_a}(P)$ infer P and from $\mathbf{GOAL_a}(Q)$ infer eventually Q, provided that A is *competent* (with respect to P and Q). That is, if you assume that A is competent, then from his belief that P you may conclude that P is indeed true, and from the fact that he has the goal of making Q true you may conclude that Q will eventually take place.

The logic that includes **BEL, GOAL, BMB, DONE,** as well as **AFTER** constitutes a basic, "atomic," layer which Cohen and Levesque then use to construct more complex concepts. In particular, they are able to define the notion of a *persistent goal* (a goal that an agent would not give up unless certain conditions are met), which is then used both in solving difficult problems in automatic planning (the "Little Nell" problem, McDermott [1982]) and in formalizing important aspects of *intending.* A formal characterization of intending, in turn, plays an important role in Cohen and Levesque's account of illocutionary acts.

I think that the concept of a persistent goal is an important one, and that Cohen and Levesque's approach to the formalization of a theory of action provides an excellent tool for modeling speech acts, including the speech act of referring. However, delving into details would take us too far afield. Therefore, in illustrating Cohen and Levesque's approach (and in modeling referring along the same lines) I will use the primitive concept of **GOAL** rather than their **P-GOAL** (persistent goal) or **INTEND.** This is, of course, a simplification but it enables us to see more clearly the general outline.

Let us turn, then, to Cohen and Levesque's account of rational communication. Following Grice, they view communication first and foremost as an expression of attitudes that are intended to affect desired changes in the hearer's mental state. According to their initial approach (Cohen and Levesque 1985), modeling this process consists of two parts. First, the model specifies the context-independent effects on the hearer's attitudes when a sentence with certain *features* (e.g., a certain grammatical mood) is uttered under normal conditions. Second, the model shows how the discourse purpose of the speaker is derived from these core effects by means of an elaborate theory of rational action and interaction (including cooperation).

In a later publication, however, Cohen and Levesque (1988) come to the conclusion that the specification of such context-independent consequences of utterances is impossible, and they change their account considerably. I think this change is not justified. Before I can argue my point, though, we need to see how Cohen and Levesque's initial approach was supposed to work in the first place. Using the concept of a *literal goal*, I will first motivate what Cohen and Levesque initially considered the context-independent consequences of uttering declarative and imperative sentences under normal conditions. I will then sketch out Cohen and Levesque's axiomatic approach. Finally, I will discuss the argument that made them revise their theory. Showing that this argument does not work should clear the way to applying Cohen and Levesque's initial approach to referring.

The prototypical illocutionary acts that can be performed by means of uttering declarative and imperative sentences are *inform* and *request*, respectively. Their typical intended effects are that the hearer adopt a belief (in the case of *inform*), or do something (in the case of *request*). These are the *discourse purposes* of these illocutionary acts, and depending on circumstances, they are either achieved or not. What we are after, however, are the *context-independent* effects of declaratives and imperatives. To uncover these effects, it is best to treat them as those changes in the hearer's mental state that occur when the *literal goal* of the utterance is satisfied. This yields a criterion for specifying the context-independent effects of a speech act: they should be those effects on the hearer's mental state that take place *as a result of the hearer's recognition of the attempt to achieve them.*

Take the literal goal of *inform*. Suppose the speaker tells the hearer that P. The discourse purpose of the speech act is to make the hearer believe that P, that is

(7.3) $\text{GOAL}_s\text{BEL}_h(P)$.

But this obviously cannot be the literal goal. The hearer may recognize that he is intended to believe P, but he may question the speaker's competence in making his judgment. Thus, a weaker goal suggests itself, namely, to make the hearer believe that the *speaker* believes that P:

(7.4) $\text{GOAL}_s\text{BEL}_h\text{BEL}_s(P)$

This still cannot be the literal goal. The hearer may recognize that the speaker wants him to believe that he (the speaker) believes that P, but the hearer may doubt the speaker's sincerity.

However, if the hearer understood the speaker at all, he cannot fail to see that the speaker has the goal that (7.4) expresses (exceptions, such as *irony* are discussed below). Hence, once the hearer recognizes the goal of making him believe that (7.4) is true, this goal is thereby satisfied. The literal goal of informing, therefore, is:

(7.5) $\text{GOAL}_s\text{BEL}_h\text{GOAL}_s\text{BEL}_h\text{BEL}_s(P)$

Given the literal goal, we derive the satisfaction of the discourse purpose as follows. The recognition of the literal goal satisfies it, and hence from (7.5) we get:

(7.6) $\text{BEL}_h\text{GOAL}_s\text{BEL}_h\text{BEL}_s(P)$.

Note that the move from (7.5) to (7.6) represents the shift from the speaker's goal to the specification of an intended *effect*.

From (7.6), on the assumption that the speaker is sincere, we get:

(7.7) $\text{BEL}_h\text{BEL}_s\text{BEL}_s(P)$.

Moreover, since $\text{BEL}_s\text{BEL}_s(P)$ implies $\text{BEL}_s(P)$, we get:

(7.8) $\text{BEL}_h\text{BEL}_s(P)$.

Finally, if the hearer takes the speaker to be competent with respect to P, we get:

(7.9) $\text{BEL}_h(P)$,

and the discourse purpose of *inform* is satisfied.

The case of *request* is somewhat more complex, but the reasoning is very similar. Take, for example, an utterance of the imperative "Close the door!" We can get the literal goal of the request by systematically weakening the discourse purpose until we arrive at a goal whose mere recognition is sufficient to satisfy this goal. Let P be the act of closing the door. Then the discourse purpose of the request is to make the hearer close the door, that is,

$$(7.10) \quad \text{GOAL}_s \text{DONE}_h(P).$$

This, obviously, cannot be the literal goal. Recognizing (7.10), in itself, won't make the door shut. So perhaps the literal goal is that the hearer at least *attempt* to do it:

$$(7.11) \quad \text{GOAL}_s \text{GOAL}_h \text{DONE}_h(P).$$

But this won't do either. The hearer may understand the request very well, but still refuse to cooperate. This leads to a weaker requirement: that the hearer believe that the *speaker* has a goal of making him (the hearer) adopt the goal of closing the door:

$$(7.12) \quad \text{GOAL}_s \text{BEL}_h \text{GOAL}_s \text{GOAL}_h \text{DONE}_h(P).$$

But (7.12) still cannot express the literal goal, since the hearer may simply not believe that the speaker is sincere in his request. However, as was the case with informing, if the hearer understands the speaker, he cannot fail to see that the speaker has the goal expressed by (7.12). Hence, the goal of making the hearer believe that (7.12) is true is satisfied by its recognition, and thus the literal goal of the request is:

$$(7.13) \quad \text{GOAL}_s \text{BEL}_h \text{GOAL}_s \text{BEL}_h \text{GOAL}_s \text{GOAL}_h \text{DONE}_h(P).$$

The reasoning that leads from the recognition of the literal goal to the satisfaction of the request is similar to the case of *inform*. Once the hearer recognizes (7.13), the literal goal is satisfied and we get:

$$(7.14) \quad \text{BEL}_h \text{GOAL}_s \text{BEL}_h \text{GOAL}_s \text{GOAL}_h \text{DONE}_h(P).$$

From this, by assuming the speaker's sincerity, we get:

Computational models

(7.15) $\text{BEL}_h\,\text{BEL}_s\,\text{GOAL}_s\,\text{GOAL}_h\,\text{DONE}_h(P)$;

and since once a speaker believes he has a goal, he actually has it, it follows that

(7.16) $\text{BEL}_h\,\text{GOAL}_s\,\text{GOAL}_h\,\text{DONE}_h(P)$.

From (7.16), by assuming that the hearer is helpful, we get:

(7.17) $\text{GOAL}_h\,\text{DONE}_h(P)$,

and by assuming that he is also competent we can conclude that the request will (eventually) be satisfied:

(7.18) $\text{DONE}_h(P)$.

Although Cohen and Levesque do not use the concept of a literal goal, their initial account has formulas similar to (7.5) and (7.13), representing the context-independent effects of declarative and imperative sentences on the hearer's mental state. These effects are incorporated into "feature" axioms, which in general have the following form:

(7.19) If conditions C hold,
then after action a effect E obtains

where conditions C specify central elements of a normal communication situation, a is the action of intentionally uttering a sentence with certain features, and E is a description of the hearer's mental state as a result of the utterance. Using this formulation, I now present simplified versions of Cohen and Levesque's declarative and imperative axioms (ignoring for the sake of simplicity the important differences between goals, persistent goals, and intentions).

If: $\text{BMB}_h^s[\text{utter}_s(u)\ \&\ \text{declarative}(u,P)\ \&\ \text{attend}_h(S)]$
then: $\text{AFTER}(\text{utter}_s(u),$
$\text{BMB}_h^s[\text{GOAL}_s\text{BEL}_h\ \text{GOAL}_s\text{BEL}_h\text{BEL}_s(P)])$

Figure 7.2: Declarative axiom

162

The *declarative axiom* states that if the hearer H believes that it is mutually believed by the speaker S and himself that (1) S has produced an utterance u, (2) u is a declarative sentence whose conditions of satisfaction are expressed by P, and (3) H is attending to S, then after the act of producing u, H believes that it is mutually believed by S and himself that S has the literal goal expressed by (7.5). The axiom itself is shown in Figure 7.2.

Similarly, the *imperative axiom* (Figure 7.3) states that if the hearer H believes that it is mutually believed by the speaker S and himself that (1) S has produced an utterance u, (2) u is an imperative sentence whose conditions of satisfaction are expressed by P, and (3) H is attending to S, then after the act of producing u, H believes that it is mutually believed by S and himself that S has the literal goal expressed by (7.13).

Given the declarative and imperative axioms, the discourse purposes of *inform* and *request* can be derived as follows: First, the mutually believed antecedent in each axiom is established (cf. Clark and Marshall 1981). As a result, the hearer can conclude that after the utterance, it is mutually believed that he has recognized the literal goal of the speech act. The discourse purposes are then derived, as we have seen, using the concepts of sincerity, helpfulness and, competence.

Since (7.5) and (7.13) represent the literal goals of *inform* and *request* respectively, their *satisfaction* — i.e., formulas (7.6) and (7.14) represent the specification of the context-independent effects of declaratives and imperatives respectively. These formulas may appear prohibitively complex for any realistic attempt at implementation. The multiple nesting of modal operators is indeed daunting. But complexity of statements in theory does not necessarily dictate a similar complexity in practice. For example, people are *usually* sincere, helpful, and competent, and if these properties are assumed by

---

If: $\mathrm{BMB}_h^s[\mathrm{utter}_s(u)$ & $\mathrm{imperative}(u,P)$ & $\mathrm{attend}_h(S)]$
then: $\mathrm{AFTER}(\mathrm{utter}_s(u),$
$\qquad \mathrm{BMB}_h^s[\mathrm{GOAL}_s\mathrm{BEL}_h\mathrm{GOAL}_s\ \mathrm{BEL}_h\mathrm{GOAL}_s\mathrm{GOAL}_h$
$\qquad\qquad \mathrm{DONE}_h(P)])$

Figure 7.3: Imperative axiom

default, the axiomatization of core effects of utterances can be simplified considerably. This is the approach taken by Perrault when he advocates applying Reiter's default logic to speech act theory (Perrault 1989; Reiter 1980). However, Perrault goes well beyond this. He argues (and Cohen and Levesque agree) that even under normal communication conditions, there simply are no speech act effects that occur *every* time the speech act is performed successfully. Thus, if Perrault is right, Cohen and Levesque's approach, as initially stated, cannot work.

Let us examine Perrault's argument more closely. First, Perrault observes that in non-serious utterances of declarative sentences (for example, irony), *none* of the effects specified in (7.6) through (7.9) are intended to be achieved. This shows, Perrault argues, that condition (7.6) is still too strong for the specification of the context-independent consequences of uttering a declarative statement. But Perrault does not take into account the fact that irony, like all non-literal uses of language, is *implicated*. That is, it is calculated on the basis of the conventional force of the utterance. If the hearer does not grasp the attitudes that are conventionally associated with the literal use of the utterance, he will not be able to grasp the non-conventional, ironical, intention either. Thus, rather than showing that (7.6) is too strong, the case of irony merely shows that the effect specified by (7.6) is an initial (and crucial) link in a chain of inferences that — when all is well — ends up with the speaker's discourse purposes satisfied. But this can hardly be an argument against Cohen and Levesque. It is the very premise that underlies their entire approach.

Perrault's second argument is potentially much more damaging. He begins by showing, correctly in my opinion, that no formula of the form

(7.20) $\mathrm{BEL_h\,BEL_s\ldots BEL_h\,BEL_s}(P)$

can be the context-independent consequence of uttering a declarative sentence. But he then proceeds to argue that the same is true for any formula of the following form as well:

(7.21) $\mathrm{BEL_h\,GOAL_s\ldots}(P).$

His argument is this: Suppose that prior to his utterance, the speaker is convinced that the hearer firmly believes that P is *not* the case, and that the hearer will not change his mind no matter what. Suppose further that the hearer knows that this is what the speaker thinks. Under such circumstances, the speaker cannot have the goal of making the hearer believe that P, because no one can have a goal he believes to be impossible to achieve. Moreover, since the hearer is aware of this, he cannot believe that the speaker has such a goal. Hence, Perrault argues, in such circumstances the consequence of asserting that P is not

(7.22) $\text{BEL}_\text{h} \text{GOAL}_\text{s} \text{BEL}_\text{h}(P)$.

Therefore, formula (7.22) cannot express the context-independent consequences of uttering a declarative sentence. This argument, Perrault continues, can be generalized to show that no formula like (7.21) can work either.

I agree, of course, that (7.22) is not the context-independent consequence of all utterances of a declarative sentence, but I think that Perrault's argument *cannot* be generalized. A rational speaker indeed may still assert that P, even if he thinks that there is no chance whatsoever that the hearer will believe it, and thus Perrault is right in claiming that under such circumstances the speaker cannot have $\text{BEL}_\text{h}(P)$ as a goal. But the same argument cannot be extended to the content of the hearer's belief in (7.6), namely, the goal that the hearer should believe that the *speaker* believes that P. The reason for this is that a rational agent will not perform an illocutionary act *unless there is at least a slim chance that the hearer will believe that the sincerity condition of that act is satisfied.* For example, suppose that nothing on earth would change your firm belief that I do not intend to wash the dishes. If I am aware of the strength of your belief, there is little point on my part in *promising* you that I will wash the dishes. Although a speaker may or may not intend to do what he promises, and the hearer may or may not believe that the speaker intends to do it, a rational promise requires at least the *possibility* that the hearer would take the speaker to be sincere. If sincerity is ruled out at the outset, a rational person would not bother to promise anything to begin with.

The same is true of assertions. If the speaker thought from the start that under no circumstances would the hearer take him to be sincere, then, being rational, he would forgo the assertion altogether. Thus, if an assertion *is* performed, we must conclude that the speaker considers it at least logically possible for the hearer to believe that the sincerity condition of the assertion is satisfied. This is all that is required for the possibility of the speaker having a *goal* that the hearer should so believe, and Perrault's argument does not apply.[8]

Cohen and Levesque do accept Perrault's argument, and their revised feature axioms stipulate that the effect of an utterance should hold *only* in contexts in which the speaker is assumed to be sincere:

> Ultimately, when everyone knows the speaker is insincere, the usual effects are not produced. We do not say specifically what *is* produced, but that is another matter. (Cohen and Levesque 1988, 30. Italics in original.)

But is that really another matter? I do not think so. By giving up the attempt to specify the context-independent effects of uttering a sentence (under normal conditions), Cohen and Levesque give up a crucial generalization. Whether a hearer takes the speaker to be sincere or not, the initial effects of hearing what was said ought to be the same. Either way, the hearer has *understood* the speaker. Now, following Grice, if we correlate understanding with recognition of propositional attitudes, then an account of speech acts that is *hearer-oriented* (as Cohen and Levesque's theory is) should strive for the specification of those propositional attitudes that are generated as effects on the hearer's mental state when he understands an utterance, *regardless* of the speaker's sincerity. This is the Archimedean fulcrum that allows all other intended effects to follow, given common rationality, cooperation, and contextual factors. This is what I take Cohen and Levesque's initial approach to be, and I see no compelling need to abandon it. It is this approach, accordingly, that I adopt below.

---

[8] I do not think that Perrault's argument is essential to his main point. As can be easily verified, the list of what we have called "normal" communication conditions is infinite. This in itself shows that an application of Default Logic to computational speech act theory is indispensable. Moreover, Perrault's central claim is that the mental states of the speaker and hearer *after* an utterance depend on their mental states *before* it, a claim I fully agree with. Since mental states can vary a great deal, it makes sense to look for a method of reasoning that would not require explicit representation of all possible mental states. But Perrault is wrong in concluding that because of such considerations, *all* the effects of uttering a sentence under normal conditions are context-dependent.

7.3.3   *Referring and rationality*

Following Cohen and Levesque's approach, Appelt and Kronfeld (1987) have sketched out a formal model of referring, in line with the general principles developed in the present study. In order to present this formal model, we need the following notation:

content(np): An open sentence with one free variable which represents the descriptive content of np (a noun phrase).

holds(F, a): F is an open sentence with one free variable. When F is interpreted as a one-argument predicate, it is true of a.

As individuating sets of presentation modes are at the heart of the view of referring presented here, we also need a mechanism that will allow us to represent formally how an agent might reason about such entities. The following is merely a convenient notation, as a formal theory of individuating sets is yet to be developed.

$\Delta(Agt, u, t)$: A function whose arguments are an agent Agt, a referring expression u, and the time of utterance t, and whose value is a *discursive* presentation mode that represents for Agt whatever individual the utterer of u had in mind. Discursive presentation modes are mental representations of objects that result from referring acts occurring in discourse (note that Agt can be either the speaker or the hearer of u).

$\Pi(Agt, p, t)$: A function whose arguments are an agent Agt, and a perceptual image p that was recorded at time t, and whose value is a *perceptual* presentation mode that results from a perceptual act (e.g., looking), and denotes the object perceived.[9]

$res(m)$: A function that takes a mode of presentation m as an argument, and returns the object that is determined by the individuating set that includes m (res is in fact a composition of two functions: the first maps presentation modes onto individuating sets that contain them, and the second maps individuating sets onto the objects that they represent).[10]

---

[9]Some representations can combine discursive and perceptual modes (e.g. the presentation mode that is acquired after hearing the description: "the painter who made this picture in front of you"), and these can be accounted for as the values of functions that take other representations as arguments.

[10]The name of the function *res* (from the Latin *res*, "a thing") is an abbreviation of REferent of an individuating Set).

Figure 7.4 shows the referring axiom, which describes the effects on the hearer's mental state when a referring expression is used under normal conditions. The similarity in structure between this axiom and the imperative and declarative ones (Figures 7.2 and 7.3 above) should be obvious. All three specify the conditions under which a literal goal is recognized. Thus, the usual preconditions that are necessary for the performance of a speech act apply here as well, namely, that the speaker should utter a sentence, and that the hearer should listen (line 1). The other preconditions, however, distinguish the referring axiom from the other two: the sentence uttered should contain a noun phrase that is interpreted as a referring expression (line 2). Being a referring expression is a "feature" of the noun phrase in the same way that being in the imperative mood is a feature of an imperative sentence. Thus, the referring axiom is as much a "feature" axiom as the axioms in Cohen and Levesque's system. There is, however, a significant difference. The "features" in Cohen and Levesque's axioms are *syntactic*, that is, they can be inferred by looking at the form of the sentence alone. Being a referring expression, by contrast, is not a syntactic property that the noun phrase wears on its sleeve, so to speak. *How* a referring expression is recognized as such is a difficult question which I do not address here.

If indeed the hearer assumes that he and the speaker mutually believe that all the preconditions are satisfied, then after the utterance (line 3), the speaker also assumes that it is now mutually believed that the literal goals of the utterance are recognized. The literal goal of *referring* is expressed in line (4): that the hearer should focus on the same object that the speaker has in mind. The literal goal of uttering a referring expression with certain descriptive con-

$$\text{If: } \text{BMB}_h^s[\text{utter}_s(u) \ \& \ \text{sentence}(u) \ \& \ \text{attend}_h(S) \ \& \qquad (1)$$
$$\text{part-of}(v,u) \ \& \ \text{np}(v) \ \& \ \text{ref-exp}(v)] \qquad (2)$$
$$\text{then: } \text{AFTER}(\text{utter}_s(u), \qquad (3)$$
$$\text{BMB}_h^s[\text{GOAL}_s(res(\Delta(S,v,t)) = res(\Delta(H,v,t))) \ \& \qquad (4)$$
$$\text{GOAL}_s\text{BEL}_h\text{GOAL}_s\text{BEL}_h\text{BEL}_s \qquad (5)$$
$$(\text{holds}(\text{content}(v), res(\Delta(S,v))))] \qquad (6)$$

Figure 7.4: Referring axiom

tent is expressed in lines (5–6): the hearer should think that the speaker intends him to believe that the speaker believes that the descriptive content of the noun phrase is true of the intended referent. The difference in the structure of propositional attitudes between the two literal goals is significant. As we have seen in Chapter 4, the mere recognition that a noun phrase is intended to be interpreted as a referring expression provides the hearer with a representation of the same object that the speaker has in mind. But the literal goal of using a referring expression with a certain descriptive content is very similar to the literal goal of using a declarative sentence for the purpose of informing. Since the speaker may be either insincere or incompetent, the hearer may not believe that the descriptive content of the noun phrase is indeed true of the intended referent. As in the case of assertions, however, the speaker will then simply adopt a weaker belief about the hearer's mental state.[11]

Once the literal goals are recognized, they are satisfied. But this, obviously, is only the first step. Now the hearer is expected to discover and satisfy identification criteria. Such criteria are derived from a variety of sources, including the syntactic and semantic properties of the utterance, the discourse, general world knowledge, and so on (cf. Appelt 1987). Within the model, however, such criteria can be represented as constraints on the relevant individuating set. For example, if visual identification is required, the identification constraint is that the individuating set should contain a perceptual presentation mode that will be acquired *after* the utterance. If we take np and t_u to be the noun phrase and the time of the utterance, respectively, this requirement can be expressed as follows:

(7.23) $(\exists t)(\exists p)[res(\Pi(H,p,t)) = res(\Delta(H,np,t_u)) \ \& \ (t \geq t_u)]$

If (7.23) obtains, identification is complete, and the referring act is successful. If not, then the hearer has to devise an appropriate plan to bring about a situation in which (7.23) is true.

Of course, mere perception of the referent is not enough. The hearer must believe that the thing he sees is the same as the one the speaker has referred to, and the descriptive content of the noun phrase often plays a major role in establishing this. It is certainly possible, however, for the hearer to figure out the correct referent even when the description used is entirely wrong. The explanation

---

[11]The axiom in Figure 7.4 modifies and combines together the Referring Schema and Activation Axiom presented in Appelt and Kronfeld (1987).

suggested in this study is that in many cases the descriptive content of the referring expression is merely a tool for identification, which the hearer is free to use at his own discretion. This is reflected in the referring axiom, since the satisfaction of the literal goal of referring depends neither on the descriptive content of the referring expression, nor on the hearer's attitudes toward its correctness.

The difference between the literal goal of referring and the literal goal of using a noun phrase with a certain descriptive content also explains why referring can be interpreted as an act of informing. As Appelt (1985a; 1985b) observes, a referring expression can be used to inform the hearer that some property holds of the intended referent. For example, a speaker may point to a tool on the table and say: "Use the wheelpuller to remove the flywheel." The speaker can rely upon the pointing action to enable the hearer to identify the referent of "the wheelpuller," while the descriptive content of the referring expression serves to inform the hearer what kind of tool it is. Given the referring axiom, this ability to inform while referring should hardly be surprising. Not only can identification succeed independently of descriptive content, but that part of the referring axiom which expresses the hearer's goals and beliefs concerning the descriptive content of the referring expression (lines 5–6) has the structure of the literal goal of *inform* (formula [7.5], p. 160 above). Thus, as a result of the referring act, the hearer believes that

$$(7.24) \quad \mathbf{GOAL_sBEL_hBEL_s}(\mathrm{holds}(cont(v), res(\Delta(S, v, t)))).$$

If the hearer believes that the speaker is sincere and competent, he may indeed be convinced that the referent has the property expressed by the noun phrase; if so, the speaker has not only referred, but informed as well.

Another aspect of referring is that it is supposed to contribute to the success of illocutionary acts. Referring acts are rarely performed in isolation. Typically, referring occurs as a step in the performance of a larger speech act, and the objectives that the referring act is expected to accomplish play a role in the agent's more general intentions and goals. Thus, it is not enough to provide the referring axiom; the model should also characterize formally the contribution of referring to illocutionary acts.

A full theoretical treatment of this problem is well beyond the scope of this study, but a modified example from our discussion in

Appelt and Kronfeld (1987) may illustrate how the effects of referring contribute to the desired effects of the request.

Suppose S tells H under appropriate circumstances: "Please replace the 300-ohm resistor." Let u be this utterance, let "the 300ΩR" be an abbreviation for the noun phrase "the 300-ohm resistor," and let $\lambda x.300\Omega R(x)$ be the descriptive content of that noun phrase. A natural way to combine the imperative and the referring axioms together is shown in Figure 7.5.

The formula in Figure 7.5 is not as complex as it seems. Lines (1) through (7) are the same preconditions as for both the referring and the imperative axioms. If these preconditions are satisfied, then after the utterance (line 8) the hearer assumes that it is mutually believed that he has recognized three literal goals: (a) the literal goal of referring (lines 9–10), (b) the literal goal of using a referring expression with certain descriptive content (lines 11–13), and (c) the literal goal of the request (lines 11, 14, and 15).

Let us suppose that all the preconditions are mutually believed to be satisfied. Given this assumption, we can conclude that following the utterance, the following holds:

$$
\begin{aligned}
&\textbf{If: BMB}^s_h[\text{utter}_s(u)\& &(1)\\
&\quad \text{attend}_h(S)\& &(2)\\
&\quad \text{imperative}(u, &(3)\\
&\qquad \text{replace}_h(res(\Delta(S, \text{'the } 300\Omega R', t))))\& &(4)\\
&\quad \text{part-of('the } 300\Omega R', u)\& &(5)\\
&\quad \text{np('the } 300\Omega R')\& &(6)\\
&\quad \text{ref-exp('the } 300\Omega R')] &(7)\\
&\textbf{then: AFTER}(\text{utter}_s(u), &(8)\\
&\textbf{BMB}^s_h[\text{GOAL}_s(res(\Delta(S, \text{'the } 300\Omega R', t)) = &(9)\\
&\qquad res(\Delta(H, \text{'the } 300\Omega R', t)))\& &(10)\\
&\quad \text{GOAL}_s\text{BEL}_h\text{GOAL}_s\text{BEL}_h &(11)\\
&\qquad (\text{BEL}_s(\text{holds}(\lambda x.300\Omega R(x), &(12)\\
&\qquad\quad res(\Delta(S, \text{'the } 300\Omega R', t))))\& &(13)\\
&\quad \text{GOAL}_s\text{GOAL}_h\text{DONE}_h(\text{replace}_h &(14)\\
&\qquad (res(\Delta(S, \text{'the } 300\Omega R', t)))))]) &(15)
\end{aligned}
$$

Figure 7.5: Referring within a request

(7.25) $\text{BMB}_{\text{h}}^{\text{s}}[\text{GOAL}_{\text{s}}(res(\Delta(S, \text{'the } 300\Omega R', t)) =$
$res(\Delta(H, \text{'the } 300\Omega R', t)))\&$
$\text{GOAL}_{\text{s}}\text{BEL}_{\text{h}}\text{GOAL}_{\text{s}}\text{BEL}_{\text{h}}$
$(\text{BEL}_{\text{s}}(holds(\lambda x.300\Omega R(x),$
$res(\Delta(S, \text{'the } 300\Omega R', t))))\&$
$\text{GOAL}_{\text{s}}\text{GOAL}_{\text{h}}\text{DONE}_{\text{h}}(replace_{\text{h}}$
$(res(\Delta(S, \text{'the } 300\Omega R', t)))))]$

The literal goals are thus recognized (and hence satisfied). Using sincerity, competence, and helpfulness, together with basic properties of **BMB** and **BEL**, it is easy to show that the following formulas are derivable from (7.25):

(7.26) $\text{BMB}_{\text{h}}^{\text{s}}[\text{GOAL}_{\text{s}}(res(\Delta(S, \text{'the } 300\Omega R', t))$
$= res(\Delta(H, \text{'the } 300\Omega R', t)))]$

(7.27) $\text{BMB}_{\text{h}}^{\text{s}}[holds(\lambda x.300\Omega R(x),$
$res(\Delta(S, \text{'the } 300\Omega R', t)))]$

(7.28) $\text{BMB}_{\text{h}}^{\text{s}}[\text{GOAL}_{\text{h}}\text{DONE}_{\text{h}}$
$(replace_{\text{h}}(res(\Delta(H, \text{'the } 300\Omega R', t))))]$

(7.26) indicates that both speaker and hearer are focusing on the same thing; (7.27) provides the information that helps the hearer identify which thing it is; and (7.28) expresses what the hearer is supposed to do once he finds it. The combination of the referring and imperative axioms, therefore, captures the intuitive idea with which this book started: that the main function of the speech act of referring is to let your audience know what you are talking about, so that you can then go on and talk about it some more.

7.4 Summary of Chapter 7

The picture of referring that has emerged from the preceding chapters is based on the notion of denotation. In referring, the speaker has a mental representation denoting what he believes to be a particular object, and he intends the hearer to come to have a mental representation denoting the same object, at least in part through the use of a noun phrase that is intended to be a linguistic representation of that object. Using the concept of an individuating set as an abstract data type, this view can be expressed as follows: when a speaker performs the speech act of referring, he has an individuating set which he believes determines a particular object, and he uses a noun phrase with the following intentions:

1. **Literal goal:** that as a result of the hearer's recognition of the noun phrase as a referring expression, the hearer generates a local individuating set that determines this very same object.

2. **Discourse purpose:** that the hearer will apply various operations on the newly created individuating set so that it meets the appropriate identification constraints.

Two computational models incorporating certain aspects of this view have been presented. The first is **BERTRAND**, a Prolog program that generates and maintains individuating sets in a dialogue. The second, which is based on the work reported in Appelt and Kronfeld (1987), outlines a computational model of referring within the framework of a general theory of speech acts and rationality.

BERTRAND is based on the dialogue program **TALK** (Pereira and Shieber 1987). Treating logical forms of referring expressions as if they were presentation modes, it constructs individuating sets by clustering together referring expressions that are interpreted as representing the same object. In constructing individuating sets, **BERTRAND** uses a combination of a logical and a pragmatic strategy. The logical strategy is based, roughly, on logical features of the identity relation. The pragmatic strategy is based on Grosz's notion of a focus stack (Grosz 1977; 1978a; 1979; Grosz and Sidner 1986).

A computational model of referring, however, should show not only how individuating sets are maintained, but also how the use of a referring expression is systematically related to changes in both the speaker's and the hearer's mental states. A central concept in this endeavor is that of *mutual belief*. Clark and Marshall (1981) have described a version of this notion that applies to referring. According to their account, in order for the speech act of referring to succeed, both speaker and hearer must mutually believe who, or what, the referent is. But Clark and Marshall's notion is not general enough. A crucial aspect of referring *in general* is not what is mutually believed about the referent, but what the speaker and hearer mutually believe about *each other*. I call this *mutual individuation*.

Equipped with mutual belief and mutual individuation, we turn to the formalization of the effects of the referring act on the hearer's mental state. One approach to modling these effects is based on two related ideas: (a) mental representations can be modeled with logical formulas, and (b) the process of planning to achieve a goal can be seen as a search for a derivation from axioms representing the world as it is to theorems that represent a world in which the goal is satisfied. Recently, Cohen and Levesque (1985; 1987; 1988) have developed a detailed formal theory in which illocutionary acts are characterized in terms of what the speaker and hearer mutually believe about each other's mental states as the result of a speech act. Moreover, Cohen and Levesque are able to show why utterances are expected to be successful given reasonable assumptions about the rationality of discourse participants.

Cohen and Levesque's initial approach was to specify the context-independent effects of utterances, and then show how, using the concepts of *sincerity*, *helpfulness*, and *competence*, other effects follow. As a result of Perrault's counterargument (1989), they conclude that such context-independent specification of utterance effects is impossible. I argue that although Perrault's argument is valid for a particular case, it cannot be generalized, and furthermore that the concept of a *literal goal* provides precisely the required context-independent effects initially called for by Cohen and Levesque.

I adopt, therefore, Cohen and Levesque's initial approach. Following Appelt and Kronfeld (1987), I present the referring axiom, which is similar in structure to Cohen and Levesque's declarative and imperative axioms.

An important feature of the referring axiom is that it distinguishes between the literal goal of referring and the literal goal of using a noun phrase with a certain descriptive content. This explains how reference can succeed even when the description used is wrong. It also explains how an act of referring can be interpreted as an act of *informing* (Applet 1985a; 1985b).

A computational model of referring also must show how the speech act of referring contributes to the success of the illocutionary act of which it is a part. I cannot provide a full theoretical treatment of this problem. However, an example is discussed, in which the imperative and referring axioms are combined together.

References

Allen, J. F. 1978. Recognizing intention in dialogue. Ph.D. diss., University of Toronto.

Allen, J. F. and C. R. Perrault. 1978. Participating in dialogues: understanding via plan deduction. In *Proceedings*, Canadian Society for Computational Studies of Intelligence.

Allen, J. F. and C. R. Perrault. 1980. Analyzing intention in dialogues. *Artificial Intelligence*, 15(3):143–178.

Appelt, D. E. 1985a. Planning English referring expressions. *Artificial Intelligence*, 26:1–33.

Appelt, D. E. 1985b. *Planning English Sentences*. Cambridge Univ. Press, Cambridge.

Appelt, D. E. 1987. Reference and pragmatic identification. In *TINLAP-3*, Computing Research Laboratory, New Mexico State Univ., Las Cruces.

Appelt, D. E. and A. Kronfeld. 1987. A computational model of referring. In *Proceedings of the 10th International Joint Conference on Artificial Intelligence*, J. McDermott, editor, pp. 640–647, Morgan Kaufman Publishers, Inc, Los Altos, Calif.

Austin, J. L. 1962. *How to Do Things with Words*. Oxford Univ. Press, London.

Barwise, J. and J. Perry. 1983. *Situations and Attitudes*. MIT Press, Cambridge, Mass.

Boër, S. E. and W. G. Lycan. 1986. *Knowing Who*. MIT Press, Cambridge, Mass.

Burge, T. 1977. Belief *de-re*. *The Journal of Philosophy*, 74:338–362.

Castañeda, H. 1977. On the philosophical foundations of the theory of communication: reference. In P. A. French, T. E. Uehling Jr., and H. K. Wettstein, editors, *Midwest Studies in Philosophy, vol. 2: Studies in the Philosophy of Language*, Univ. of Minnesota,

Morris.

Chastain, C. 1975. Reference and context. In K. Gunderson, editor, *Language, Mind and Knowledge*, pp. 194–270, Univ. of Minnesota Press, Minneapolis.

Clark, H. H. and C. Marshall. 1981. Definite reference and mutual knowledge. In A. Joshi, I. Sag, and B. Webber, editors, *Elements of Discourse Understanding*, pp. 10–63, Cambridge Univ. Press, Cambridge.

Cohen, P. R. 1978. On knowing what to say: planning speech acts. Ph.D. diss., University of Toronto, Toronto.

Cohen, P. R. 1984. Referring as requesting. In *Proceedings of the 10th International Conference on Computational Linguistics*, pp. 207–211, Association for Computational Linguistics.

Cohen, P. R. and H. Levesque. 1985. Speech acts and rationality. In *Proceedings of the 23rd Annual Meeting*, pp. 49–59, Association for Computational Linguistics.

Cohen, P. R. and H. Levesque. 1987. *Persistence, Intention, and Commitment*. Technical Report 415, Artificial Intelligence Center, SRI International.

Cohen, P. R. and H. Levesque. 1988. *Rational Interaction as the Basis for Communication*. Technical Report 433, Artificial Intelligence Center, SRI International.

Cohen, P. R. and C. R. Perrault. 1979. Elements of a plan-based theory of speech acts. *Cognitive Science*, 3:117–212.

Dahl, Deborah A. 1984. Recognizing specific attributes. Presented at the 59th Annual Meeting of the Linguistic Society of America. Baltimore.

Donnellan, K. S. 1970. Proper names and identifying descriptions. *Synthese*, 21:334–358.

Donnellan, K. S. [1966]1971. Reference and definite descriptions. In J.F. Rosenberg and C. Travis, editors, *Readings in the Philosophy of Language*, pp. 195–211, Prentice Hall, Englewood Cliffs, N.J.

Frege, G. [1892]1975. Sense and reference. In D. Davidson and G. Harman, editors, *The Logic of Grammar*, pp. 116–128, Dickenson, Encino, Calif.

Grice, H. P. 1957. Meaning. *Philosophical Review*, 66(3):377–388.

Grice, H. P. 1968. Utterer's meaning, sentence meaning, and word meaning. *Foundations of Language*, 4:225–242.

Grice, H. P. 1969. Utterer's meaning and intentions. *Philosophical Review*, 78:147–177.

Grice, H. P. 1975. Logic and conversation. In D. Davidson and G. Harman, editors, *The Logic of Grammar*, pp. 64–75, Dickenson, Encino, Calif.

Grosz, B. J. 1977. The representation and use of focus in dialogue understanding. Ph.D. diss., University of California, Berkeley.

Grosz, B. J. 1978a. Discourse analysis. In D. Walker, editor, *Understanding Spoken Language*, pp. 235–268, Elsevier North Holland, New York.

Grosz, B. J. 1978b. Focusing in dialogue. In *TINLAP-2*, pp. 96–103, University of Illinois, Urbana-Champaign.

Grosz, B. J. 1979. *Focusing and Description in Natural Language Dialogues.* Technical Report 185, Artificial Intelligence Center, SRI International. Also in *Elements of Discourse Understanding*, A. Joshi, I. Sag, and B. Webber, editors, Cambridge Univ. Press, Cambridge, 1981.

Grosz, B. J. and C. L. Sidner. 1986. Attention, intentions, and the structure of discourse. *Computational Linguistics*, 12(3):175–204.

Grosz, B. J., A. K. Joshi , and S. Weinstein. 1983. Providing a unified account of definite noun phrases in discourse. In *Proceedings of the 21st Annual Meeting,* pp. 44–50, Association for Computational Linguistics.

Halliday, M. A. K. and R. Hasan. 1976. *Cohesion in English.* Longman, London.

Hintikka, J. 1962. *Knowledge and Belief.* Cornell Univ. Press, Ithaca, N.Y.

Hintikka, J. 1967. Individuals, possible worlds, and epistemic logic. *Nous,* 1:33–62.

Kamp, H. 1984. A theory of truth and semantic representation. In J. A. G. Groenendijk, T. M. V. Janssen, and M. B. J. Stokhof, editors, *Truth, Interpretation, and Information*, pp. 277–322, Foris, Dordrecht.

Kaplan, D. [1968]1975. Quantifying in. In D. Davidson and G. Harman, editors, *The Logic of Grammar*, pp. 160–181, Dickenson, Encino, Calif.

Kaplan, D. 1977. Demonstratives. Department of Philosophy, Univ. of California, Los Angeles. Photocopy.

Kaplan, D. 1978. Dthat. In P. Cole, editor, *Syntax and Semantics, Vol. 9*, pp. 221–243, Academic Press, New York.

Kasher, A. 1976. Conversational maxims and rationality. In A. Kasher, editor, *Language in Focus*, pp. 197–216, Reidel, Dordrecht.

Kasher, A. 1977. What is a theory of use? *Journal of Pragmatics*, 1:105–120.

Kasher, A. 1982. Gricean inference revisited. *Philosophica*, 29(1):25–44.

Kasher, A. 1985. Philosophy and discourse analysis. In Teun van Dijk, editor, *Handbook of Discourse Analysis, Vol. 1*, pp. 231–248, Academic Press, New York.

Kasher, A. 1987. Justification of speech, acts, and speech acts. In E. LePore, editor, *New Directions in Semantics*, Academic Press, New York.

Kratzer, A. 1977. What "must" and "can" must and can mean. *Linguistics and Philosophy*, 1(1):337–335.

Kratzer, A. 1979. Conditional necessity and possibility. In R. Bäuerle, U. Egli, and A. Von Stechow, editors, *Semantics for Different Points of View*, pp. 117–147, Springer, Berlin.

Kratzer, A. 1981. The notional category of modality. In H. J. Eikmeyer and H. Rieser, editors, *Words, Worlds, and Contexts: New Approaches in Word Semantics*, pp. 38–74, Walter de Gruyter, Berlin.

Kripke, S. 1977. Speaker reference and semantic reference. In P. A. French, T. E. Uehling Jr., and H. K. Wettstein, editors, *Contemporary Perspectives in the Philosophy of Language*, pp. 6–27, Univ. of Minnesota Press, Minneapolis.

Kripke, S. [1972]1980. *Naming and Necessity*. Harvard Univ. Press, Cambridge, Mass.

Kronfeld, A. 1986. Donnellan's distinction and a computational model of reference. In *Proceedings of the 24th Annual Meeting*, A. W. Biermann, Editor, pp. 186–191, Association for Computational Linguistics.

Kuhn, T. 1962. *The Structure of Scientific Revolutions*. Univ. of Chicago Press, Chicago.

Lakatos, I. 1970. Falsification and the methodology of research programmes. In I. Lakatos and A. Musgrave, editors, *Criticism and the Growth of Knowledge*, pp. 91–196, Cambridge Univ. Press. Cambridge.

Loar, B. 1976. The semantics of singular terms. *Philosophical Studies*, 30:353–377.

McDermott, D. 1982. A temporal logic for reasoning about processes and plans. *Cognitive Science*, 6(2):101–155.

Milne, A. A. [1928]1965. *The House at Pooh Corner.* Methuen, London.

Moore, R. C. 1980. *Reasoning about Knowledge and Action.* Technical Report 191, Artificial Intelligence Center, SRI International.

Pereira, F. and S. Shieber. 1987. *Prolog and Natural Language Analysis. Lecture Notes,* Center for the Study of Language and Information, Stanford University.

Perrault, C. R. 1989. An application of default logic to speech act theory. In P. R. Cohen, J. Morgan, and M. E. Pollack, editors, *Intentions in Communication,* MIT Press, Cambridge, Mass.

Perrault, C. R. and P. R. Cohen. 1981. It's for your own good: a note on inaccurate reference. In A. Joshi, B. Webber, and I. Sag, editors, *Elements of Discourse Understanding,* pp. 217–230, Cambridge Univ. Press, Cambridge.

Perrault, C. R., J. F. Allen, and P. R. Cohen. 1978. Speech acts as a basis for understanding dialogue coherence. In *TINLAP-2,* pp. 125–132, University of Illinois, Urbana-Champaign.

Perry, J. 1977. Frege on demonstratives. *Philosophical Review,* 86:474–497.

Perry, J. 1979. The problem of the essential indexical. *Nous,* 13:3–21.

Popper, K. R. 1959. *The Logic of Scientific Discovery.* Hutchinson, London.

Putnam, H. 1975. The meaning of "meaning". In K. Gunderson, editor, *Language, Mind, and Knowledge,* pp. 131–193, Univ. of Minnesota Press, Minneapolis.

Quine, W.V. [1956]1972. Quantifiers and propositional attitudes. In D. Davidson and G. Harman, editors, *The Logic of Grammer,* pp. 153–159, Dickenson, Encino, Calif.

Reiter, R. 1980. A logic for default reasoning. *Artificial Intelligence,* 13:81–132.

Rosenschein, S. J. 1985. Formal theories of knowledge in AI and robotics. *New Generation Computing,* 3(4):345–357.

Russell, B. [1910]1953. Knowledge by acquaintance and knowledge by description. In *Mysticism and Logic,* Penguin, Harmondsworth, G.B.

Schiffer, S. R. 1972. *Meaning.* Oxford Univ. Press, Oxford.

Schiffer, S. R. 1978. The basis of reference. *Erkenntnis,* 13:171–206.

Searle, J. R. 1958. Proper names. *Mind,* 67, No. 266:166–173.

Searle, J. R. 1969. *Speech Acts: An Essay in the Philosophy of Language.* Cambridge Univ. Press, Cambridge.

Searle, J. R. 1971. What is a speech act? In J. R. Searle, editor, *The Philosophy of Language*, pp. 39–53, Oxford Univ. Press, Oxford.

Searle, J. R. 1979a. Indirect speech acts. In *Expression and Meaning: Studies in the Theory of Speech Acts*, Cambridge Univ. Press, Cambridge.

Searle, J. R. 1979b. Referential and attributive. In *Expression and Meaning: Studies in the Theory of Speech Acts*, Cambridge Univ. Press, Cambridge.

Searle, J. R. 1979c. A taxonomy of illocutionary acts. In *Expression and Meaning: Studies in the Theory of Speech Acts*, Cambridge Univ. Press, Cambridge.

Searle, J. R. 1983. *Intentionality: An Essay in the Philosophy of Mind*. Cambridge Univ. Press, Cambridge.

Searle, J. R. and D. Vanderveken. 1985. *Foundations of Illocutionary Logic*. Cambridge Univ. Press, Cambridge.

Sidner, C. L. 1983. What the speaker means: the recognition of speakers' plans in discourse. *International Journal of Computers and Mathematics*, 9(1):71–82.

Sidner, C. L. 1985. Plan parsing for intended response recognition in discourse. *Computational Intelligence*, 1(1):1–10.

Sosa, E. 1970. Propositional attitudes de dicto and de re. *Journal of Philosophy*, 67:883–896.

Strawson, P. F. 1959. *Individuals*. Methuen, London.

Strawson, P. F. 1971. Intention and convention in speech acts. In J. Searle, editor, *The Philosophy of Language*, pp. 23–38, Oxford Univ. Press, Oxford.

Strawson, P. F. [1950]1971. On referring. In J.F Rosenberg and C. Travis, editors, *Readings in the Philosophy of Language*, pp. 175–195, Prentice Hall, Englewood Cliffs, N. J.

Walters, R. S. 1967. *The Encyclopedia of Philosophy*, Volume 4, pp. 410–414. Macmillan, New York, s.v. "laws of science and lawlike statements".

Webber, B. L. 1983. So what can we talk about now? In M. Brady and R. Berwick, editors, *Computational Models of Discourse*, pp. 331–371, MIT Press, Cambridge, Mass.

Wettstein, H. 1981. Demonstrative reference and definite descriptions. *Philosophical Studies*, 40(4):241–257.

Wettstein, H. 1986. Has semantics rested on a mistake? *Journal of Philosophy*, 83(4):185–209.

Index

AFTER, 157
AI (artificial intelligence), 4, 14, 15, 36, 148n
Allen, J. F., 8, 69, 70
Appelt, D. E., 8, 110, 144, 167–174 passim
attentional state, 147
attributive use. *See* Donnellan's distinction.
Austin, J. L., 10, 70

Barwise, J., 47, 148n
BEL, 157
belief. *See de re* belief; *de dicto* belief.
    content of, *sec.* 2.4, 46
    and the descriptive research program, 22
    in Frege's theory, 23
    and the philosophical problem of reference, 19
BERTRAND, *sec.* 7.2
BMB, 157
Böer, S.E., 60
Burge, T., 32

Carnap, R., 116, 117
Castañeda, H., 47
causal chain, 19, 26, 40–45, 86, 113
causal theory of reference. *See* reference, new theory of.
Chastain, C., 47
Clark, H.H., 151–156 passim, 163, 173
Cohen, P. R., 8, 11, 47, 70n, 150, 153, 155, 157–168 passim, 174
communication intentions, 7–8, 10, *sec.* 4.1
    Grice's theory of, 71–72,
    and mutual belief, 150
    and rationality, *sec.* 7.3.2
    in referring, *ch.* 4

competence, 158, 160, 163, 172, 174
constitutive rules, 8n
conversational implicature, 99–100, 106, 108, 109, 127
    Grice's theory of, 97–99
conversational referring, 96–97
conversational relevance, *sec.* 5.2
    and modes of presentation, 93n, 135–136
conversationally relevant description, *ch.* 5, 132, 135, 140
    implicating necessity, 105–106, 114
    indefinite, 111–113
    and intensional justification, *sec.* 5.3.3
    in non-assertives, 110–111
    recognition of, *sec.* 5.3.1
    and universal generalization, 101–106
cooperative principle, 97

Dahl, D.A., 112
declarative axiom, 162–163, 168, 174
declarative sentence, 12, 159, 163, 165, 169
    context-independent effects of, 159, 162–166
    non-serious utterance of, 164
de dicto belief, 19–20, 32, 50, 125
    and "having a particular object in mind," *sec.* 3.2
default logic, 164, 166n
definite description. *See* Donnellan's distinction.
    abbreviated, 24, 25
    ambiguous, 29n
    disguised, 22
    "essential," 28

181

expressing a universal
generalization, 7, 102
functionally relevant, 91–92
and relevance, *sec* 5.2
and rigid designation, 55–56
Russell's theory of, 24–25
used to inform, 110
value-loaded interpretation of,
47, 47n
denotation, 21, 22, 25, 45, 87, 141
de re belief, 19–20, 22, 25, *sec.* 2.3.4,
36n, 65, *ch.* 6, 154
content of, *sec.* 2.4
de re report of propositional attitudes,
32n, *sec.* 6.2
and the epistemic intuition,
51–52
and the modal intuition, 52–57
truth conditions of, 126–134
two goals in, 127–129, 138
descriptive approach. *See* descriptive
research program.
descriptive content, 19, 20, *sec.* 2.2,
26, 28–29, 35, 36n, 45,
85–86, 91, 95, 113, 114, 118,
121, 122, 125, 143, 170, 171
of a noun phrase, 167, 169–170,
174
of a referring expression, 49, 63,
65, 67
descriptive research program, *ch.* 2,
121–122. *See also*
descriptive theory of *de re*
thought.
cornerstone of, 116
and Donnellan's distinction,
28–33, 64,
limiting cases of, 131-132
main postulates of, 20–22
and Russell, 23–26
and the twin earth argument,
122–123
descriptive theory of *de re* thought,
ch. 6
and individuating sets, *sec.* 6.2.4
Fregean view, 117
Russellian view, 122
discourse entity, 5, 74
discourse purpose, 69–70, 83
distinct from illocutionary point,
70
of informing and requesting,
159–164
of referring, *sec.* 4.2, 84, 86, 143
discourse segment, 147
discourse-level intentions, 70
DONE, 157

Donnellan's distinction, *sec.* 2.3.1, *ch.*
3
criteria for, *sec.* 3.1, 56–57
denotational aspect, 62, 65, 87,
88, 114
epistemic aspect, 60, 65,
and having a particular object in
mind, *sec.* 3.2
Kripke's interpretation of, 32n,
87, 90–91
as a methodological tool, 28, 45,
64
modal aspect, 52–56, 65
paradigmatic examples of, 63–65,
66, 102, 106, 109
and referent identification, 77
Searle's interpretation of, 87–90
as a test case, 64
used in arguments against the
descriptive program, 28–33
Donnellan, K.S., 26, 27, 26n, 29,
32n.7, 33, 38n, 44, 118, 138.
See also Donnellan's
distinction.
DTHAT, 55–56

Eeyore, 75
existential generalization, 50–51,
53–54, 123
extensional context, 127, 133
external perspective, *sec.* 1.1, 13, 15,
16

feature axioms, 162
fixing the referent, 53, 55
focus space, 147–148, 148n, 149, 173
focus structure, 75
Frege, G, 19, 23, 25, 35, 45, 116, 121,
Frege's theory of sense and reference,
23
Fregean dictum, 29
Fregean principle, 42
functionally relevant description, 93,
114

general proposition, 19, 85, 113
general term, 117, 122 141–142
GOAL, 157
Grice, H.P., 7–8, 10, 68, 70, 71–74, 87,
97–99, 127, 150, 156, 159,
166. *See also*
communication intentions;
conversational implicature,
Grice's theory of; meaning,
Grice's theory of.
Grosz, B.J., 47, 69, 70, 75, 147, 148n,
173

Halliday, M.A., 80n
Hasan, R., 80n
helpfulness, 158, 163, 172, 174
Hintikka, J., 32, 52
horn clause, 144

identification, 33, 76–81, 91, 93, 94,
    114, 169, 170
    degrees of, 78
    epistemic, 76–77, 83, 154
    hearer's sense of, 76, 83
    and indefinite descriptions, 112
    pragmatic, 76–77, 79, 83–84, 142
    speaker's sense of, 76, 83
    specified in terms of presentation
        modes, 79, 84
    under a presentation mode, 95
    visual, 78, 169
identification constraints, 79–82, 84,
    86, 90, 93, 143, 169, 173
identifying description, 19, 22, *sec.*
    2.3.5, 116, 138
illocutionary act, 9–12, 16, 70, 72–73,
    78, 157, 158, 165, 170, 174
illocutionary force, 10, 78
illocutionary point, 10, 12, 70
imperative axiom, 162–163, 168, 171,
    172, 174
imperative sentence, 12, 159, 161, 163,
    168
    context-independent effects of,
        159, 162, 163
indefinite description, 24n, 111-113,
    115
indexicals, *sec.* 6.1
    "I," 118–121, 142
    "now," 119, 142
    "you," 123, 129
individual concept, 116, 117, 119, 120
individuating principle, 40, 58
individuating representation, 20,
    21–22, 25, 30, 32, 42, 44,
    86, 138, 139
    necessary for a *de re* belief, *sec.*
        6.1
    sufficient for a *de re* belief, *sec.*
        6.2
individuating set, *sec.* 3.3.1, 61n, 62,
    64, 66, 74-75, 79–80, 84, 86,
    90, 140, 142
    abstract data type, 142–143,
        172–173
    in, **BERTRAND** 146–149
    and *de re* thought, 142
    and the descriptive view, *sec.*
        6.2.4
    determining an object, 59
    formalization of, 167

local, 74, 146
and pragmatic identification,
    80–82, 142
quasi-permanent, 74, 146
representing the modal intuition,
    142–143
inform, 159–161, 163, 170
intensional context, 51, 53, 54,
    123–124
intentional content, 132. *See also*
    descriptive content; belief,
    content of.
internal perspective, *sec.* 1.1, 15, 80n

justification:
    causal element in, 132–133
    extensional and intensional, *sec.*
        5.3.3
    "folk theory" of, 104

Kamp, H., 74
Kaplan, D., 26n, 31, 39, 51, 54, 55, 56,
    125–126, 130–131, 132
Kasher, A., 8, 10n, 11, 157
knowing who, 51–52, 60, 76, 77, 83,
    126, 142
knowledge, by acquaintance and by
    description, 23–25, 119–122,
    124, 135n, 137, 138,
    141–142
Kratzer, A., 107–108
Kripke, S., 19, 26n, 28, 32n, 37, 52–53,
    55, 87–88, 90, 114, 136
Kronfeld, A., 144, 167, 169n, 171, 173,
    174
Kuhn, T., 14

Lakatos, I., 14
Levesque, H.J., 8, 150, 157–168
    passim, 174
literal goal, 10–11, 69–70, 82, 83, 86,
    143, 162, 168, 170, 171, 173,
    174. *See also* referring,
    literal goal of.
    of informing, 159–160, 163
    of a request, 69, 161, 163
literal purpose, 10n
Loar, B., 49n, 119–120
Lycan, W.G., 60

McDermott, D., 158
Marshall, C., 151–156 passim, 163, 173
maxims of conversation, 97–98, 128,
    132, 157
meaning, 11, 22, 28–29, 37, 68–69,
    Grice's theory of, 70, 71–72
    of "must," *sec.* 5.3.4

Index

speaker's vs. sentence, 87–88, 91,
   95, 96, 114
Milne, A.A., 75
modal intuition, 52–56, 142–143
mode of presentation, 23, 39–44,
   58–63, 66, 80, 167
Moore, R.C., 38n
mutual agreement, 153
mutual individuation, *sec.* 7.3.1,
   173–174
mutual knowledge and belief, 99n,
   149–156, 173–174

Pereira, F., 144, 173
perlocutionary act, 70
Perrault, C.R., 8, 11, 69, 70, 153,
   164–166 passim, 174
Perry, J., 26n, 39, 47, 118, 120–121,
   138, 148n
persistent goal, 158, 162
physical object, 6–7, 24, 25, 30, 119,
   120, 121, 132
Piglet, 75–76
plan-based account of communication,
   8–9, 70, 76, 83, 100
Pooh, Winnie the, 75–76
Popper, K.R., 14
pragmatic presuppositions, 11–12
presentation mode. *See* mode of
   presentation.
primary aspect, 88–91
proper name, 19, 22, 25n3, 31, 37, 95,
   143, 144
   and subsumption, 148
   Russell's theory of, 24
proposition, 17–22, 30–31, 45
   constituent of, 18, 24, 31, 45
   as content of belief, 22, 117–118
   as content of utterances, 22,
      117–118
   general, 19
   "incomplete," 43
   in Russell's theory, 24–25
   singular, 19, 22, *sec.* 2.3.3, 32,
      35, 38–39, 61, 65, 66, 85–86,
      95, 96, 113, 118, 120–121,
      143
propositional act, 9
propositional attitudes, 17–18, 32, 34.
   See also de re beliefs.
propositional content, 10, 17, 18
propositional function, 25, 35, 116
Putnam, H., 26n, 122–123

quantifying-in, 124
Quine, W.V., 50

REFER, 12

reference
   direct, 31, 32
   new theory of 26, 34–44, 45, 46,
      86, 122
   philosophical problem of, 13–14,
      sec. 2.1, 45
referential/attributive distinction. *See*
   Donnellan's distinction.
referential use of definite descriptions.
   See Donnellan's distinction.
referring, 20
   contribution of to illocutionary
      acts, 12, 16, 170, 174
   conversational, 96
   different from illocutionary acts,
      10–13, 15–16
   discourse purpose of, *sec* 4.3,
      143, 173
   effects of, 9, 12, *sec.* 7.3
   functional, 95–96, 117
   and identifying descriptions, 21,
      33
   and informing, 170, 174
   literal goal of, 10, 12, 16, *sec.*
      4.2, 79, 80, 81, 82, 83, 84,
      143, 168, 170, 171, 174
   to non-physical objects, 6
   and planning, *sec.* 1.2, 15, 58,
      149
   pragmatic theory of, 9
   problem of, 13, 16
   and rationality, *sec.* 7.3.3
   speech act of, 9–13, 15, 22, 23,
      35, 45, 88, 90, 113, 141, 173
referring axiom, 168, 170–172, 174
referring expression, 7, 9, 13, 15, 18,
   19, 21, 22, 23, 25, 26, 28,
   30, 33, 86, 88, 91, 100, 110,
   111, 112, 144–146, 149, 173
   choice of, *sec.* 3.3.3, 95–96, 114,
      128, 139
   descriptive content of, 75, 85–86,
      95, 117, 168–169, 170
   logical form of, 146, 173
referring intention, *sec.* 3.3.2, 87–91,
      113, 114
   two types of, 60, 66, 91, 95-96,
      135
Reiter, R., 164
request, 159, 161–163, 171
research program, 14, 16. *See also*
   descriptive research
   program.
rigid designation, 31, 53–57, 61, 63,
   65, 66, 143
Rosenschein, S.J., 36
Russell, B., 23–26, 45, 102, 116, 119,
   120, 121, 138,

184

Russellian principle, 141, 145

Schiffer, S., 41, 119–120, 134, 137,
        150–151
Searle, J.R., 8–10 passim, 17, 19, 23,
        33, 45, 70, 76, 87-91 passim,
        101, 114, 120, 121, 150
self, 24, 119–121, 123, 135n, 138, 142
sense and reference, Frege's theory of,
        23
Shieber, S., 144, 173
Shortest spy argument, *sec.* 6.2.2
Sidner, C.L., 69, 70, 147, 148n
sincerity, 158, 160, 161, 163, 165–166,
        172, 174
singular proposition. *See* proposition,
        singular.
situation theory, 148n
Sosa, E., 125–127, 131
speaker's reference, 86–87, 90–91
speech act, 8–12, 86, 88, 166
Stalnaker, R., 44n
standard name, 4, 142
standard-name assumption, 4, 81–82
Strawson, P. F., 6, 23, 33, 91, 101,
        116, 120, 121, 123, 150
subsumption, 148

TALK, 144, 145
twin earth argument. *See under*
        descriptive research
        program.
two-squares argument, 118, 119–120,
        138

uniqueness condition, 101–102, 105
universal generalization, 101–105
        accidental, 103–104
        implicated, 112
        intensional and extensional
                justification of, 104–105
universality condition, 101–102, 105

visual experience, 119–121 passim
vivid name, 125–126, 133-134

Walters, R.S., 103
Webber, B.L., 74
Wettstein, H., 39, 49n

Lightning Source UK Ltd.
Milton Keynes UK
UKOW04f0925110913

216995UK00001B/98/A